Unfair Housing
How National Policy
Shapes Community Action

Mara S. Sidney

University Press of Kansas

© 2003 by the University Press of Kansas

All rights reserved

Published by the University Press of Kansas (Lawrence, Kansas 66049), which was organized by the Kansas Board of Regents and is operated and funded by Emporia State University, Fort Hays State University, Kansas State University, Pittsburg State University, the University of Kansas, and Wichita State University

Library of Congress Cataloging-in-Publication Data

Sidney, Mara S., 1964–
    Unfair housing : how national policy shapes community action / Mara S. Sidney.
        p. cm. — (Studies in government and public policy)
Includes bibliographical references and index.
    ISBN 0-7006-1275-0 (cloth : alk. paper) — ISBN 0-7006-1276-9 (pbk. : alk. paper)
    1. Discrimination in housing—United States. 2. Discrimination in housing—Government policy—United States. 3. Housing policy—United States. 4. Housing policy—United States—States. 5. Community development—United States—States. I. Title. II. Series.
    HD7288.76.U5S53 2003
    363.5'5'0973—dc21

                                                                    2003008802

British Library Cataloguing-in-Publication Data is available.

Printed in the United States of America

10 9 8 7 6 5 4 3 2 1

The paper used in this publication meets the minimum requirements of the American National Standard for Permanence of Paper for Printed Library Materials Z39.48-1984.

Unfair Housing

STUDIES IN GOVERNMENT AND PUBLIC POLICY

Contents

Tables

Preface

Several experiences during my field research for this book capture the questions and concerns that motivated me to write it. The first happened one afternoon in south Denver on a quiet block with fairly large 1960s-era homes. I was touring a spacious and comfortable split-level with an open living room and dining room, high ceilings, good-sized bedrooms, a nice yard, and an attached garage. The monthly rent was $2,500. I had told the agent that I worked for a local insurance company, and that my family and I were looking for a larger house to rent. The agent had almost completed the tour, and we stood in the foyer talking about the security deposit, the cost of utilities, and other details when we saw a black woman walking up the path toward the front door. The agent, a white woman, turned to me, also white, and said, "Don't discuss the terms in front of this person." I nodded and headed back toward the bedrooms, lingering in the hall to hear some of the next tour. When the woman had seen the house, she asked about the application procedure. The agent told her that the application form required a detailed income and employment history. When the woman asked for one to take with her, the agent couldn't find it, although she had an office in the house. The woman left without an application, and a little later the agent walked me to my car. I asked her what we would do if I decided I wanted the house. "Sign the lease, give me some money, and I'll give you the keys. It's simple—keys for money." She didn't mention anything about an application. As I drove home, my heart was pounding. I had lied to the agent: I was not looking for a house, I didn't work for an insurance company, I didn't have one child. I was working as a tester for a local fair housing group and had just witnessed discriminatory treatment. I wrote a narrative of my experience—what I was told and shown, what I observed—and submitted it to the testing coordinator. Because testing results are not shared with testers, I never knew what happened in this particular case.

This incident occurred in the midst of my field research, while I was inter-
viewing a range of government officials and housing and civil rights activists
about housing discrimination. I also talked about my work with friends. These
discussions taught me that many people don't realize that housing discrimination
remains a problem for people of color, regardless of income. Although I was sur-
prised by their ignorance, it makes sense to some extent. One might notice that a
city's neighborhoods are racially segregated, but the process of discrimination is
usually invisible to an individual home seeker. Most people have not had the
chance to see discrimination occur, as I did that afternoon in Denver. While conducting my research, I was struck by the gap between the large body of work
showing the pervasiveness of housing discrimination and the low place of housing discrimination in the public mind and on the political agenda. As a political
scientist, I knew agendas to be political creations, so I wondered what was keeping housing discrimination off of them.

The second set of pivotal experiences occurred during a four-month period
in 2000 when I attended the national conferences in Washington, D.C., of two
community reinvestment groups, National People's Action (NPA) and the
National Community Reinvestment Coalition (NCRC), and a fair housing group,
the National Fair Housing Alliance (NFHA). At each conference, I heard about
current efforts to fight housing and lending discrimination, updates on policy
implementation, and ideas for reform. But the moods, the presentations, and the
strategies were strikingly different. During NPA panels, community organizers
told of creative ways they were using the Community Reinvestment Act (CRA)
to rid neighborhoods of slumlords, they described efforts to fight the harmful
effects of FHA loans, and in one session they taught about predatory lending with
a skit featuring a lender dressed in a shark costume. They planned demonstrations to be held around the district. During the sessions, audience members
cheered successes, booed opponents, and chanted for social justice.

At the NFHA conference, attorneys and other fair housing activists talked
about filing lawsuits and calculating damages. They heard from HUD officials
and staff at Fannie Mae. In one well-attended session, a panel of attorneys dis-
cussed each fair housing case litigated that year, describing the circumstances,
the rulings, and the remedies. In another, groups receiving federal grants had the
chance to question HUD staff about problems with applications, requirements,
and the slow pace of receiving funds. One session was about grassroots organizing for fair housing. It was held in a small room, and few people were in the audience. One panelist, a woman from Montgomery, Alabama, had begun working
for a fair housing center after twelve years of organizing. "We're trying to create
a bond between fair housing and community work," she said of her group. "Fair
housing isn't a movement. There's no mass organizing. We're not in the streets
in our communities. Fair housing centers should reach out to neighborhood
alliances and religious organizations. We're not trained to go door-to- door; we
need people with those skills to go out into the community."

During the third conference, held by NCRC, staff of community development corporations and other community organizations, banking watchdog groups, and fair housing groups heard legislative briefings from congressional staff and bank regulators and attended sessions on using and understanding Home Mortgage Disclosure Act data. They talked about community economics and learned about nontraditional lending institutions such as Community Development Financial Institutions and credit unions. Buses took them to Capitol Hill to visit their representatives in Congress. In a panel on the insurance industry, activists from California and Massachusetts described how they achieved CRA-like disclosure and regulatory standards for insurance companies. They mobilized constituents to press for state legislative changes, and after years of work, they were successful. They described the importance of strong community coalitions, technical knowledge about the insurance industry, and the ability to negotiate with industry representatives. During the question and answer session, a well-known fair housing activist stood up and spoke in a chastising tone to the panelists: "You're overlooking the Fair Housing Act as a tool and as an influence over the insurance industry. There is a $100 million lawsuit pending in Virginia. Many cases have brought huge settlements that go back into the community."

These snapshots of three housing conferences illustrate the different, and separate, worlds of action that fair housing and community reinvestment advocacy have become despite their overlapping goals. As I learned more about these movements, I wanted to understand why they had taken such different directions, whether there could be value in bridging them, and what stood in the way. I suspected that the structures of fair housing and community reinvestment policies would be part of the answer. I first began to compare these policies in graduate school. I started with fair housing, writing research papers on its politics and history for a series of courses. Literature on fair housing is depressing. Authors lament the decline of advocacy, call fair housing the stepchild of the civil rights movement, and complain that the country's leaders lack the political will to tackle housing discrimination in a serious way.

The next year, when reading accounts of community reinvestment advocacy for another course, I was struck by their optimism. Case studies recounted stories of advocacy groups standing up to banks and winning, and the stories implied that this was happening across the country. I saw that both fair housing and community reinvestment movements were fighting racial inequalities in housing, but that one seemed to be thriving and the other to be declining. I wondered why, and the comparative idea was born. Once in the field, I expected to see vibrant community reinvestment movements and weak fair housing movements. Instead, both community reinvestment movements I studied were struggling. But in Minneapolis, the fair housing movement was growing, and in Denver, groups actively pursued fair housing with innovative ideas, although they relied on a small set of activists and their work was largely invisible to the general public. These unexpected findings became another puzzle I tried to unravel.

Another surprise from my field research was the realization that compliance with fair housing policy sometimes means keeping silent about the intersection of race and housing. I attended several training sessions for real estate agents on fair housing law. To a real estate agent, fair housing law is primarily a series of rules to keep in mind as one does one's job. Training often includes multiple-choice questions about what one is, and is not, allowed to do or say. During these sessions, brokers describe how they handle questions about the racial composition of neighborhoods by referring clients to the census bureau or the city government. Their logic is that the realtor should not indicate racial composition to be a legitimate determinant of housing choice, and that even beginning a discussion of race would put the agent at risk of violating the law. This contemporary approach differs significantly from the ideals of 1950s- and 1960s-era activists who founded fair housing movements with the goal of creating racially integrated neighborhoods.

One motivation for writing this book was my (perhaps naive) belief that talking about race relations and racial inequality is necessary for positive change. Although I try to keep an open mind, I am skeptical that skirting issues of race, focusing instead on other types of inequality such as economic inequality, or working for universal policies will move our nation forward. These efforts may well be part of a strategy for racial equality. Yet it seems to me that the basis for advocacy of racial justice must be open discussion about racial inequality. I hope this book contributes, even if in a small way, to that discussion.

Many dedicated activists and government officials in Washington, Denver, and Minneapolis took time to talk to me about their experiences with fair housing and community reinvestment advocacy, policy making, and policy implementation. Without their generosity, there would be no book. The staff of Denver's Housing for All, Donna Hilton, Clyda Stafford, and Terrance Turner, were especially welcoming. Walter Mondale granted me permission to consult his papers at the Minnesota Historical Society, where librarians and staff were helpful and friendly. The U.S. Department of Housing and Urban Development, the Aspen Institute's Nonprofit Sector Research Fund, and the Graduate School at the University of Colorado each provided funding for this research. I am grateful to the expert staff of the University Press of Kansas. Fred Woodward, Susan Schott, and Dorothea Anderson managed the transformation of this project from manuscript to book with care, skill, enthusiasm, and kindness.

A number of excellent scholars helped to make this book better, and I appreciate their contributions. Helen Ingram and Peter Dreier read the manuscript and offered enthusiastic and detailed suggestions for improvements. Helen, along with Anne Schneider, encouraged me to pursue this project from its first iteration as a conference paper. Faculty in the political science department at the University of Colorado also helped in the early stages and as the project became my dissertation. My adviser Susan Clarke still helps me organize my thoughts, think about data in fresh ways, and evaluate and link theories. Her willingness to read and quickly comment on numerous drafts was generous and invaluable. Sam Fitch and Anne Costain offered useful suggestions and important alternative perspectives. Rodney Hero has been a constant source of support, and our wide-ranging conversations remind me to return to big ideas. Willem van Vliet-- continues to share his depth of knowledge about housing issues, his sense of social justice, and his unique sense of humor.

Ed Goetz at the University of Minnesota introduced me to social science and to housing policy; when I was in the thick of my field research, he listened patiently as I tried to make sense of what I was learning. At Rutgers-Newark, Kim DaCosta Holton and Max Herman commented on repeated drafts of the prospectus, helping me to conceptualize the project as a book. My colleagues in the Department of Political Science also have been supportive. In Boulder, Judy Ball worked quickly to produce precise transcriptions of my interviews. In Newark, Katalin Dancsi offered research assistance during the final stages of manuscript preparation.

During my field research in Minneapolis, Marilou and Mark Cheple, Sue and Gerry Weisberg, and Suzanne Bring provided homes away from home. Jeff Henig and his family offered a spare bedroom in Washington. Michele Betsill kept my spirits up during another D.C. trip. Sarah Henderson's empathy, healthy perspective, and good humor kept me going from the early stages of writing the dissertation to the final manuscript revisions. All members of my family have been consistently understanding and caring. My father tolerated unreturned phone calls, my mother followed instructions not to ask about my book and provided a unique clipping service on fair housing, and Dana supplied cheerful office decorations at key moments. I am most grateful to B., whose unwavering encouragement and love sustain me.

1

Housing Discrimination: Problems, Politics, Policies

In a Chicago public housing project, LaJoe Rivers and her young children find that home and neighborhood pose daily challenges to their survival.[1] Few businesses or services exist in the predominantly poor, black community, with its overcrowded, fiscally strapped schools and frequent eruption of gunfire from warring gangs. Their apartment amounts to "a dark dank cave" with cinder block walls, rusted kitchen cabinets, a bathtub hot-water faucet that does not turn off, and a heating system with broken controls.[2] The family strategically places furniture near windows to stop stray bullets, and the children know to run to the hallway and stay low when they hear the sound of guns. Farther south in the same city, Mary Pattillo-McCoy describes the daily lives of middle-class African-American families in Groveland, a neighborhood that "buffers" middle-class white families from poor black families.[3] Groveland youth navigate conflicting examples of life choices. Adults work as teachers, entrepreneurs, bureaucrats, and social workers, sometimes holding two jobs or juggling work and school to get ahead. Drug dealers and gang members drive fancy cars and wear stylish clothing, but also perpetrate or become victims of violent crime. The juxtaposition is less common in white neighborhoods, leading Pattillo-McCoy to describe black middle-class life as a unique blend of "privilege and peril."

Perhaps these are worst-case examples of the racial segregation and concentrated poverty that millions of people experience in American cities. But in the twenty-first century, as the U.S. population becomes more racially and ethnically diverse than ever before, white people continue to live in different neighborhoods than people of color. These divisions matter because in the United States, housing shapes life chances and prospects for social mobility; one's neighborhood influences where one attends school and looks for work. Regardless of income, people of color continue to live in neighborhoods with lower quality services and schools.[4] Thus for families such as LaJoe's, housing is a trap

1

instead of a vehicle to success. In our society, homeownership is "a powerful symbol of independence and civic virtue, of family life and personal success";[5] it also represents the primary source of wealth for most Americans. But for millions of families, housing is a far cry from the American dream. Why? I argue that national policies against housing discrimination weaken local advocacy groups. As a result, local government agendas are not likely to include housing discrimination, little enforcement of existing law occurs, and racial segregation continues.

The story I tell begins in Washington, where legislators crafted two national solutions to housing discrimination, the 1968 Fair Housing Act and the 1977 Community Reinvestment Act. But housing is also a local matter, so my story moves to advocacy groups in two cities. It turns out that national policies set up hurdles for local housing advocates. I describe the many ways in which these laws stack the deck against local housing groups, but I also show that groups can cultivate community resources to overcome the difficulties. My comparative study of housing advocacy in Minneapolis and Denver shows some of the ways in which this process unfolds. In Minneapolis, local fair housing groups beat the odds, succeeding in developing political strength. They pushed their agenda much farther than groups in Denver did. Yet community reinvestment movements floundered in both cities, first gaining but then losing influence over local government and local banks. In sum, my analysis shows that national policies have critical, though not uniform, effects on local advocates struggling to achieve equality in housing. I argue that understanding this link between national policy and local groups sheds light on our failure to reduce discrimination and segregation.

More generally, this book identifies the pathways through which public policies shape political landscapes and the prospects and capacities of groups acting within them. My research focuses on three specific and important aspects of the relationship between policies and politics. It looks across levels of government to analyze how national policies interact with urban politics. It examines how public policies transform advocacy groups. Some groups become stronger when they use a public policy, while others become weaker. These interactions are particularly important to examine in our contemporary context of devolution, marked by government's increasing reliance on nonprofits for policy implementation. Finally, the cases I examine here demonstrate more generally how inequality becomes rooted in the American political system. By tracing the policy process from legislative struggles through implementation, I show that when legislators strike compromises to win votes for policies that benefit weak groups, such as racial minorities or poor people, these compromises can have long-lasting harmful political and social consequences for those groups. As our society grows increasingly diverse and polarized, understanding the constraints our political system places on marginalized groups becomes especially critical.

HOUSING INEQUALITY: DIMENSIONS OF THE PROBLEM

Local advocacy groups working to decrease inequalities in housing are neither as numerous nor as strong as they could be. Whether this deficiency is a cause for concern depends on one's beliefs about the prevalence of discrimination. Many people think that racial discrimination in housing markets occurs infrequently. During my field research, some respondents expressed the belief that income drives opportunities and choices in the housing market regardless of one's race or ethnicity, or that having dark skin constrains housing opportunities only for the poor. Thus, a Latino city official in Denver said, "If you can afford a $250,000 to $300,000 apartment, like these condos that are being built [in downtown Denver], they'll grab you in a minute." A white civil rights professional said that although there were impoverished neighborhoods in Denver with large black populations, those black families who could afford to live in the suburbs were able to do so. "If the minority, instead of moving with the horde, has enough money to jump it, I think there's not very much discrimination." Several middle-class African-American professionals I interviewed echoed the sentiment of a black fair housing trainer: "I live where I want to live."

Other respondents were more convinced of the prevalence of racial discrimination in housing. A longtime African-American activist in Minneapolis said, "On the one hand, you have all of the good will of people who want to do the right thing. And then you have on the other hand those deep-seated fears that keep a community from being truly integrated and healthy." As a black civil rights professional in Denver put it, "Racism is still alive and well, even here." A white fair housing trainer in Minneapolis described her sense that encounters with discrimination occur "on a daily basis" for racial minorities: "A lot of people in the majority who have a fairly active social conscience really believe we've addressed the problems and they're pretty minor. I think in reality that's not the case."

Survey data show that people of color are more likely than white people to believe that discrimination continues to shape life chances, regardless of one's individual efforts to get ahead.[6] Hochschild found that middle-class blacks were less likely to think that individually they had suffered from discrimination but more likely to think that, in general, blacks frequently encounter such treatment.[7] A recent survey in the Washington, D.C., metro area found that 58 percent of white respondents thought that blacks and whites had equal opportunities in the housing market, but only 16 percent of black respondents thought so.[8] Blacks were three times as likely to report that they had experienced discrimination while seeking housing and twice as likely to report knowing someone who had experienced discrimination.

The United States does not have a comprehensive system to monitor the levels and forms of housing discrimination, but when studies are done, they find evidence of discrimination. Research consistently demonstrates that discrimination occurs at every stage of the housing search process, from looking for a home to securing financing to acquiring insurance. Studies document the negative consequences of this treatment for racial minorities.

The Prevalence of Housing Discrimination

A large body of research shows that discriminatory practices occur frequently and persistently in all U.S. cities. Current research on housing discrimination relies primarily on audits, paired-comparison studies in which individuals similar in all ways but race or ethnicity seek to buy or rent a home. These "testers" complete reports about their experiences—how they were treated and the information they were given. Comparing these reports can identify differential and discriminatory treatment. Audit reports read like X rays, showing what is not visible to any one home seeker. Below are a few examples from an audit in selected Minnesota communities:

> White tester was shown several units. The African American was shown only one unit.

> White tester was offered a $25 discount on the rent for the first six months as "food for thought." African American was not offered a discount. White tester was given an application. African American was not given an application.

> African American was required to show ID for "security reasons." White tester was not required to show ID. White tester was told that "we would love to have you live here." . . . African American was not so encouraged.[9]

Reviewing results of a 1989 national audit and other studies, Yinger reports that when looking for housing, minorities tend to learn about fewer housing units than whites.[10] Agents are less likely to ask them about their housing needs but more likely to ask about their income. Minorities are less likely to hear positive comments about the units they see. Agents are less likely to invite them to call back or to place a follow-up call to them, and are less likely to offer special incentives such as reduced security deposits or one month's free rent. Although blacks almost never hear negative comments about a neighborhood, one in four whites will hear negative comments when viewing a unit in a neighborhood that is at least 50 percent black. Indeed, minorities and whites often are shown housing in different locations. Agents tend to show blacks homes in neighborhoods with higher percentages of black residents or in neighborhoods closer to largely black neighborhoods. Houses in largely white neighborhoods typically are marketed through different channels than homes in black or integrated neighborhoods.

Yinger concludes that a minority home seeker visiting several agents will probably encounter discrimination at least once. He summarized the large body of research this way: "African American and Hispanic households are very likely to encounter discrimination when they search for housing. This discrimination

occurs throughout the country; it severely limits the information minority households receive about available housing; and it adds annoyance, complexity, and
expense to their housing search process. The evidence to back up these claims is
overwhelming."[11] HUD has sponsored audit studies in more than twenty large
metro areas every ten years since the late 1970s. The 1989 study led to the esti-
mate that 54 percent of racial minorities face discrimination of one kind or another when seeking housing.[12] Results of the 1999 audits showed again that
black and Hispanic home seekers experience adverse treatment in more than half
of their visits to sales and leasing agents. Yet consistent adverse treatment is estimated to occur about 22 percent of the time, a lower figure than that reported
in 1989. The study found that Hispanic renters faced the highest prospect of discrimination, and that geographic steering of prospective buyers based on their
race occurred more often than in previous studies.[13]

Racial and ethnic minorities also experience discrimination in acquiring
mortgages; studies document significant gaps between whites' and minorities'
access to mortgage credit.[14] Racial differences in loan denial rates have been
found across all markets and loan types.[15] A 2002 study of lending patterns in
sixty-eight cities found blacks rejected for mortgage loans at twice the rate of
whites, and Latinos at one and a half the rate.[16] One well-known Boston study
found that blacks and Latinos were 82 percent more likely to be denied a loan
than comparable white applicants.[17] Evidence exists that secondary market enti-
ties (such as Fannie Mae and Freddie Mac) disproportionately buy loans made to
white borrowers,[18] and that their underwriting guidelines may be biased against
minority borrowers.[19]

Studies identify numerous forms of differential treatment in mortgage lending. In research prepared for fair lending litigation, the Department of Justice dis-
covered that loan officers advised white applicants on how to provide
explanations for credit flaws and told them how to reduce their debt-to-income
ratios, whereas they did not counsel black applicants in such matters. In this particular case, whites with credit flaws were more likely to receive mortgages than
their black counterparts.[20]

Discrimination in loan pricing also occurs. Investigating the records of one
California lender, the Department of Justice found that black women paid much
higher loan costs than any other group of borrowers. More generally, the subprime lending market, in which lenders charge more points and higher interest
rates, receives a disproportionate share of minority mortgage applications.[21]
Such lending, where loan rates can reach 30 to 35 percent, also occurs disproportionately in inner-city areas; many inner-city residents have paid subprime
lending rates their whole lives.[22] Finally, disproportionate numbers of minorities
have government-insured FHA loans, which require lower down payments but
ultimately are more costly for borrowers.[23]

Some evidence suggests that discrimination occurs in other sectors of the
housing industry such as homeowners and private mortgage insurance and home

appraisals. The availability and cost of insurance as well as the location of agent offices can be associated with the racial composition of a neighborhood.[24] A 1991 nine-city audit study found that about 53 percent of the time, minority testers, or testers with property in minority neighborhoods, encountered practices or policies that denied or restricted their access to homeowners insurance.[25] Although less research exists on the private mortgage insurance industry and the appraisal industry, limited studies have found evidence of differential treatment.[26]

Linking Discrimination to Inequality

The unfavorable treatment that racial and ethnic minorities receive because of their skin color or background violates principles of justice and thus is problematic on its own. Discrimination also creates and magnifies other inequalities across racial groups. Housing discrimination contributes to lower levels of wealth among minority households, to racially segregated housing patterns, and to restricted life chances for those minority families trapped in declining inner-city neighborhoods.

Because homeownership is the most important means of accumulating wealth in American society, those with constrained access to homeownership are disadvantaged.[27] Although minority homeownership rates have risen in the past several years, wide differentials remain, with 74 percent of whites owning their homes compared to 48 and 46 percent for black and Latino households.[28] Black-owned homes tend to have lower values, thus black people are less able to use their homes as collateral for business or education loans.[29] And since wealth is passed down from generation to generation, restricted access to homeownership among blacks and Latinos has intergenerational consequences.[30]

Discrimination is one of a range of factors that contribute to patterns of racial residential segregation[31] and concentrated poverty. From 1970 to 1990, the number of high-poverty areas in metropolitan areas doubled.[32] Racial and ethnic minorities are more likely than whites to live in these places, where more than 40 percent of the population earn incomes below the poverty line. Of the 3.9 million poor residents of high-poverty neighborhoods in 1990, 56 percent were black, 26 percent were Latino, and 18 percent were non-Latino white.[33] Racial segregation cuts across income levels, however. Today, a black person is likely to live in a neighborhood where 51 percent of the households are black, 33 percent are white, 11 percent are Latino, and 3 percent are Asian. This distribution contrasts with the typical white person's neighborhood, where 80 percent of households are white, 7 percent are black, 8 percent are Hispanic, and 4 percent are Asian.[34] The black-white segregation index for metropolitan areas in 2000 was 65, meaning that on average, 65 percent of black people would have to move to achieve more even housing patterns.[35] This level has dropped somewhat over the past twenty years, but at a slow rate. Asians and Hispanics are less residentially segregated from whites, although their segregation increased between 1980 and 2000.[36] Whether they live in cities or suburbs, these groups are more isolated from whites today than they were twenty years ago.

Segregated living generates inequality because residential location affects children's opportunities to attend quality schools and adults' access to high-paying jobs, both of which contribute to a person's ultimate earning potential. Segregated housing patterns thus contribute to education, employment, and income disparities between groups.[37] Again, many people of color have difficulty accessing quality neighborhoods, despite their income levels. Logan reports that white and Asian people can translate higher incomes into better neighborhoods, whereas black and Hispanic people cannot; the gap in neighborhood quality between these groups grew during the 1990s, especially so between affluent blacks and Hispanics compared to whites.[38] An indirect effect on life chances emerges from the way segregation influences consumer perceptions and judgments about neighborhoods.[39] These judgments have tangible and often self-fulfilling effects when they depress property values, guide development decisions, influence residential choice, and ultimately shape attitudes toward social policy.[40]

LAWMAKERS AND ADVOCATES
RESPONDING TO HOUSING INEQUALITY

Despite widespread and persistent inequalities in housing, few elected officials focus on these problems. Indeed, housing issues create dilemmas for elected officials because they raise value conflicts and involve powerful industry and constituency interests. As one state legislator told me, "Housing is the most visceral issue in American politics. I don't think there's anything that's even close to it. Particularly when the issue of race becomes involved, there's nothing that even approaches it." Housing discrimination violates principles of equal opportunity and fair treatment, core aspects of American political culture. But regulating housing can threaten the individualist, liberal traditions of our political culture, which revere individual initiative, bootstrapping, and self-sufficiency, and which highly prize free-market processes and property rights. Despite longstanding government intervention in U.S. housing markets,[41] policies that would increase or change regulations to secure benefits for marginalized groups will always be a hard sell. The real estate and financial services industries are among the most wealthy and politically organized in Washington. Each has well-established trade associations and political action committees, and major firms have their own lobbyists in the capital as well. Because banks and real estate offices can be found everywhere, these industries reach into the home districts of all elected officials. Thus, this is not an industry where some officials may be immune to political pressure. Finally, the finance–insurance–real estate sector is the top contributor of campaign funds in the country. Its PACs and individual donors contributed $305 million during the 2000 election season; since

1990, the sector has given $1 billion, split between the Republican and Democratic parties.[42]

Legislators concerned about housing equality have twice overcome these formidable obstacles by enacting the Fair Housing Act in 1968 and the Community Reinvestment Act in 1977. The Fair Housing Act prohibits racial discrimination in housing, establishing a civil right to nondiscriminatory treatment. The bill faced strong opposition even with statutory precedents guaranteeing civil rights in voting, public accommodations, employment, and education. Supporters of fair housing still expected it to fail. Legislators, activists, and scholars, then and now, consider passage miraculous, even of what they judge to be a relatively weak statute; strengthening amendments took twenty years to pass.[43] By contrast, Congress adopted the Community Reinvestment Act (CRA) without incident. This law, which addresses racial discrimination only by stealth, seeks to reduce discrimination against neighborhoods (redlining) by stating that lenders have an affirmative responsibility to serve their entire communities, including the low-income people living in them. In practice, this means minority neighborhoods receive attention.

The social movements pressing for fair housing and for community reinvestment are historically linked together. Fair housing activism emerged in response to the rapid racial transition of neighborhoods that occurred across U.S. cities, especially in the postwar period. Neighborhood activists identified the real estate practices that drove this transition—e.g., racial covenants, racial steering, blockbusting—effectively keeping blacks out of developing suburbs and confined to transitional or black neighborhoods. Legislators finally responded with the 1968 law. As fair housing's limited impact became clear, the community reinvestment movement emerged in black and integrated (transitional) neighborhoods. Residents worried about the declining property values and neighborhood quality of their inner-city neighborhoods, and community activists recognized that banks' redlining practices contributed to this decline. Banks (and appraisers and insurers) deemed minority and integrated neighborhoods to be poor credit risks and denied applications for mortgage and home improvement loans to people living in them. Residents' reliance on more expensive alternative sources of credit strapped household finances, and the inability to borrow money to pay for home repairs meant that neighborhood structures deteriorated. Activists developed strategies to limit redlining. Legislators responded with the 1977 Community Reinvestment Act. Although CRA formally targets low-income rather than minority or racially integrated neighborhoods, advocates have always been motivated by concern about racial, as well as class, discrimination.[44]

Fair housing and community reinvestment laws set in motion a range of programs and activities, and subsequent amendments, designed to reduce discrimination. Since 1968, progress is evident. Most Americans know about civil rights protections in the housing market, and HUD receives thousands of complaints every year.[45] The Department of Justice's litigation in fair lending cases has brought $33.4 million in relief; its fair housing cases have brought $1.2 million in civil penalties and $6.3 million in relief to individuals; from 1990 to 1998, non-profit fair housing organizations have worked on nearly 1,400 private lawsuits, resulting in a total of $116 million in recovery.[46] The most recent national audit study found a lower incidence of discriminatory treatment than a similar study found ten years earlier. Home loans to minority and low-income borrowers are rising, as are homeownership rates. Studies link CRA to regulated banks' higher rates of lending and service to low- and moderate-income people and neighborhoods.

HOUSING POLICIES MAKE HOUSING POLITICS

Despite signs of progress, why do housing discrimination and segregation remain serious problems? Political observers and analysts typically take one of two approaches to answering such questions. They focus either on the content of public policies or on the balance of power between the groups pressing for reform and the groups who are satisfied with the status quo. That is, analysts argue that policies are too flawed to diminish a problem, or they point out that the interests who would benefit are too weak to press for change. Along these lines, housing scholars and activists lodge many complaints against fair housing and community reinvestment policies. For example, they note that fair housing law places the enforcement burden most heavily on victims, who may not know when they have experienced discrimination because of the subtle tactics that housing agents use. They point to a lack of confidence in the enforcement system and its relatively slow speed. In the case of community reinvestment law, researchers and activists point to the law's partial coverage of the financial services industry and the reluctance of regulatory agencies to implement the law aggressively. To explain why lawmakers do not strengthen these weak laws, observers typically lament the lack of political will on the part of elected officials reluctant to confront the housing and banking industries in Washington as well as perhaps the majority of white Americans.

These explanations for the low political salience of housing inequality, and the consequent persistence of housing problems, are valid. In part, discrimination persists because we have imperfect laws and we lack the political will to improve them. In a democratic political system, without strong voices pressing for change, little change is likely to occur. But I argue that we have missed a key link between weak policy and weak interests: fair housing and community reinvestment laws actually erode political will. That is, they weaken the actors who use the laws to work for change. Generating political pressure to improve flawed policies therefore becomes harder over time.

My analysis focuses on the connection between policies and advocacy by closely examining policy designs and tracing how they influence advocates' work and political strength. Policy designs are the frameworks of ideas and instruments contained in every public policy. They capture ideas about problems and groups of people, and these ideas guide how a policy distributes benefits and burdens. This theoretical approach places policy designs at the center of analysis: Designs "capture" prior political processes, then channel future political battles in particular directions. Theorists call attention to the ways that ideas interact with interests in the policy formation process, and then to how policy institutionalizes sets of interests and ideas as it distributes resources, thereby structuring the implementation and advocacy that follows.[47] Using a policy design approach brings out the irony that a particular package of ideas and tools, forged to gain votes in a specific political context, has enduring consequences as it shapes politics and problem solving for decades to come. When I bring this approach to the study of housing policies, I shed new light on housing politics and show the political barriers two policies create for advocacy groups. Over time, groups fighting housing inequality grow weak unless they find ways to beat the odds.

The policy design perspective fits within a series of important philosophical and theoretical developments in political science and policy studies. Postmodern or postpositivist work calls attention to the role of discourse in political life. Politics consists of competing efforts to make meaning as much as to win votes. Indeed, the pursuit and exercise of power include constructing images and stories and deploying symbols. Critical approaches to political and policy studies explore how government and policy create and maintain "systems of privilege, domination, and quiescence among those who are the most oppressed."[48] Scholars take an explicitly normative stance, exploring ways to make political life truly democratic. Schneider and Ingram develop the policy design perspective in these directions. They theorize that policy designs reflect efforts to advance certain values and interests, that they reflect dominant social constructions of knowledge and groups of people as well as power relations. Moreover, policy designs influence not merely policy implementation but also political mobilization and the nature of democracy. They see policies as "the principal tools in securing the democratic promise for all people"[49] and argue for evaluating policy designs not only on the basis of their effectiveness at mitigating social problems but also in terms of their impact on democratic citizenship—the degree and the nature of political participation policies inspire, and whether policy exacerbates or remedies social divisions.

Besides incorporating key ideas from postmodern and critical policy analysis, the policy design perspective answers calls for integrative approaches to policy research. Lasswell and other policy scientists have consistently emphasized the importance of integrative approaches to policy scholarship,[50] and political scientists also have begun to acknowledge the limitations of analysis that focuses exclusively on interests, ideas, or institutions.[51] As Heclo puts it, "Interests tell institutions what to do; institutions tell ideas how to survive; ideas tell interests what to mean," so partial analyses produce partial explanations.[52] The policy design perspective offers a framework to guide empirical research that integrates these three dimensions: Ideas and interests interact within an institutional setting to produce a policy design. This policy design then becomes an institution in its own right, structuring the future interaction of ideas and interests.

Core Elements of Policy Design Analysis

In their book *Policy Design for Democracy,* Schneider and Ingram articulate the elements of policy design analysis. They theorize an evolutionary process, from predecision struggles, to the choice of a design, to the design's impact.[53]

Policy Designs. Central to the policy design perspective is the notion that every public policy contains a design—a framework of ideas and instruments—to be identified and analyzed. Rather than a "random and chaotic product of a political process," policies have underlying patterns and logics.[54] For Dahl and Lindblom writing in 1953, an emphasis on policy designs challenged the prevailing focus of political scholarship on ideologies as critical aspects of political systems. They argued that broad debates about the merits of capitalism versus socialism were less important to the well-being of society than was careful consideration of the myriad designs (what they termed "techniques") that might be used to regulate the economy and to advance particular social values.[55] Later scholars advocated studying policy designs as a corrective to implementation studies that held bureaucratic systems responsible for policy failure. These design theorists argued for looking farther back in the causal chain, noting that original design processes and the designs themselves were primarily responsible for the outcomes of policy implementation.

Policy design analysis conceptualizes policies as institutional structures and therefore is linked to institutionalist theories of politics. Institutional scholars analyze the effects of laws, constitutions, and the organization of the political process on political behavior and choices. They argue that institutions shape actors' preferences and strategies by recognizing the legitimacy of certain claims over others and by offering particular sorts of opportunities for voicing complaints.[56] Schneider and Ingram offer a comprehensive framework of the institutional elements of policies, suggesting that policy designs consist of goals, target groups, agents, an implementation structure, tools, rules, rationales, and assumptions.[57]

Policy-Making Process: Context and Agency. To understand and explain why a policy has a particular design, one must examine the process leading to its selection. Here, policy design analysis draws on institutional and ideational theories as well as theories of stages in the political process, such as agenda setting, and theories of decision making, such as bounded rationality. Policy making occurs in a specific context, marked by distinctive institutions and ideas. Institutional arenas, whether Congress, the courts, or other venues, come with rules, norms, and procedures that affect actors' choices and strategies. Additionally, policy making takes place at a particular moment in time, marked by particular dominant ideas related to the policy issue, to affected groups, to the proper role of government, and so on. These ideas will influence actors' arguments in favor of particular solutions, and their perceptions and preferences when they take specific policy decisions.

Analysis of a particular context might lead to broad predictions about the policy design that will emerge from it. But because designs have so many "working parts" (goals, problem definitions, target groups, tools, agents, and so on), such analysis cannot specify in advance the particular package of dimensions that actors will build at a particular point in time. Policy making has a human side, too, in that actors might reimagine the meaning of a context or reframe the structure of opportunities as they attempt to create policy solutions to pressing problems. In considering agency—leadership, creativity, debate, and coalition-building—we can turn to the insights of agenda-setting and problem-definition literature, which characterize policy making as interested actors struggling over ideas.[58] We thus examine not only who participates but also whether actors succeed in expanding or restricting such participation, and how this mobilization affects the policy choice.[59] Adding attention to the problem definitions that these actors hold offers a richer understanding of what political support and "interest" mean in a given policy process.[60]

Part of the agenda-setting process involves delimiting the alternative policy designs that decision makers consider prior to making a choice. Some see the process of generating alternatives, rather than the policy choice itself, as the crux of problem-solving activity.[61] The set of alternatives bounds choice by focusing decision makers' attention on a limited number of attributes of the policy problem. Humans' bounded rationality ensures that actors will take into account only a limited range of a problem's dimensions;[62] actors engaged in agenda-setting essentially seek to control which of these dimensions will receive attention.

Consequences of Public Policy. Policy designs act as institutional engines of change, and analysis can trace how their dimensions influence political action. Policy implementation distributes benefits to some groups while imposing burdens on others. In doing so, designs establish incentives for some groups to participate in public life and offer them resources for doing so. Other groups receive negative messages from policies. For example, if benefits are distributed in a stigmatizing way, individuals may be intimidated by government, withdraw from public life, or feel alienated from it.[63] This approach is consistent with arguments about policy feedback, which suggest a number of ways through which policies shape the course of future politics. Groups receiving benefits from government programs are likely to organize to maintain and expand them. Mobilization is facilitated when policies provide resources to interest groups such as funding, access to decision makers, and information.[64] Consequently, target groups whose understanding of the problem differs from the one in the policy or who lack the expertise needed to use a policy's administrative procedures will not receive the same degree of support or legitimacy from the policy; they will have greater barriers to overcome in order to achieve their goals. Another element of policy feedback is what Pierson calls "lock-in effects."[65] Once a choice of policy is taken, the cost of adopting alternative solutions to the problem increases. A policy persists because the investments in its programs and commitments to its ideas cumulate over time.

Schneider and Ingram are particularly concerned about the impacts of policy designs that result from "degenerative" political processes.[66] During such processes, political actors sort target populations into "deserving" and "undeserving" groups as justification for channeling benefits or punishments to them. Although political gain can be achieved this way, policies that result from such arguments undermine democracy and hinder problem solving. The language and the resource allocation stigmatize disadvantaged groups, reinforce stereotypes, and send the message—to group members and to the broader public—that government does not value them.

Building on the Policy Design Perspective: Urban Politics and Social Movements

When applying the policy design framework to policies aimed at housing discrimination, two limitations of the approach emerge. Community reinvestment and fair housing are policies that cross government scales. That is, they are national policies governing the operation of housing markets, which are inherently local arenas. In addition, these policies rely on nonprofit advocacy groups for enforcement; indeed, observers credit such groups with enforcing the laws in the absence of vigorous government action. The policy design perspective considers neither the role of crossing scales nor the role of advocacy groups in mediating the consequences of policy designs. That is, the model anticipates that all groups, regardless of their location, will respond to policy incentives in the same way. And it ignores the role that nonprofit groups play in conditioning policy's impact on target groups. This book shows that the policy design framework can be fruitfully extended to incorporate intergovernmental relationships and to understand the behavior of advocacy groups.

Incorporating Scale. National policy designs provide an initial set of opportunities and constraints—a playing field—for local action and therefore represent a starting point for inquiry. But in the American political system, national policies cross scales when state and local governments implement them. In a federalist system, local conditions are likely to affect local response to national policies. As a particular national policy meets a variety of local contexts, we would expect to see variation in group activity. Urban scholars have long studied the connections between national policy and group action. Mollenkopf argues that federal-level political actors used national urban policy to reconfigure local-level political coalitions, which in turn gave rise to new forms of conflict and changed social conditions in U.S. cities.[67] More recently, Gregory documents the impact that War on Poverty programs had on African-American political activism in one New York neighborhood.[68] Other work examines variations in how cities use federal programs as well as how they respond to external constraints such as economic restructuring and globalization.[69]

Scholars of federalism and implementation also show how local factors mediate implementation of federal policy. Derthick, for example, finds that "domestic programs are neither 'federal' nor 'local,' but a blend of the two," this "blend" arising from "a process of adjustment to local interests."[70] Ingram describes implementation of federal policy as a bargaining process between national and state actors.[71] These metaphors imply a dialogue between political groups across national and local scales. On the one hand, as Schneider and Ingram theorize, national policy's power to structure local action will reflect its design and the actions of federal-level agents, e.g., the level of resources appropriated, the nature of the tools, the level of discretion that agents have. On the other hand, as urban and federalism scholars reveal, national policy's power also depends on how it fits into the existing political landscape. This book therefore begins with an investigation of national policy-making processes, then moves to case studies of advocacy in two cities. Incorporating national and local analyses leads to insights about how national policies interact with local politics.

Incorporating Advocacy Organizations. In this era of devolution, local-level actors implement or enforce many national policies, from social service programs to housing programs to transportation policies. Increasingly, nonprofit organizations rather than local governments take on these roles.[72] Yet policy design theory focuses on policy's impact on target, or social, groups—the groups that policies are intended to benefit or burden. When government does not allocate resources directly to groups, nonprofits often perform this task. How policy designs influence the capacity and orientation of nonprofits is therefore a critical issue.

Scholarship on nonprofit organizations recognizes that government importantly shapes the development of these groups, attributing the growth of the nonprofit sector to a range of postwar government policies.[73] Studies also document the threats that government contracting arrangements pose to an independent nonprofit sector.[74] They explore how the tax code and other regulations shape group behavior, including their goals, strategies, and advocacy activities.[75] Social movement scholars also do empirical and theoretical work on the interaction of policy and advocacy. Adherents of the "resource mobilization" school have long recognized that the state can facilitate or impede advocates' ability to mobilize resources into a movement; policy is one of the mechanisms through which this mobilization occurs. There are many ways in which the "architecture" of a policy might affect a social movement.[76] Policies can provide a target for movements, something to focus their opposition on; the administration of a policy provides specific sites for protests or arenas for action.[77]

Another way of thinking about sites is the notion of "habitats," safe spaces for particular ideas within mainstream institutions.[78] Policies inspire movements to adopt certain strategies; draft policy supplied cards that could be burned, files that could be defaced, and so on.[79] Policies also can create movements by delineating a target group for government benefits or burdens. Alternatively, policy can divide groups or silence them as it allocates resources.[80] In sum, policies constitute an important source of resources for social movement organizations and affect their ability to mobilize the resources into effective initiatives for change. Policy design analysis can place these insights in a framework that enables comparative, multidimensional analysis of public policies' impact on nonprofit groups. It encourages attention to the impact on groups of a range of policy elements, from the more obvious funding mechanisms, to the tools and arenas policy offers, to the intangible problem definitions that they promote.

POLICY DESIGNS AND THE STRUGGLE FOR HOUSING EQUALITY

Evaluating the activities of local fair housing and community reinvestment movements is important because while critics diagnose the flaws of fair housing and community reinvestment policies and their federal implementation, few studies systematically analyze political action on fair housing and community reinvestment, particularly by advocacy organizations. Yet these groups not only mediate policies' effectiveness at solving problems but also take part in the struggles to change policy designs.

Fair housing and community reinvestment policies offer an ideal opportunity to consider how policies shape politics, because they share broad goals but differ in design. That is, each aims to address housing discrimination, but with different institutional structures; they define the problem differently and offer different incentives and tools to local actors. Thus, I use a comparative research design to analyze the development of the two policies, and their impact on local advocacy groups. To date, scholars have not empirically applied the full policy design framework, stretching from the genesis of policy through to its consequences.

The Plan of the Book

The book has two sections, first focusing on national policy processes, then on patterns of local advocacy.

Crafting National Policies. In Chapters 2 and 3 I compare the legislative processes leading to the Fair Housing and Community Reinvestment Acts and analyze the policy designs contained within them. Legislators fighting for fair housing and CRA acted in dramatically different political contexts and developed distinctive arguments to support their positions. Fair housing supporters faced a hostile environment marked by urban riots, black militancy, and a powerful conservative coalition in Congress. To combat opponents' portrayal of blacks as lawless rioters, supporters created a new target group of beneficiaries: a small cadre of deserving black professionals. They argued that fair housing would allow only this relatively small group to escape the ghettos and move to white neighborhoods, since "ability to pay" would continue to govern the housing market. By contrast, supporters of community reinvestment held powerful positions in Congress enabling them to keep the issue out of the limelight and thus avoid conflict. Part of this strategy was to avoid explicit discussion of the low-income people and the racial minorities whom the law would help. Instead, they emphasized that deteriorating neighborhoods—places—would benefit and presented CRA as a minor adjustment to existing banking laws that would not burden banks or banking regulators. These divergent legislative strategies shaped the policies that emerged.

In Chapter 3 the perspective shifts from that of the lawmakers who enacted antidiscrimination policy to that of local advocacy groups working to solve housing problems in their cities. I analyze how each policy's distinctive resource mix might influence the types of groups who participate, how they define discrimination, their actions, and their political relationships. For example, fair housing groups are likely to be legal specialists who investigate individual claims of discrimination in the private housing sector. Few policy resources exist to pursue housing integration or to fight discrimination in the public housing sector, so we should see less activity along these lines. In general, fair housing groups will partner with government, though in a relatively unstable relationship. On the other hand, community reinvestment advocacy groups are likely to be multi-issue organizations that define discrimination in terms of lending rates to specific neighborhoods. This place-based definition invites the use of community organizing strategies because groups can show neighborhood residents that they have a common interest in working for change. Groups can try to change lending practices by intervening in the banking regulatory process, but because CRA does not give them a formal role, and because regulatory agencies are traditionally allied with the industry, groups are likely to have an adversarial relationship to government.

Analyzing Local Action. In Chapters 4 and 5 I draw from extensive field research in Denver and Minneapolis to outline the history of advocacy on fair housing and community reinvestment at the local level and to analyze whether and how groups responded to national policies. These are interesting cases because scholars have paid little attention to them as sites of racial struggles, even though racial minorities experience problems related to discrimination. Instead, housing is well studied in older, industrialized cities with deeply segregated populations, such as

Chicago, Cleveland, or Detroit. Nonetheless, housing problems exist everywhere; discrimination in housing and mortgage lending, and redlining, have been documented in both cities.[81] In both places, low-income blacks experience segregation most severely, and affordable housing is concentrated in the central cities of both metro areas.[82] The cities are well matched as cases in terms of population size and levels of economic growth. They each have a history of progressive economic development and social policies and of multi- or biracial political coalitions. Yet housing advocates in Minneapolis contend with a newly multiethnic city, while Denver has historically been home to black, white, and Latino people.

In both cities, groups used some policy resources, but not others. In Minneapolis, I found a growing fair housing movement focused on public housing; in Denver, a small, stable movement focused on private housing. The community reinvestment movements in both cities grew, then shrunk. An initial burst of activity and achievement was followed by the disintegration of coalitions and the decline of oppositional politics.

In Chapter 6 I build a comparative analysis of fair housing movements and community reinvestment movements from the case studies. The analysis paints a more complex picture than extant portraits of the fair housing and community reinvestment movements, which depict the fair housing movement as stagnant in contrast to a vibrant community reinvestment movement. I find that community reinvestment movements face critical obstacles to success, especially over the long term, and that fair housing movements can achieve local strength in particular contexts.

The chapter confirms that each policy design corresponds to a distinct advocacy movement in the cities, and that community reinvestment and fair housing advocates rarely work together. I examine differences in the fair housing movements in Minneapolis and Denver, tracing these to local contextual factors that support different sorts of goals and activities. The cities vary in the recent growth of minority and poor populations, in the liberal or conservative state political context, and in the presence or absence of historic fair housing networks. These factors explain why a small set of fair housing advocates in Denver work to protect civil rights in private-sector housing through partnerships and educational strategies rather than litigation. But in Minneapolis, advocates work to increase publicly subsidized affordable housing through strategies of mass mobilization and confrontation with government, both in the courts and the legislative process.

I suggest that CRA's set of policy resources induces movement activity but hinders groups from sustaining it. Its focus on places and its lack of specificity in defining "community reinvestment" enable different kinds of advocacy groups to form coalitions in pursuit of housing equality. When banks respond to some groups and not to others, coalitions break apart and groups' different definitions of "reinvestment" become evident. For some groups, bank loans for affordable housing constitute "reinvestment," but other groups want low-cost banking services for the poor. The lack of a distinct and explicit role for community groups in the policy design means that government and banks can portray groups as troublemakers when they intervene in the regulatory process.

Struggling for Housing Equality in the Twenty-First Century. Chapter 7 steps back from the empirical details to reflect on their broader implications. I consider the political consequences of policies against housing discrimination, arguing that these are equally important to the more technical aspects of fair housing and community reinvestment laws. I also suggest that compromises struck to enact a law can negatively affect advocacy for social justice over the long term. This research contrasts theoretically with more typical analyses of interest-group politics, which focus on groups' internal resources to explain their activity. Although group resources certainly are important in housing politics, I argue that structural factors such as public policies do much to shape the nature and level of resources that groups will be able to muster. By offering a distinctive mix of resources to advocacy groups, policies influence which goals and strategies groups pursue, their relationships with government and the private sector, and their prospects for political strength.

For more than thirty years, fair housing and community reinvestment policies have shaped the activities, goals, and political strength of advocacy groups working at the local level on issues of housing discrimination and segregation. In doing so, the two policy designs separate potential allies and create obstacles for groups who try to advance alternative definitions of discrimination. In three of the four local movements for housing equality, groups were weak by the end of the study period. Where greater strength was evident — in Minneapolis — advocates relied primarily on local resources rather than on national policy resources. More specifically, fair housing policy resources promote the legitimacy of advocacy groups and enable some adaptability, but create difficulties for building alliances. Community reinvestment policy resources create obstacles for legitimacy and adaptability and promote short-term coalitions at the expense of long-term ones.

Identifying the obstacles that policies pose to advocacy groups suggests avenues for reform. This chapter thus suggests that groups consider how policies might be changed to help them politically and organizationally. For example, groups can support reforms that would help them build and maintain coalitions and that would bolster their legitimacy in a policy arena. Despite their linked history and the common concerns of fair housing and community reinvestment activists, the fair housing and community reinvestment movements have diverged, as has the scholarship about each issue. Indeed, many now understand the two as quite separate. I argue that differences in the two policy designs have driven this divergence. Yet in recent years, some advocates and scholars have begun to recognize political and instrumental advantages of joining forces. In a sense, advocates are searching for ways to overcome the limitations and challenges that either the fair housing or the community reinvestment policy design imposes on their groups.

This research contributes in a number of ways to theoretical development in political science and to substantive research on housing discrimination. It empirically applies the policy design framework and extends this theoretical approach by testing it across scales and exploring its usefulness in understanding the mobilization of advocacy groups, their orientation to particular policy issues, and the strategies they employ. Substantively, this research begins to fill a gap in literature on housing discrimination politics by assessing the local movements that have emerged around fair housing and community reinvestment policies. It offers an analysis of these two laws that suggests they have political consequences that matter as much as their effectiveness at solving problems. I argue that these laws, whose implementation has relied critically on advocacy groups, have shaped such groups in important ways.

2
Crafting Housing Policy
in Spotlight and Shadow

On Monday, March 4, 1968, when voting began on a measure to stop debate on fair housing, the Senate floor and galleries were full of people. Three previous attempts to stop the filibuster had failed, falling short of the sixty-five votes needed. Without cloture, the "open housing" bill would never come to a vote. Seasoned politicians, both supporters and opponents of civil rights laws, doubted the bill had a chance; it had failed many times to attract support, including during the previous congressional session in 1966. As the roll call proceeded, the number of votes for cloture climbed. Anticipation rose. Two Republican senators had switched their position, voting in favor. At the very last moment, three Democrats did the same, realizing their votes were critical. Senator Cannon from Nevada said he had "examined his conscience" and changed his position that morning. When Senator Bartlett of Alaska switched his position and cast the final vote in favor of cloture, "gasps of surprise and waves of applause broke out in the galleries," while liberal senators thronged the cloakroom to cheer their colleagues, shaking hands and slapping backs. Vice President Humphrey, presiding officer, banged the gavel again and again trying to restore order.[1]

Nearly ten years later, senators debated a second landmark housing bill. But on June 6, 1977, no crowds watched from the galleries, and only seven legislators spoke. In fact, very few senators heard the short debate on the community reinvestment title of the Omnibus Housing Act; at one point, only three were in the chamber. Republicans on the Senate's banking committee strongly opposed the title, and Washington's political observers thought that community reinvestment's "prospects in the Senate [were] grim, and in the House, nil."[2] Still, the full Senate defeated an amendment to strike the title from the bill; judging from the 31–40 vote, a fairly large number of senators decided not to take up the issue at all. The House never debated the title, and both chambers passed the final version of that year's housing bill, including community reinvestment, by wide margins.

20

Once enacted, these two laws moved the nation closer to equality in housing. The Fair Housing Act prohibited racial discrimination, outlawing a range of common real-estate practices that limited minorities' access to housing. No longer would landlords or real estate agents be able, legally, to refuse to rent or sell to a person because of his or her color or national origin. The Community Reinvestment Act focused on redlining (discrimination against neighborhoods). It conferred on lenders an affirmative responsibility to serve low-income communities. Both laws imposed burdens on powerful and politically organized industries—housing and banking—generally regarded as important elements of the nation's economy. The odds for enactment therefore were low. But in each case, supporters in Congress developed strategies to beat them. This chapter traces the two legislative strategies, showing that their impact went beyond securing passage. These strategies shaped the two housing policies in important ways. The arguments legislators made, and the compromises they struck, became inscribed into each housing policy, setting boundaries on how advocates and policy makers would think about and act on housing problems in the future.

Supporters of fair housing and community reinvestment legislation strategized in dramatically different political contexts; different sorts of policies were possible at each juncture and required different kinds of persuasive approaches. In the case of fair housing, supporters faced a hostile context, struggling against opponents in Congress who deployed highly negative images of black people rioting in city streets. Fair housing advocates fought back by describing an honorable group of black people, middle-class professionals, and by emphasizing that fair housing policy would help them, not the poor (and rioting) black people. The high profile of civil rights, race relations, and urban riots during the late 1960s meant that fair housing was crafted in the spotlight of public scrutiny. But when members of Congress began pushing for community reinvestment law, this spotlight was gone, and supporters worked to keep it that way. Legislators holding key positions in Congress kept the issue out of the public eye, arguing that the new law would change an existing regulatory framework only marginally. Rather than evoking images of the low-income people or the racial minority groups who would benefit from the law, supporters described the deteriorating neighborhoods—the places—that would improve as credit became available.

These two rhetorical strategies took institutional form in the Fair Housing and Community Reinvestment Acts, from there shaping the landscape for local advocacy on issues of housing discrimination. Both policies tempered benefits to minorities, and burdens to industry, such that their effectiveness at changing housing patterns and conditions was always limited, fulfilling legislators' arguments during debate. The Fair Housing Act targeted discrimination in private-sector housing with tools of greatest use to middle-class households. The Community Reinvestment Act gave federal regulators much discretion to carry out new responsibilities; it neither authorized appropriations nor named community organizations as enforcement partners. In the analysis that follows, I link the ideas that legislators struggled over during congressional debates to each law's distinctive features and flaws.

ANALYTIC CONCEPTS AND DATA

To analyze these legislative processes and the public policies emerging from them, I use a conceptual framework to deconstruct them into their parts. I draw on a theory of policy making that sets out general expectations for policy designs based on the nature of the legislative process in which policies are crafted. A summary of the framework and the expectations is useful before moving to the analysis.

Any political struggle, such as a legislative process, occurs in a unique context. Important dimensions of the context include the following:

(1) *Social constructions of problems and people.* Particular understandings of problems prevail at a given point in time. These include images and ideas about the groups of people who suffer from the problems, and those who cause them. More specifically, public perceptions exist about the objects, or targets, of specific public policies—for example, homeowners in the case of fair housing or banks in the case of community reinvestment.

(2) *A distribution of power.* Actors and groups vary in the amount of power they enjoy; some relevant players in a political struggle are weak while others are strong. A group's power might derive from a structural advantage, such as the privileged position of the business sector in a free-market economy. Power may derive from the large number of people (and votes) in a group, the level and kind of resources it has, including the degree to which the group is politically organized or mobilized.

(3) *An institutional arena.* A political struggle typically occurs within a particular institution. Institutions have formal and informal rules, standard practices, and norms of behavior. These influence the behavior of people working within them, affecting their decisions about what is important, and when and how to act.[3] Because I look at congressional battles, the rules and procedures governing Congress are important to my analysis.

These elements are not independent of one another. That is, a group's power may depend on which institution it is working in as well as the prevalent social constructions of the group. Together, these contextual elements set the stage for politics, the struggles between actors over policy ideas, the crafting of policy, policy choice, and implementation. Thus, any legislator taking up an issue will contend with a unique context and will seek to use it to his or her advantage. A legislator's perception of what is possible derives from his interpretation of this context.

Once we understand the contours of a specific context, we can analyze how legislators maneuver within it. We can make sense of the target-group images, the problem definitions, and the rationales that legislators use as they try to achieve their policy goals. And we can consider how these arguments show up inside a bill or law. That is, the policy design that emerges—its instruments, its allocation of resources, its definition of who gains and who receives sanctions— is likely to reflect the rhetorical strategies legislators developed with the hand they were dealt, the context in which they worked.

Schneider and Ingram theorize about the kinds of policies that emerge from particular contexts and particular strategies. Their work on "degenerative" policy making is most relevant to my analysis.[4] Social constructions of target populations become the primary fodder that legislators use to pursue their policy goals. Building on existing perceptions of groups and cognizant of the power these groups hold, legislators create images of target groups, portraying them as either deserving or undeserving of policy benefits. But Schneider and Ingram suggest that power differences constrain how effective this strategy can be. They predict that when legislators succeed in channeling benefits to weak groups, even if legislators have used positive images to describe the group, the benefits will be undersubscribed—that is, provided at levels insufficient to remediate the group's problems. If a policy design channels burdens to powerful groups, even when portrayed in negative terms, Schneider and Ingram predict the burdens will be undersubscribed—that is, conferred at levels insufficient to change behavior to an extent that would remediate the problem these groups are causing. In this way, "attention to the deservedness of the target populations by policymakers can seriously hamper the ability of policies to remediate complex social problems."[5]

Schneider and Ingram also theorize about the types of benefits and burdens that different kinds of target groups are likely to receive from policy. For example, they suggest that policy tends to deliver burdens to powerful groups in the form of incentives rather than punishment. Weak groups may receive benefits, but policy is likely to deliver them in a stigmatizing form, or in a way that requires groups to work for them. The form of a group's benefits and burdens sends messages to members about their value, letting them know "whether they are atomized individuals who must deal directly with government and bureaucracy to press their own claims, or participants in a cooperative process joining with others to solve problems collectively."[6]

These concepts and theories ground the analysis that follows. I tell the story of how fair housing and community reinvestment laws were enacted by setting out the two contexts and analyzing the strategies legislators created to achieve success within them.[7] I then show how the policies themselves evolved during the process, changing in ways consistent with legislators' rhetorical strategies and consistent with theoretical expectations noted here.

FAIR HOUSING POLICY: CONTEXT, STRATEGY, AND DESIGN

As the first national law to address racial discrimination in housing, the 1968 Fair Housing Act was truly a landmark piece of legislation. It prohibited homeowners, real estate agents, lenders, and other housing professionals from engaging in a range of practices they had commonly used to keep neighborhoods racially segregated, such as refusing to sell or rent to a person because of his or her race, lying about the availability of a dwelling, or blockbusting (inducing white owners to sell by telling them that blacks were moving into the neighborhood).[8] The last of the 1960s-era civil rights laws, the Fair Housing Act tackled the arena long felt to be the most sensitive to whites. Intense controversy, demonstrations, and violence over fair housing issues had occurred in many cities and states since at least the 1940s.[9] John F. Kennedy promised during his presidential campaign to end housing discrimination "with the stroke of a pen"; once elected, however, he waited two years to sign a very limited executive order.[10] In 1966, a fair housing bill supported by President Johnson failed in Congress. Unlike other civil rights bills, the issue of housing evoked opposition not just from the South but also from the North. Opponents claimed it challenged basic American values such as "a man's home is his castle"; but to supporters, the symbolism of homeownership as "the American Dream" only underscored the importance of ensuring that housing was available to all Americans, regardless of race.

How Congress finally came to pass a fair housing law in 1968 is a fittingly dramatic story, with sweeping events, tense floor votes, and backroom negotiations. The House of Representatives voted to pass the bill that became the Fair Housing Act on April 10, six days after Martin Luther King's assassination and in the midst of unrest in the capital city. The murder had prompted blacks in Washington and many other cities to riot; during House debate, National Guard troops were assembled in the Capitol basement, preparing to go out into the streets.[11] The Senate had passed the same bill a month earlier, after the fourth attempt to cut off a filibuster succeeded, garnering not one vote more than the required two-thirds; "gasps of surprise and waves of applause broke out in the galleries" at the close of the roll call vote.[12] Just a few days earlier, the Kerner Commission Report on the causes of urban riots had been issued, describing the emergence in the United States of two separate societies, "one black, one white—separate and unequal"; its recommendations included adoption of national fair housing legislation.

The Context for Fair Housing Politics

As legislators worked to build support for fair housing law in 1967 and 1968, civil rights politics was changing. The civil rights movement was increasingly understood by white people as a volatile and threatening nationwide effort rather than as the nonviolent pursuit of justice in the South. Additionally, blacks' political power as a group of swing voters was declining. And southerners' entrenched power in Congress meant that fair housing supporters would have to break a filibuster to succeed.

Social Construction of the Civil Rights Movement. In the late 1960s, three changes in the civil rights movement prompted new understandings of civil rights issues and new images of the actors involved: the emergence of the Black Power movement, the proliferation of urban riots, and the shift of activism to the North. These developments conflicted with what had been the prevailing message of civil rights leaders such as Martin Luther King, who emphasized the goal of achieving integration through nonviolent means; they also brought to American citizens new images that stood in contrast to those of southern whites, police officers, and dogs attacking peacefully protesting black activists. The radical activists emerging within the civil rights movements in the late 1960s cared more about economic and social justice than racial integration, doubted that the formal political system would be the mechanism to achieve change, and supported direct action tactics, violent if necessary.[13]

The growing visibility of these Black Power leaders coincided with the increasing incidence of riots in ghetto neighborhoods. Between 1966 and 1968, 290 "hostile outbursts" occurred, during which 169 people were killed, 7,000 wounded, and 40,000 arrested.[14] In July and August 1967, riots erupted in sixty cities, including Newark and Detroit.[15] Additionally, the attention of civil rights activists was shifting to the North as leaders began to decry the poor living conditions that blacks experienced throughout the country rather than focusing on conditions linked to Jim Crow laws in the South. In 1966, for example, Martin Luther King moved into a black slum neighborhood in Chicago and initiated a summerlong campaign against housing and job discrimination.[16]

These changes within the civil rights movement led to changes in the white public's perceptions of blacks, their demands, and their problems. By 1966, 70 percent of white people believed that "Negroes were trying to move too fast."[17] As Sundquist puts it, "The image of the Negro in 1966 was no longer that of the praying, long-suffering, non-violent victim of southern sheriffs; it was of a defiant young hoodlum shouting 'black power' and hurling 'Molotov cocktails' in an urban slum. And the white neighborhoods that might have opened their doors to a Martin Luther King in 1964 would only bar and shutter them at the thought of Stokely Carmichael as a neighbor."[18]

Distribution of Political Power. In addition to changing images and understandings of civil rights issues, the degree of political power held by blacks was decreasing. The housing industry, on the other hand, was highly mobilized against fair housing policy. Housing industry lobbyists and other fair housing opponents often spoke for the largest unorganized constituency—white homeowners—to whom each legislator was accountable in his district.

In the late 1960s, blacks were losing national political power. Their increasing loyalty to the Democratic Party decreased their attractiveness as swing voters,[19] and the civil rights movement was undergoing the fragmentation described earlier.[20] Civil rights leaders from the Leadership Conference on Civil Rights, the coalition of civil rights organizations, supported the legislation, testified in hearings, and worked with legislators behind the scenes in negotiations with opponents. But this effort paled in comparison to the large-scale mobilization that had taken place in support of previous civil rights bills, such as those covering public accommodations, employment, and voting rights.[21]

White homeowners and the housing industry clearly held the most political power—whites through their status as the majority population, and the housing industry through its political mobilization against fair housing and its historic privileged status in federal housing policy dating from the Great Depression era.[22] The real estate industry was the most vocal opponent. In 1966, the National Association of Real Estate Boards (NAREB), representing eighty-five thousand brokers, prompted thousands of real estate agents to write their members of Congress expressing opposition to fair housing. NAREB was less prepared when fair housing hit the Senate floor two years later, so senators did not receive this flood of mail, but they certainly knew the industry generally opposed the bill.[23]

Finally, groups opposed to fair housing held legislators accountable throughout the country, not just in the South. Because fair housing law would affect their constituents, northern legislators' decision calculus on fair housing proposals was likely to differ from that used on previous civil rights bills. Indeed, consideration of fair housing ordinances at both state and local levels had occurred in many locations, from Massachusetts to California, from New York to Albuquerque.[24] Legislators across the country were familiar with the vociferous opposition that fair housing provoked.

Institutional Arena: Congress. The institution of the U.S. Congress—its operating procedures and organizational structure—was the arena in which proponents of fair housing strategized and struggled to win support. Party affiliation was less important to civil rights issues than ideology and regional identity; coalitions of northern Democrats and moderate Republicans had provided the votes to pass previous civil rights laws.[25] In the 1966 elections, Republicans gained four seats in the Senate and forty-seven in the House. Those elected in the House shifted the body toward a more conservative stance, whereas new Republican senators actually were more moderate than the Democrats they had replaced, and their presence increased the pool of possible swing voters on the issue of fair housing.[26] Nonetheless, Senate Minority Leader Everett Dirksen had shown his ability to control the votes of many Republicans in past civil rights battles, and he strongly opposed fair housing.[27]

Attention to potential swing voters was especially important because on civil rights issues, the Conservative Coalition frequently took advantage of the Senate rule enabling filibusters. In 1966, Senator Dirksen had led a successful filibuster against a fair housing bill, and he threatened to do so again in 1968. Fair housing supporters therefore needed more than a majority to win passage, because they would first need two-thirds of the members to vote in favor of cloture, stopping debate on the bill. Also, 1968 was an election year for the Senate, making argumentation especially important to those legislators up for reelection, who would have to defend their votes to constituents.[28] The persuasive strategies used by fair housing proponents and opponents were likely to be repeated to constituents during the campaign season. Some accounts suggest that moderate Republicans wanted to improve the party's civil rights record for the election year, but others emphasize the successful "law and order" conservative stance that had increased the Republican ranks in 1966.

Debating Fair Housing Law

Nearly all accounts of the legislative process leading to fair housing law emphasize that no one thought fair housing had any chance of success in 1968. Pessimists ranged from Attorney General Ramsey Clark to senior Senate leaders on civil rights such as Philip Hart (D-Mich.) and Jacob Javits (R-N.Y.). Indeed, some were worried that including a fair housing bill on the civil rights agenda would limit the chances of less controversial civil rights bills that were also under consideration.[29] The preceding analysis of the fair housing context shows why expectations were so low, and why supporters were so overjoyed at their success, calling passage "the legislative upset of the century";[30] to sponsor Senator Mondale, it was "a miracle."[31] This highly emotional issue came to the floor during an election year in which blacks' political power was waning. It raised the issue of racial segregation during a period of increasingly frequent riots in black neighborhoods across the country. And despite the addition of a handful of moderate Republicans in the Senate, the House had grown more conservative since passing a version of fair housing law in 1966 (which died in the Senate). Additionally, the key player in past civil rights legislative efforts, Senator Dirksen, had voiced his opposition to fair housing.

In a context that stacked the deck against passage of fair housing law, supporters would have to develop a political strategy that could turn a political risk into an opportunity. Opponents exploited the risks well, emphasizing during congressional debate images of white homeowners as upstanding and truly "American" citizens whose rights would be trampled by fair housing law; the housing industry, they argued, would be subject to frivolous claims and the heavy hand of government. Supporters did not refute images of whites but focused instead on describing the injustice suffered by blacks as long as housing discrimination persisted. More important, supporters adapted their rhetorical strategy to the new context of civil rights, which they had failed to do in 1966.[32] They created a narrative about fair housing that helped secure passage, but at the cost of a policy design that would limit the prospects for change.

Analysis of the *Congressional Record*'s transcript of fair housing debate, summarized in Table 2.1, shows the persuasive strategy that supporters developed. Three aspects of it demonstrate how they adapted to their difficult context.

Table 2.1. Fair Housing Debate, 1968 (Senate): Target Group Images and Policy Arguments (percents are column percents)

	Legislators	
	Supporters	Opponents
Target groups		
Blacks	26% of statements	10% of statements
	Victims of discrimination, Rioters	Rioters
	Valence: Positive	*Valence: Negative*
Middle-class blacks	24%	2%
	Portraits of individual black professionals who can afford to leave ghetto but face discrimination	Law would give black soldiers returning from war privileges that discriminate against white soldiers
	Valence: Positive	*Valence: Neutral*
Low-income blacks	9%	0
	Law would provide hope of upward mobility	
	Valence: Neutral/positive	
White homeowners	14%	56%
	Individual homeowners would be exempt	Upstanding, worked hard to achieve homeownership; fair housing would rob them of property rights, freedom of choice; victimize them with false claims
	Valence: Positive	*Valence: Positive*
Housing industry	12%	8%
	Most want to behave fairly; problems come from actions of unscrupulous few; law would "shield" good industry members	Law would burden industry members, making them subject to false claims and the heavy hand of government
	Valence: Mixed	*Valence: Positive*
Agent: federal government (HUD)	3%	19%
	Opponents overstate; federal power is needed to address problems of housing discrimination	Too powerful; ready to usurp individual and states' rights; bureaucracy is eager to expand power
	Valence: Positive	*Valence: Negative*

	Legislators	
	Supporters	Opponents
Rationale	26%	15%
	Riots prove fair housing is needed; battle between black moderates and extremists; government needs to show that moderates are right	Fair housing law would reward blacks for lawlessness and violence
Policy logic	24%	0
	Free-market frame: Law would allow equal opportunity to housing, but income inequality will prevent drastic change in residential patterns	
Number of statements	58	48

Source: Congressional Record.

First, supporters transformed the significance of the urban riots. Second, they constructed a new target group, middle-class blacks, depicted as deserving of better housing. Third, they used rhetoric of the free market to weave together conflicting narratives about fair housing aimed at different constituencies—whites and blacks. Each part of this strategy had consequences for the policy design that the Senate adopted.

Riots: Creating a Sense of Urgency. In earlier fair housing debates, supporters had portrayed blacks as noble victims of discrimination, trapped in ghettos by forces beyond their control. This was a typical image used in civil rights politics, advancing the notion that blacks relied on whites' goodwill for dignity and freedom. But as riots erupted summer after summer across the country, civil rights opponents began to depict blacks as violent and destructive, "deviants" in Schneider and Ingram's terms rather than "dependents." Opponents argued that passing fair housing law would reward blacks for lawlessness and endanger other Americans. In 1966, an opponent characterized the fair housing debate as about "whether [we] are going to surrender further to the so-called revolution of the Negro race."[33] As Rep. Bennett (D-Fla.) succinctly put it, fair housing would be "just another splash of gasoline on the embers of unrest."[34]

But in 1968, fair housing supporters fought back, making the riots a key component of their persuasive strategy and invoking them nearly twice as often as opponents (26 percent versus 15 percent of statements). They used the riots to create a sense of urgency about addressing the problems of the ghettos, which they described as products of housing discrimination. The riots demanded rather than precluded congressional response. Supporters also addressed fears aroused

by Black Power activists by claiming that the riots symbolized a larger battle taking place between a group Senator Mondale (D-Minn.) called "black racists" and
the rest of society (including "moderate" blacks): "There is a critical debate now
underway in the ghetto. The issue is quite simple—whether there is any basic de-
cency in white America and whether white America ever really intends to permit
equality and full opportunity to black Americans. . . . We believe that our continuing failure to put an end to segregated housing lends a powerful argument to
the black separatists and black racists, and can only speed the process of separation and alienation."[35]

Fair housing cosponsor Senator Brooke (R-Mass.) elaborated on this theme
that fair housing law would remedy riots by restoring faith in the political system: "Most important, in my judgment, this legislation on so vital a matter will
offer desperately needed evidence that the American political process remains
the most viable and responsive institution yet conceived by man. When the rele-
vance and potency of our institutions come into question, as they have in many
quarters, there is no other way to restore public confidence than by demonstrat-
ing the capacity and willingness of political leaders to act."[36]

A Deserving Target Group: The Black Middle Class. Although the riots provided
a sense of crisis, they created a problem of deservedness that fair housing supporters solved by constructing a new target group. They distinguished blacks
along class lines and described a small group of middle-class professionals who
deserved to escape the ghettos and could afford to do so. Although hardly anyone in previous fair housing debates had referred to middle-class blacks, nearly
a quarter of advocates' statements in 1968 referred to this group, often through
references to witnesses who had testified in Senate hearings the previous year.
These stories brought individual faces into the debate. During the 1967 hearings,
a black U.S. Navy lieutenant and a black college professor testified about how
discrimination thwarted their efforts to find decent housing for their families.
When Lieutenant Campbell sought housing in Washington, D.C., thirty-six leasing agents turned him down.[37]

Other witnesses told the stories of two sisters, a welfare worker and a nurse,
who were prepared to offer the asking price for a two-family house when the
owner learned they were black and raised the price;[38] a black doctor, who read
the real estate ads each week describing the pleasures of the suburbs and knew
he could not move there despite his income and education;[39] and a newly hired
black research technician who found an apartment for his family in a suburb near
his lab, only to have his application rejected despite the intervention of his company's directors, community leaders, and local religious organizations.[40] Senators drew on such stories during floor debate to personalize the plight of the black
middle class. These accounts were conscious efforts to allay white fears that rioters would invade their neighborhoods if fair housing became law. Supporters
emphasized that fair housing would enable members of the black middle class to

escape the ghetto, while low-income blacks would gain only the hope of escaping in the future; middle-class blacks could live the American dream, low-income blacks could only dream it. Sen. Brooke's remarks capture this line of reasoning: "Fair housing does not promise to end the ghetto; it promises only to demonstrate that the ghetto is not an immutable institution in America. It will scarcely lead to a mass dispersal of the ghetto population to the suburbs, but it will make it possible for those who have the resources to escape the stranglehold now suffocating the inner cities of America. It will make possible renewed hope for ghetto residents who have begun to believe that escape from their demeaning circumstances is impossible."[41]

In the following statement, Mondale's description of the hope that fair housing would offer to low-income blacks emphasizes the middle-class tenet that hard work brings success, the very value that fair housing opponents credited white homeowners with exhibiting: "Open occupancy will have great practical psychological significance to the Negro who has 'tried harder' and yet remains trapped in the ghetto for a lifetime. He can tell his child growing up in the ghetto that he can get out if he wants—if he is willing to study and to work."[42]

Emphasizing Modesty: Reliance on the Free Market. Prior to 1968, civil rights opponents had challenged the logic of fair housing proposals, which always exempted categories of housing from coverage. Critics called these proposals hypocritical for condemning discrimination, but enabling so many individuals to practice it. They noted that states and cities with fair housing laws still had ghettos, thus challenging supporters to explain how the modest bills they proposed would begin to solve the problems of housing discrimination and deteriorated neighborhoods. In the past, supporters responded weakly by noting that the bill's exemptions were political compromises.

In 1968, however, when fair housing supporters constructed the target group of the black middle class, they could build a policy rationale using free-market rhetoric to bring the parts of their argument together and to incorporate arguments of the opposition. Using the free-market concept enabled advocates to tell two stories at once: that fair housing law *would* and *would not* bring social change. In particular, they could say (to blacks): Removing race from the housing transaction will make housing available to all. But they also could say (to whites): Economic inequality means that few black families will move into white neighborhoods.

In stating that fair housing law was insufficient to break up the urban ghettos, supporters answered the critique that fair housing law would not work—they made the proposal's promise of ineffectiveness a reason to support the legislation. Senator Mondale articulates this nontransformative story: "The basic purpose of this legislation is to permit people who have the ability to do so to buy any house offered to the public if they can afford to buy it. It would not overcome the economic problem of those who could not afford to purchase the house of their choice."[43] Here, Mondale tells both stories back to back, starting with the nontransformative one: "There will not be a great influx of all the Negroes in the ghettos into the suburbs—in fact, the laws of supply and demand will take care of who moves into what house in which neighborhood. There will, however, be the knowledge by Negroes that they are free—if they have the money and the desire—to move where they will; and there will be the knowledge by whites that the rapid, block-by-block expansion of the ghetto will be slowed and replaced by truly integrated and balanced living patterns."[44]

The notion of the free market thus pulled two narratives together in a meaningful way, creating a plausible policy rationale. Indeed, Table 2.1 shows that about a quarter of supporters' statements articulated this logic. On the one hand, supporters could emphasize that fair housing law would correct the problem of housing segregation and discrimination by eliminating the dual housing market, enabling blacks and whites to have equal opportunity to all housing. They argued that this change in the terms of housing supply was a crucial step toward addressing the problems of the ghetto. On the other hand, supporters also acknowledged that removing race from the housing transaction would leave in place the economic inequality that existed between whites and blacks. Characteristics of housing demand would remain untouched, and only those blacks who could afford to leave the ghetto would be able to do so; supporters claimed this was a small group. Opponents offered no alternative: They restated earlier arguments about burdening white homeowners and proposed no solution to the riots and ghettos.

The Fair Housing Policy Design

How did these arguments, crafted to achieve success in a difficult political context, matter for fair housing policy? We may be tempted to consider them "just words," successful in garnering votes, but nothing more. Yet when we examine fair housing law, we can see congruence between supporters' arguments and specific features of the policy. Ideas that supporters expressed are built into the policy design in several ways. First, the design focused attention on the private housing market, reflecting the discourse on free-market processes, and on middle-class blacks. Second, the design included mechanisms that actually hinder the policy from addressing housing discrimination and segregation, bearing out the story told by fair housing supporters that fair housing law would not lead to drastic change. Also consistent with theoretical expectations, the design reflected the political risks of channeling burdens to powerful groups and benefits to weaker groups.

Broadly, the 1968 Fair Housing Act prohibited racial discrimination in housing transactions, from rental and sales to lending, insurance, and appraisals. It specified and prohibited a set of practices and directed the U.S. Department of Housing and Urban Development (HUD) to establish a process for taking, investigating, and conciliating claims. It authorized the Department of Justice to intervene in cases that display a "pattern and practice of resistance" to the law. The act also established the right of private citizens to file suit in federal court. Below I analyze the statute in more detail, tracing elements of the law that reflect the discourse supporters used to promote passage.

Private Sector Housing and Middle-Class Minorities. The fair housing policy design offered more resources to middle-class than to low-income minorities, and it targeted discriminatory practices in private-sector housing more directly than public-sector housing practices. This emphasis is consistent with the free-market rhetoric that fair housing proponents used as well as their construction of middle-class blacks as the target group who would benefit from fair housing law.

The bulk of the statute consisted of rules and tools designed to minimize racial discrimination against individual home seekers by working to eliminate bias from housing transactions in the private sector, such as broker-client relations and mortgage lending decisions. Sections 804–806 specified the practices that were prohibited, and sections 810–811 directed HUD to establish a process to receive, investigate, and conciliate complaints. Section 812 authorized individuals to file lawsuits in federal, state, and local courts. Structurally, middle-class blacks stood to benefit more from these rules and tools than low-income blacks; they were likely to have the resources, both educational and financial, to engage in the complaint process or to file a civil lawsuit.

One section of the statute addressed public-sector housing practices. Section 808 required HUD to integrate "fair housing" into its existing housing programs "in a manner to affirmatively further the purposes of this title," thus directing attention to the operating procedures and outcomes of federal programs such as public housing and FHA loan guarantees. Whereas the fair housing statute was quite detailed in its delineation of the enforcement process for remedying discrimination in the private sector, it offered no guidance on how HUD was to incorporate fair housing into its own housing programs. This higher level of discretion has meant more variation over time, and by presidential administration, in how HUD and others define "fair housing" and the "affirmatively further" requirement relative to its own affordable housing programs. The degree to which fair housing law has benefited low-income minorities who rely on subsidized housing thus varies according to federal commitment and leadership.

Ensuring Gradual and Minimal Change. The double narrative of stasis and change told by legislators supportive of fair housing emerged in the policy design. On the one hand, the statute asserted the message of equal opportunity by covering most housing and by outlawing practices that obstructed access to housing. Legislators argued that persistent income inequality would limit change, but several structural elements of the policy also served that purpose. First, the policy offered neither adequate sanctions to coerce those engaging in discriminatory practice to cease doing so nor adequate resources to minorities or to HUD to enforce the provisions aggressively. A staged introduction of covered dwellings also served to ensure that little would change, that no "deluge" of blacks into white neighborhoods would occur. Initially, only housing already covered by a previous executive order (federally funded housing such as public housing) would be subject to the law. After one year, coverage was extended to multifamily housing and housing that was not owner-occupied. By the third year, all housing save a small set of exempted dwellings would be covered. Finally, the law's judicial and administrative enforcement processes would not result in immediate remedial action but would take time to move forward. Thus, the likelihood of quickly solving a complainant's existing housing problem was low. This delay also would contribute to the act's ineffectiveness, ensuring that no immediate or drastic change in segregated living patterns would occur.

Undersubscribed Benefits and Burdens. Fair housing debate framed the bill as pitting the interests of blacks against the interests of whites and the housing industry. Although supporters' creation of a new target group—middle-class blacks—justified provision of benefits to them, white homeowners and the housing industry remained politically powerful and tended to be portrayed in positive terms, so imposing burdens would be difficult. Aspects of the Fair Housing Act's design bear out Schneider and Ingram's predictions about undersubscribed burdens and benefits, which was especially clear when comparing elements of the design with alternatives that Congress considered. Table 2.2 summarizes the contents of five versions of fair housing proposals and notes the relative strength of each one's goals, coverage, and enforcement structure.

The Fair Housing Act's goal statement is ambiguous compared to earlier versions. It states: "It is the policy of the United States to provide, within Constitutional limitations, for fair housing throughout the United States." This differs significantly from goal statements in prior versions. For example, the Johnson administration sent a version to the House in 1966 with the following goal statement: " It is the policy of the United States to prevent, and the right of every person to be protected against, discrimination on account of race, color, religion, or national origin in the purchase, rental, lease, financing, use and occupancy of housing throughout the Nation."[45]

This version directly states the benefits blacks would receive from the legislation: a right and government protection of that right. On the other hand, the statement in the final version did not explicitly define fair housing, and it suggested that fair housing might conflict with constitutional rights. Ambiguity can be a positive aspect of legislation because interested groups may be able to assert their own definitions of terms as implementation proceeds. Still, this ambiguous statement burdened whites and benefited blacks much less directly than prior versions.

Antidiscrimination provisions of the Fair Housing Act applied to most housing except owner-occupied multifamily dwellings with up to four units ("Mrs.

Table 2.2. Five Versions of Fair Housing Policy Designs

	Version 1 H.R. 14705 (1966)	Version 2 1966 Civil Rights Act (Title IV)	Version 3 S. 1358 (1967)	Version 4 1968 Mondale-Brooke Amendment	Version 5 1968 Civil Rights Act (Title VIII)
Policy statement	"It is the policy of the United States to prevent, and the right of every person to be protected against, discrimination on account of race, color, religion, or national origin in the purchase, rental, lease, financing, use and occupancy of housing throughout the Nation." *Strong*	"It is the policy of the United States to prevent discrimination on account of race, color, religion, or national origin in the purchase, rental, financing, and occupancy of housing throughout the United States." *Slightly less strong*	Same as Version 2	Same as Version 2	"To provide, within constitutional limitations, for fair housing throughout the United States." *Ambiguous*
Coverage	Coverage is not mentioned. Implies all housing is covered. *Broad*	Covers actions of real estate professionals only. (Owners can instruct agents to discriminate.) Covers all housing except Mrs. Murphy's boardinghouse. *Narrow*	Three-year staggered program that by 1969 would cover all housing. *Somewhat broad*	Same as previous, but with Mrs. Murphy exemption. *Somewhat broad*	A three-year staggered program would by 1970 cover all housing except: • Mrs. Murphy's boardinghouse • Single-family homes sold by the owner without use of real estate agent or discriminatory advertising. *Somewhat broad*

Table 2.2. continued

	Version 1 H.R. 14705 (1966)	Version 2 1966 Civil Rights Act (Title IV)	Version 3 S. 1358 (1967)	Version 4 1968 Mondale-Brooke Amendment	Version 5 1968 Civil Rights Act (Title VIII)
Enforcement	• DOJ can initiate "pattern and practice" suits and intervene in private suits if of "general public importance." • Individuals can file civil suits. *Weak*	• Establishes Fair Housing Board to investigate and initiate complaints. Holds hearings and in case of violation has powers similar to National Labor Relations Board. • DOJ can initiate pattern and practice suits and intervene in private suit if "of general public importance." • Individuals can file civil suits. *Strong*	• "The [HUD] secretary is empowered . . . to prevent any person from engaging in any discriminatory housing practice." • HUD can investigate complaints and can initiate complaints; can issue temporary restraining orders and hold formal hearings. • HUD can issue cease and desist orders and order party to take affirmative action. • DOJ can initiate pattern and practice suits. *Strong*	Same as Version 3 *Strong*	• HUD may investigate complaints and seek conciliation; may refer cases to attorney general. • DOJ may pursue "pattern and practice" cases or "general public importance" cases. • Individuals can file civil suits. *Weak*

Murphy's boardinghouse") and single-family homes sold without the use of a real estate agent. Coverage was broader than that in the House-passed 1966 bill, which essentially had allowed homeowners to discriminate but not housing professionals. It was only slightly less broad than the Mondale-Brooke version immediately preceding it. But coverage proceeded in three stages, as noted above. Although minorities benefited from the Fair Housing Act's relatively broad coverage, this benefit was tempered by the gradual implementation process; only after three years would most housing be covered. This mechanism benefited whites and the housing industry by giving them three years to continue current practices.

The Fair Housing Act provided two avenues for enforcement, one judicial and one administrative, whereas the original Johnson bill relied solely on judicial remedies. The benefit to minorities of two enforcement options was tempered by HUD's limited authority to administratively enforce the law. The 1966 version had established a new regulatory body, a Fair Housing Board modeled after the National Labor Relations Board, with broad powers to investigate and force compliance. The 1968 version assigned administrative enforcement authority to HUD, allowing the agency to investigate complaints received but not to initiate an investigation on its own. Agency officials had to rely on "conference, conciliation, and persuasion" with the guilty party to correct discriminatory practices. The agency's power to issue injunctions and restraining orders against offenders, and to use the courts to enforce them, had been removed in negotiations with Dirksen. Also in the final version, HUD was directed to "immediately" convene with representatives of the housing industry to discuss implementation procedures.

Stronger enforcement authority for HUD would have benefited minorities by enabling the agency to seek out and strongly sanction discriminatory behavior; conversely, these mechanisms would have burdened whites by subjecting them to legal action and punishment. The Fair Housing Act, then, undersubscribed burdens on whites by limiting the government's enforcement powers and undersubscribed benefits to minorities by limiting the government's ability to prevent and correct discriminatory housing practices. Minorities also had the burden of essentially enforcing the law themselves; they had to bring claims to HUD or to the courts.

This legislation that purportedly addressed the problem of housing discrimination took care not to overburden the people whose behavior it was attempting to change. The housing industry, and whites more generally, had three years to get used to the idea of open housing. They would be held accountable essentially only when an individual brought a claim to HUD or to court, or when the Department of Justice found a "pattern and practice" of discrimination. Charges would be resolved through conciliation. In court, the complainant would shoulder the burden of proof. The price blacks paid for legislation prohibiting housing discrimination was the burden of enforcing it themselves.

COMMUNITY REINVESTMENT POLICY:
CONTEXT, STRATEGY, DESIGN

By the early 1970s, with fair housing law in place, the racial transition of neighborhoods continued in cities across the country. Lending institutions continued to deny loans to neighborhoods they deemed "susceptible to racial change."[46] People living in neighborhoods where racial minorities occupied most homes, in neighborhoods with integrated populations, and in predominantly white neighborhoods near minority neighborhoods all had trouble accessing credit from private lenders. In many cities, neighborhood groups were formed to protest the withdrawal of private financial institutions from their communities, arguing that it triggered a self-fulfilling prophecy of property devaluation and blight.[47] Several states began to adopt antiredlining legislation, including California, New York, New Jersey, and Connecticut. The banking industry opposed these measures, arguing it was being scapegoated for "fundamental forces at work in many older cities."[48] But by 1975, Congress had passed the Home Mortgage Disclosure Act, requiring banks to report loan activity by neighborhood, and in 1977, Congress held hearings on the antiredlining law that would become the Community Reinvestment Act (CRA).

The CRA is Title VIII of the 1977 Housing and Community Development Act.[49] The statute focuses primarily on intergovernmental urban development programs, including the Community Development Block Grant (CDBG) program and public housing. Much of the deliberation and controversy that occurred during the legislative process focused on changes proposed to the CDBG program, which had existed for only three years and represented a major shift in federal funding to cities. At first, the community reinvestment title appeared only in the Senate version of the bill; it became a part of the conference committee's final version that was passed by both chambers and signed into law by President Carter in October 1977.

The Context for Community Reinvestment Politics

In 1977, legislators faced a distinctive political landscape as they worked to build support for the community reinvestment law. A new urban America was emerging, characterized by deepening regional and metropolitan disparities, while a new regime of federal urban policy emphasized the importance of the private sector to the public welfare. Political supporters of CRA were localized rather than nationally powerful, but their Democratic allies in Congress enjoyed strong majorities and held key positions within Congress. They could build on the success of a banking disclosure law that had raised the issue of redlining two years earlier.

Social Construction of Urban Decline. Community reinvestment policy was debated not in terms of civil rights and in the midst of urban riots, but in the midst of profound changes in the American urban landscape, as metropolitan areas in the Northeast and Midwest lost population and jobs while southern and especially southwestern cities grew.[50] This trend was unsettling (especially to those in the declining areas) because it followed one hundred years of "consistent expansion" in urban areas.[51] Accompanying these changes in the U.S. system of cities was continued and accelerated suburbanization within metro areas; northern and midwestern central cities especially suffered.[52] During the 1970s, many central cities lost population; groups remaining in the cities tended to be poorer and less educated than their suburban counterparts. The recession of 1973–1975, the worst economic decline since the Great Depression, compounded the problems of northeastern and midwestern central cities.[53] Central city governments in the 1970s found themselves with a declining tax base and a needier population.[54]

Uneven and unequal development patterns deepened within the central cities as well. Federal urban and housing policies, combined with local officials' desire to attract middle-class residents and business to the city, resulted in the demolition of low-income housing and its replacement with office complexes or luxury housing or both, although some cleared lots remained vacant for years.[55] In the 1970s, gentrification began to occur in some urban neighborhoods, also displacing poor people and creating tensions between old and new urban residents.[56]

Federal urban and housing policy was in flux in the mid-1970s; a new role for the federal government was emerging that focused on local decision making and public-private partnerships. The Nixon administration had directed the consolidation of a range of categorical urban and housing programs into a block grant that emphasized local discretion. President Carter focused on community development and neighborhood solutions.[57] His Urban Development Action Grant program sought to encourage partnerships between business and local government. Policy makers, scholars, and activists were beginning to emphasize the role of the private sector in shaping the urban landscape.

Finally, passage of the Home Mortgage Disclosure Act (HMDA) in 1975 had placed the issue of redlining on the federal agenda. Whereas legislators in the fair housing battle were trying to pass a bill that had failed repeatedly in Congress, legislators supportive of community reinvestment policy were building on the success of HMDA. This disclosure law was controversial, and the votes were close.[58] At that time, legislators linked financial institutions' lending decisions to neighborhood deterioration and argued that consumers had a right to know when choosing a bank what its lending patterns were. If a bank used neighborhood residents' deposits to make loans in the suburbs, legislators argued, consumers might choose to put their deposits elsewhere, such as into a bank that "reinvested" in their community. While lenders denied that they redlined—denied loans, regardless of borrower qualifications, in neighborhoods they considered poor risks—by 1977 they were less able to make that claim, as the first rounds of disclosure data were becoming available and showing uneven lending patterns.[59] The HMDA debate introduced to Congress the notion that lending patterns were linked to trajectories of neighborhood decline.

Distribution of Political Power. The groups who would be affected by community reinvestment policy had different degrees of political power and different allies in government. Civil rights and neighborhood advocates had raised the issue of redlining. Civil rights groups worked through the court system and had sued bank regulators in 1971 for not complying with the Fair Housing Act. In general, the community reinvestment movement was not as visible or widespread as the civil rights movement had been in the 1960s. It emerged in particular neighborhoods in a handful of states when advocates began to protest banks at the local and state levels; several states adopted antiredlining legislation. In 1975 these groups, led by Gale Cincotta's National People's Action, based in Chicago, took the issue to Congress and found allies among Democratic legislators from urban districts; most notably, they convinced Senator Proxmire (D-Wis.), chair of the Senate Committee on Banking, Housing, and Urban Affairs, to support antiredlining proposals.[60] He became the primary spokesperson for CRA.

In contrast to grassroots activists, financial institutions enjoy a privileged structural position because they are understood as critical engines of the U.S. free-market economy. From the start then, any regulation that would intervene in the free market is initially suspect.[61] Bankers tend to view consumer regulation as burdensome and invasive,[62] and federal regulators have come to share this perspective. These agencies consider consumer protection issues secondary to their critical mission of ensuring the economic viability of financial institutions.[63] As self-funded agencies, the regulators are more autonomous than other executive branch agencies, with no need to seek appropriations each year from Congress.[64] Regulators forcefully opposed CRA in letters to the Senate Committee on Banking, Housing, and Urban Affairs.[65] The banking lobby did not spearhead a major campaign against the bill, although when it was debated on the Senate floor, senators received phone calls from their own bankers who expressed their opposition. Additionally, the U.S. League of Savings Associations claimed that the public was not interested in the issue, because its member survey found that financial institutions had received very few requests for the newly available HMDA data.[66]

Institutional Arena: Congress. By the mid-1970s, Democrats had won back congressional seats lost to Republicans in a civil rights electoral backlash starting ten years earlier. They enjoyed strong majorities in both chambers of Congress. In the 1974 elections, they gained 4 seats in the Senate, moving to 61 of 100, and 49 seats in the House, increasing to 291 out of 435.[67] In the 1976 elections, Democrats retained 61 Senate seats and added 1 House seat. Also important for CRA was the nature of the congressional committee system, where specialization and norms of deference mean that small sets of senators and representatives can control particular policy arenas.[68] This situation is especially true for banking regulation. Policy on banking regulation tends to have low visibility; it is perceived as technical and complex, so relatively few congressional representatives are eager to work on the issue or develop expertise,[69] which means that those who do specialize may have a higher degree of influence over their peers than specialists in more visible and less technical issues. Also, the chairpersons of congressional committees wield more power than other members of Congress.

Supporters of CRA benefited from this uneven distribution of power within Congress. In 1975, Senator Proxmire became chair of the Committee on Banking, Housing, and Urban Affairs. His home state of Wisconsin was one in which organized activity against redlining had occurred. Soon after he took the chairmanship, a delegation of community groups visited his staff to discuss redlining. Senator Stevenson of Illinois, also on the committee, had advocated for more urban lending in the state government during the 1960s; other Democrats on the Senate committee also supported the legislation.[70]

Members of Congress can use rules governing the legislative process to expand or to limit debate and participation. With CRA, supporters clearly chose the latter route. The bill was debated in only one chamber, with very few legislators present. Rules and procedures enabled CRA supporters to limit debate to the Senate and to embed the issue in a bill in which other titles attracted attention. The CRA title was part of the 1977 Housing and Community Development proposal and received little attention during congressional debate. Other aspects of the bill, primarily changes in the allocation formula for the CDBG program, received more attention. It is not surprising that, given the incentive structure facing members of Congress, they chose to focus on the CDBG allocation formula, which would determine the amount of grant money flowing to their districts. Indeed, disagreement over this title caused a deadlock in the conference committee that required Congress to pass two stopgap funding measures. By the time the conference committee reported the Housing and Community Development Act, there was little interest in further delay to reconsider the CRA provision, even though a handful of members continued to oppose it.[71]

Debating Community Reinvestment

Although congressional supporters of community reinvestment certainly faced the political challenge of channeling benefits to weak groups and burdens to strong ones, the 1977 issue context held greater prospects for success than that of fair housing in the late 1960s. Supporters could frame the policy to mesh with an emerging concern about urban decline. The key positions of power they held in a Democratic Congress enabled them to use institutional rules to their advantage, offsetting the systemic power enjoyed by the banking industry and federal regulators. In particular, they were able to restrict the scope of conflict by limiting the community reinvestment proposal's visibility inside Congress and thus to the broader public. The Senate Banking, Housing, and Urban Affairs Committee attached CRA to the Housing and Community Development Act, which included major changes to the Community Development Block Grant program and to public housing programs. The result was to deflect attention from community reinvestment because the CDBG changes were so controversial. The committee vote suggests that if the CRA title had received more attention, it may have attracted more opposition. The committee reported the bill by a 7 to 7 vote, and four senators appended additional views stating their opposition to CRA.[72] Their statement refers to the strategy of keeping CRA invisible; they complain that the title was added to the larger bill quickly, without giving members of Congress the chance to consider it carefully. Hearings had been held in late March, and the title was appended to the community development bill in May.

Senate debate on the community reinvestment title of S. 1523, the Housing and Community Development Act, took place on June 6, 1977. This was the only floor debate on community reinvestment because the House version of the bill had no CRA title, and both chambers passed the conference version without debating it. The issue did not draw attention from legislators outside the reporting committee. Only seven senators spoke—two in favor of CRA, five against it—and all were committee members. Most remarks were made when Senator Morgan (D-N.C.) introduced an amendment to strike CRA from the bill. Few legislators were present; Morgan refers to three.

Although limited, the debate does offer the chance to examine the rhetorical strategy supporters used to promote CRA and to consider how the stories they told influenced the policy design that emerged. Table 2.3 presents summary data for the coded debate. Supporters nested the issue within the larger problem of urban decline and portrayed the bill as a small clarification to the existing regulatory framework governing the banking industry. Most statements concerned the regulators or lenders; senators talked less about the neighborhoods that would benefit from the law. They did not mention the groups of people who would benefit or the advocacy organizations poised to use CRA as a tool to improve their communities. Each of these choices influenced features of the policy design.

Focus on Regulators. The politically powerful groups whom the law would burden received the most attention during congressional debate. As Table 2.3 shows, speakers referred in nearly every statement to the regulatory agencies who would enforce the law. A cornerstone of supporters' rhetorical strategy was to portray CRA as a modest alteration of the existing framework of regulations governing financial institutions that would require regulators to make only limited changes to their examination and charter-approval procedures. Law dating from 1935 governs the bank charter approval and renewal processes, requiring regulators to ensure that financial institutions meet "the convenience and needs" of local communities.[73] CRA supporters emphasized that their bill clarified rather than changed this policy by specifying that Congress defined "convenience and needs" as credit needs in addition to the depository needs that examiners routinely assessed. According to Senator Proxmire, "The law *already provides* that banks are chartered to meet the convenience and needs of their communities. . . .

Table 2.3. Community Reinvestment Debate, 1977 (Senate): Target Group Images and Policy Arguments (percents are column percents)

	Legislators	
	Supporters	Opponents
Target Groups Financial Institutions	44% of statements	38% of statements
	Neglect local communities; take money from community and invest elsewhere (engage in redlining). Resource-rich; ignore responsibility; need "encouragement."	Financial institutions already reallocate money from affluent neighborhoods to poor ones. Should not be forced to make risky loans.
	Valence: Negative	*Valence: Positive*
Neighborhoods	33%	23%
	Older, urban neighborhoods suffer from denied credit; resource-poor.	Older urban neighborhoods suffer from multiple problems emerging from complex process.
	Valence: Positive	*Valence: Neutral/Positive*
Agent: regulatory agencies	89%	69%
	CRA simply asks regulators to consider reinvestment as one part of application process. They do not do this now despite "convenience and needs" requirement; reluctant to address redlining issues.	Agencies already assess responsiveness to community ("convenience and needs"). CRA would overburden with more regs and work.
	Valence: Negative	*Valence: Positive*
Rationale	33%	69%
	Low-cost solution; government needs private sector to solve inner-city problems; government grants privileges to financial institutions with charter and financial institutions have public responsibilities.	CRA would overburden financial institutions and regulatory agencies with a "mountain of paperwork"; government should not undertake credit allocation; existing laws address issue; ambiguity of language is problematic.
Policy logic	11%	31%
	Disinvestment by financial institutions causes neigh-borhood decline; reinvestment will lead to neighborhood revitalization.	CRA would further deprive neighborhoods by dis-couraging banking activity within them. Sanctions not severe enough to change behavior.
Number of Statements	9	13

Source: Congressional Record.

But unfortunately many bankers and bank regulators have forgotten the meaning of those words." CRA would "reaffirm" that "convenience and needs does not just mean drive-in teller windows and Christmas Club accounts"—that is, diversified depository products and services—"it means loans."[74]

Opponents cited letters from agency directors who contended that CRA was unnecessary for the same reason supporters promoted it: Existing law authorized agencies to assess credit flow; they claimed they already did so.[75] Opponents maintained that the legislation would overwhelm agencies with "a mountain of paperwork." Supporters disagreed and accused regulators of failing to hold banks accountable for uneven lending patterns and thus perpetuating redlining. They cited regulators' earlier opposition to the Home Mortgage Disclosure Act, which was meant to identify redlining, as evidence of their reluctance to address the problem.

Linking Banks and Neighborhood Decline. Supporters' rationale for CRA's allocation of burdens and benefits rested on a negative portrayal of financial institutions and the depiction of urban neighborhoods as victims who would benefit from the law. The story drew on then-familiar ideas and images described earlier: the emerging landscape of urban America, with its declining northern cities, and the emerging paradigm of urban policy that brought together the public and private sectors. Although supporters blamed banks for neighborhood decline, they emphasized that the CRA remedy was meant to encourage change through incentives rather than to harshly punish infractions. As Senator Proxmire said, "Bankers sit right at the heart of our economic system. . . . the record shows we have to do something *to nudge them, influence them, persuade them* to invest in their community."[76]

Supporters contrasted rich financial institutions with poor, older, urban communities, and they claimed that banks caused urban blight by redlining these neighborhoods. In 44 percent of their statements, supporters claimed that banks' refusal to make loans in old neighborhoods brought deterioration and decay; especially unjust was banks' willingness to accept deposits from the same community where it refused to extend credit. Supporters sometimes noted that U.S. banks loaned money in foreign countries; Senator Proxmire read a letter from a banker defending his institution's loans to developing countries with "urgent economic development needs." "What about the urgent economic development needs in Detroit, Philadelphia, Baltimore, and Boston?" Proxmire asked. "The banking industry must be encouraged to reinvest in local needs rather than continuing to favor speculative loans to shaky foreign regimes."[77] Focusing on lenders made sense from a practical perspective as well; according to Proxmire, "The banks and savings and loans have the funds. . . . If we are going to rebuild our cities, it will have to be done with the private institutions."[78] Offering state-level antiredlining policies as examples, supporters claimed that CRA would address the persistent problem of redlining without burdening lenders.

When legislators debated the Home Mortgage Disclosure Act two years earlier, opponents could deny that redlining occurred,[79] but in this debate, supporters referred to analyses of the first round of disclosure data that documented redlining problems. Opponents could not deny the existence of redlining, but contested its role in urban decline and characterized CRA as unacceptable intervention in the free market. They described bank lending policies as rational market responses to a complex set of forces. Senator Tower blamed local government for blight, noting that inner-city neighborhoods did not receive adequate public services, such as schools, street maintenance, garbage removal, and public transportation.[80] Opponents charged that CRA would chase banks out of urban neighborhoods; forced to make risky loans, banks would choose to pull out of the community altogether. The community reinvestment title smacked of "credit allocation," opponents claimed, a practice antithetical and dangerous to the free market. But the solutions they preferred tended to depend on government subsidy and thus were out of sync with new ideas about solving urban problems; they mentioned tax and interest-rate incentives for making inner-city loans, shared-risk programs backed by government, or simply development dollars that would revitalize declining neighborhoods.

A Strategy of Omission. As supporters and opponents of CRA argued over the role of banks in urban decline and whether federal banking regulators were adequately assessing the lending records of banks and thrifts, they kept silent about two groups who would benefit from the proposed legislation: community activists and racial minorities. This silence likely contributed to the proposal's low visibility. Neighborhood organizations and civil rights groups had put redlining on the political agenda, both at the local and national levels.[81] Grassroots activists had testified at Senate hearings on the proposal and had helped Proxmire's staff draft the bill. They anticipated using the law in their communities and offered suggestions to the Senate committee about how to make it more effective. They had been active in the legislative effort that led to the Home Mortgage Disclosure Act in 1975. Yet nowhere in the Senate debate did legislators mention the work of community organizations who were likely to monitor the activities of banks in their neighborhoods; rather, legislators focused on the government agents who would be charged with implementing the law—the federal regulators.

Discourse about CRA also tended to emphasize class over race. Activists understood the redlining problem to derive from racial and class bias.[82] Activists themselves were racially diverse, including working-class whites who lived in neighborhoods experiencing racial change and suffering from redlining. Unlike civil rights issues, then, CRA could not be categorized as a black or Latino issue, even though minorities stood to benefit from it. Low and moderate incomes were what constituents had in common. In Senate hearings, activists talked about class and race. Their testimony described the neighborhoods suffering from redlining as racially diverse, and their stories of struggles with banks in their cities described the individuals, many of them black, who were denied loans by local banks.[83]

On the Senate floor, however, legislators referred to race only once.[84] By framing the beneficiaries of CRA as places rather than people, senators avoided discussion of the deservedness of individual beneficiaries that had marked fair housing debates. CRA would contribute to revitalizing declining cities and neighborhoods, according to legislators; they did not speak of it as a special program that would channel loans to poor people and minorities. Nesting CRA into an existing regulatory framework enabled this depersonalization of the program because the language of banking regulations required chartered financial institutions to meet the convenience and needs of communities, not individual citizens. The Home Mortgage Disclosure Act similarly had required banks to report lending data by neighborhood (census tract), not by individual.

The Community Reinvestment Policy Design

Features of the Community Reinvestment Act reflect the stories supporters told about the bill during Senate debate and to some extent address the concerns raised by opponents. Supporters claimed that the law would clarify the existing regulatory framework without imposing burdens on regulators or lending institutions. They argued that lenders needed encouragement to contribute to the revitalization of deteriorating neighborhoods, emphasizing the places that would benefit rather than the people. They were silent on the role of community groups and the law's prospects for reducing racial discrimination in lending. Each version of the Community Reinvestment Act conformed more to these arguments. The first version included an explicit role for community organizations. The second version eliminated that language. The final version offered the most discretion to regulators and lenders and few sanctions; it targeted places by class, with a focus on low-income neighborhoods.

Like the debate itself, CRA lacked visibility; it is a short title in a long piece of legislation focused primarily on housing and community development programs. The act includes no funding authorization and no specific mandates or sanctions, each of which might have attracted more attention and provoked stronger opposition. Its six short sections direct federal regulatory agencies to include in their bank examinations an assessment of how well an institution meets the credit needs of low-income neighborhoods and to take this record into account when considering applications for branches, insurance, mergers, and acquisitions. Table 2.4 compares three drafts of the legislation. The first, S. 406, was introduced by Senator Proxmire in January 1977, and hearings were held on it in March. The second, S. 1523, is Title IV of the proposed Housing and Community Development Act, the version reported out of the Senate Banking, Housing, and Urban Affairs Committee in May and debated in June on the Senate floor. The third, Public Law 95-128, was signed into law in October; it is the product of the conference committee convened to reconcile the Senate and House versions. The House version did not have a community reinvestment title.

Table 2.4. Three Versions of Community Reinvestment Policy Designs

	Version 1 S. 406 (January 1977)	Version 2 S. 1523 (May 1977)	Version 3 Public Law 95-128 (October 1977)
Goal	"To encourage financial institutions to help meet the credit needs of the communities in which they are chartered . . . consistent with safe and sound operation of such institutions."	Same as Version 1	Same as Version 1
Target groups	Primary Savings Service Area (PSSA)	Same as Version 1	Low- and moderate-income neighbor-hoods
	Depository institutions	Same as Version 1	Same as Version 1
Lenders must:	Delineate a PSSA, analyze its deposit and credit needs, specify how to meet them, indicate the proportion of consumer deposits from PSSA residents that will be reinvested there, and report periodically to regulators and the public on the amount of credit extended in the PSSA.	No reporting requirements for lenders	Same as Version 2
Regulators must:	Use the above record as a factor in approving applica-tion; permit and encourage consumer or similar organiza-tions to present testimony at hearings on applications for deposit facilities on how well the applicant has met or is proposing to meet the credit needs of the communities served by or to be served by the applicant or subsidiaries.	In connection with its examination, assess the institu-tion's record of meeting the credit needs of its PSSA consistent with the safe and sound operation of such institution; and take such record into account in its evaluation of an application.	In connection with its examination, assess the institu-tion's record of meeting the credit needs of its entire community, includ-ing low- and moderate-income neighborhoods, consistent with the safe and sound operation of such institution; and take such record into account in its evaluation of an application.
Effective date	180 days after enactment	Same as Version 1	390 days after enactment
Resources	None	None	None

An Inherited Design. The Community Reinvestment Act used a preexisting regulatory framework to address the problem of lending discrimination, or redlining. In doing so, it inherited several features of that framework, including the orientations and priorities of regulators and a set of target groups. As emphasized by supporters during debate, CRA modified the framework governing nationally chartered or insured financial institutions. The act used the language of previous banking regulation as it clarified the definition of "convenience and needs" to mean credit needs and directed regulatory agencies to encourage community lending "consistent with the safe and sound operation" of local banks. These phrases derive from 1930s-era banking law.

CRA assigned responsibility for implementation to the four agencies that already were responsible for banking regulation: the Comptroller of the Currency, the Federal Reserve Board, the Federal Deposit Insurance Corporation, and the Federal Home Loan Bank Board (now the Office of Thrift Supervision). These agencies since at least the Great Depression have worked to guarantee the "safety and soundness" of banks and thrifts. They undertake regular examinations of the banks under their jurisdiction, assessing management practices and balance sheets and essentially judging whether banks are economically viable or whether they operate with too much risk.[85] Banks must apply for permission to receive federal insurance, to add branches, and to merge with or acquire other banks. CRA folds one more task into the existing processes of bank examinations and of consideration of applications for charters, deposit insurance, branches, and mergers and acquisitions.

Across the agencies, regulators have tended to view consumer compliance issues such as CRA as secondary to their purpose and even bothersome to enforce.[86] Although the agencies tend to share a basic mission—and a negative view of regulations—they vary in management and oversight styles, in examination cycles, and in their autonomy from elected officials.[87] Assigning implementation of CRA to four regulatory bodies meant that the law would be enforced in four ways and that subsequent efforts to modify enforcement must change the behavior of four sets of civil servants. A final implication of using the existing banking regulation system to address redlining was that only banks falling under the jurisdiction of these four agencies had to comply with the law; CRA thus applied to depository institutions but not to other financial institutions including mortgage companies and credit unions.

Undersubscribed Burdens and Benefits. Although the Community Reinvestment Act can be understood as a victory for constituencies concerned about redlining, the rhetorical strategy supporters used, and the effort to limit the visibility of the title, entailed a policy design that minimized burdens on financial institutions (and on regulators) and benefits to poor neighborhoods. Rather than debating how to ensure maximum benefits for deteriorating neighborhoods, legislators argued about whether the law would impose unacceptably high burdens on lenders and regulators. Supporters claimed that CRA only clarified existing law without requiring additional reporting or regulatory procedures. With each version of the bill, this argument became more true.

The original version had directed lenders to delineate a "primary savings service area," to analyze its credit and deposit needs, to indicate the percentage of deposits that would be reinvested in the area, and to demonstrate what it was already doing to meet credit needs. Lenders would have had to report the amount of credit extended in the service area. Regulators were directed to use these reports when considering applications from banks for branches, mergers, and so on.

In Senate hearings on the original bill, community advocates had objected to what they saw as a high level of regulatory discretion, asking for more specific direction to regulators about what to look for and what to demand of banks. But in the second version of CRA, lenders' reporting requirements were eliminated, as was reference to calculating the portion of deposits that would be reinvested in the community. This latter deletion helped bolster supporters' claims that CRA would not allocate credit, understood by opponents as a direct threat to free-market processes. In Version 2 and the final version, the regulators received the burden of assessing an institution's lending record and were directed to take that record into account when evaluating applications. However, CRA minimized this burden by leaving considerable discretion to regulators. Nothing in the law's text indicated what would constitute such an assessment or the weight regulators should give it when considering a bank's request to branch, merge, and so on. Finally, CRA contained no funding authorization. Regulators would receive no special appropriations to carry out this new responsibility, consistent with congressional supporters' assertions that it was neither new nor onerous so regulators could use data already disclosed by banks.

CRA minimized burdens on lenders and regulators by lacking explicit sanctions for noncompliance. The implicit threat to lenders was that regulators could decide to deny an application for a charter or a merger if an institution had a poor record of community lending, but CRA did not include any specific rules about such an outcome. Rather, the language of the law directed regulators to "encourage" lenders to attend to the credit needs of low- and moderate-income neighborhoods. Additionally, by the third version of the law, the effective date was changed from 180 days to 390 days after enactment.

Beneficiaries. During legislative debate, supporters made clear that CRA was intended to help deteriorated inner-city neighborhoods; advocates described these as poor and working-class racially diverse communities. The initial version of the law identified the beneficiary as a "primary savings service area" defined by each lending institution. Opponents complained that the concept was vague and that defining such an area would be a difficult task for lenders. In the third and final version of CRA, as legislators reduced reporting requirements, they defined the beneficiary more explicitly and chose a class-based definition. Regulators were required to consider banks' lending records to the low- and moderate-income neighborhoods within their communities.

Despite their awareness of the work of community organizations on redlining issues, CRA supporters chose to keep silent about these groups during Senate debate. The first version of the law, however, directed regulators to permit and to encourage consumer organizations to testify on the lending records of local banks. During the Senate hearings, activists urged legislators to go further and to expand the role that groups could play by giving them authority to sue lenders and regulators for failure to comply with the law. Instead, this early mention of community groups was eliminated from subsequent versions of the proposal. Rather, advocacy groups would have to use channels that the existing regulatory framework provided.

LEGISLATIVE STRUGGLES FOR ANTIDISCRIMINATION HOUSING LAWS

Both the 1968 Fair Housing Act and the 1977 Community Reinvestment Act represent legislative victories in the effort to reduce housing discrimination. In each case, supporters were able to overcome the structural bias against passage. They succeeded in channeling benefits to politically weak groups and burdens to politically powerful industries, broadly understood as important players in the private economy. But in each case, passage came at a price, producing two modest policies with designs that limited the prospects for social change.

On the one hand, this outcome is consistent with coalitional models of politics that predict competing players will strike compromises. In the case of fair housing, strong antidiscrimination statements and enforcement mechanisms were removed from the proposed legislation. Versions of community reinvestment law increased the discretion of banking regulators. Still, compromises are not random. And it was not clear at the time whether some of the design changes that members of Congress made to the bills would "weaken" the laws or not. So in the final version of CRA, community groups received an implicit role in enforcement rather than an explicit one. And fair housing enforcement responsibility went to an existing agency rather than to one that would have been newly established for the purpose.

Analysis of political contexts and persuasive strategies thus sheds light on the particular nature of the compromises that were struck. As I have shown, in many respects, the two policy designs were consistent with the discursive strategies used by proponents to gain support. The policy designs, then, institutionalized the ideas behind the interests in legislative struggles against housing discrimination.

3

Linking Housing Policy to Advocacy

Enacting policy to fight housing inequality, no matter how difficult, is only a first step. Whether and how policies actually change conditions or solve problems depends on how actors both inside and outside government use them. A scan of the Internet on any given day can find numerous examples of groups using fair housing and community reinvestment laws to work for housing equality. For example, the *National Fair Housing Advocate* reports an award of about $250,000 in damages, costs, and attorney's fees to a California family in August 2002.[1] The Fair Housing Council of San Fernando Valley investigated the family's claim that a prospective landlord refused to rent them a house because their son is black. The group referred them to fair housing attorneys, who filed suit in federal court and won. On another Web site, the Toledo Fair Housing Center announces its federal fair housing lawsuit, filed with five other fair housing groups, against Citigroup, Travelers Property and Casualty, and Aetna.[2] The groups conducted a series of tests and found that these companies' policies, practices, and underwriting standards denied or limited homeowners' insurance coverage on homes in black, Latino, and racially integrated neighborhoods. In Tucson, the Southern Arizona Housing Center trains landlords and property managers on fair housing requirements.[3] And in Washington, D.C., the National Fair Housing Alliance reports the results of its study estimating that only 1 percent of illegal housing discrimination is reported.[4]

On the community reinvestment front, New Jersey Citizen Action boasts of CRA agreements with nearly all New Jersey banks that provide $8 billion in commitments for low-cost mortgages and home improvement loans, financing for affordable housing, and small business loans for women- and minority-owned businesses.[5] It describes an "informational picket" at J. P. Morgan Chase Bank over the 2001 holiday season, in which members portrayed the bank as the "Grinch" who stole Christmas by resisting resolution on the loans of twenty-three victims of predatory lending. The Center for Community Change in Washington, D.C., describes its CRA Sunshine Checklist that helps advocacy groups comply with the law's reporting requirements.[6] The Association of Community Organizations for Reform Now (ACORN) announces the results of its analysis of 2001 HMDA data, showing that African Americans were more than twice as likely to be turned down for a conventional mortgage compared to whites and that Latinos were one and a half times as likely to be denied.[7] In the Bronx, Inner City Press reports on the CRA protests it filed with federal regulators in recent merger and acquisition reviews, including Citigroup's acquisition of Golden State, Wells Fargo's acquisition of Marquette Bank, and many others; it reports on the ins and outs of the review processes and gives examples of the probank attitudes of regulators and of banks' resistance to release information to advocates.[8]

Across the country, advocacy groups have become key implementers of fair housing and community reinvestment laws.[9] Fair housing advocates are working daily in courtrooms and classrooms, filing lawsuits, and training real estate agents. They are investigating claims of discrimination, conducting fair housing tests, preparing complaints, and guiding clients through the administrative enforcement process. Community reinvestment advocates are at work crunching the lending data available from bank regulators, learning about the practices of specific banks, and writing detailed, technical briefs protesting banks' performance and advising against mergers. They are training future homeowners on how mortgage lending works and developing affordable housing in their communities. And they bring out the picket signs from time to time, drawing public attention to "the bad guys" of the banking world.

Squires calls community organizations the "driving force" behind all CRA successes, and studies have shown that when regulators do deny mergers on CRA grounds, they refer to advocates' claims in the record.[10] Even though regulators approve most mergers, it is likely that without nonprofit advocacy, CRA-based denials or compliance conditions placed on merger approvals would rarely occur. As for fair housing, Smith writes that "without the ingenuity of the private movement, housing discrimination would go virtually unchecked in the United States."[11] If we want to understand the implementation of key housing policies in American cities, we must consider the work of these advocacy groups.

In Chapter 2, I recounted how supporters of fair housing and community reinvestment policies maneuvered in difficult political environments. These lawmakers argued that their proposals were modest but necessary steps to fight racial discrimination (in the case of fair housing) and urban decline (in the case of community reinvestment). Claims of modesty, captured in the two policy designs, set in motion inherently limited implementation frameworks, partly through constraining the benefits that racial minorities and low-income neighborhoods would gain from the law. But individuals, whether racial minorities or residents of poor neighborhoods or both, rarely use these laws directly. Rather, advocacy groups aid them or act on their behalf. In this chapter I examine the policies from the perspective of local advocates, asking what opportunities the two policy designs provide for action and what constraints they place upon it. I ask what sorts of political landscapes the fair housing and community reinvestment policy designs create and what resources they make available to groups who want to fight for housing equality.

THE ROLE OF ADVOCACY GROUPS
IN POLICY IMPLEMENTATION AND CHANGE

Advocacy groups and public policies are linked together in many ways. First, advocacy groups participate in the policy process, working to shape and to change public policies. In the cases of fair housing and community reinvestment policies, their features reflect lawmakers' strategies, as documented earlier, but advocacy groups contributed ideas as the laws took shape. As groups participate in the laws' implementation, they again influence the nature of housing policy. But just as advocacy shapes policy, so policy shapes advocacy. Fair housing and community reinvestment policies chart the course of housing advocacy by offering resources and channeling activity in particular directions. Evidence of advocates' efforts to change policy, and of their activity to implement it, is fairly easy to find. Yet little analysis of policy's impact on advocacy exists.

Advocates' efforts to improve fair housing law began almost immediately after the original statute took effect, as groups grappled with the limitations the law placed on their efforts to fight housing discrimination.[12] The public record contains numerous research reports and congressional hearings in which civil rights and fair housing groups testified about these problems and recommended changes.[13] They complained that rates of segregation and discrimination persisted in the face of a fair housing law without significant administrative enforcement and with caps on court damages. HUD could neither initiate investigations nor punish violations of the law, and even the existing process was too slow to result in relief for victims.[14] In 1984, groups began to work for a grant program for fair housing organizations. Officers of twenty-five such groups adopted a resolution urging HUD to seek enabling legislation to provide direct funding to nonprofits.[15] A demonstration project was established in 1987 and a permanent one in 1992.

Civil rights and fair housing groups took part in the legislative process leading to passage of the 1988 Fair Housing Amendments Acts. A compromise they struck with real estate industry groups broke a stalemate and prompted passage in both chambers of Congress by large majorities.[16] The compromise created a two-track enforcement process, in which any party to a complaint could elect, and receive, a jury trial rather than resolve the dispute through what would be a new administrative law process.

Groups working for community reinvestment also have consistently sought to improve and to defend CRA since its enactment, lobbying members of Congress, testifying at hearings, and mobilizing community groups across the country who benefit from the law. These efforts generally are spearheaded by two national organizations, the National Community Reinvestment Coalition and ACORN. In 1988 oversight hearings, "a crescendo of [advocates'] complaints" testified that CRA was "fail-safe" due to rating inflation—only about 2 percent of examined banks received poor grades.[17] These hearings established the justification for changes in the 1989 Financial Institutions Reform, Recovery, and Enforcement Act (FIRREA), improving public information related to CRA. President Clinton's administration was friendly to CRA, and advocates participated in, and generally approved of, the revision of the law's regulations regarding the criteria used in bank examinations. National organizations worked to defend CRA, which came under attack when Congress crafted financial modernization legislation in 1999. They lobbied supporters in Congress, mobilized letter-writing campaigns, and met with executive branch staff. Advocates characterized the changes to CRA exams and the disclosure requirements for nonprofit groups as retrenchment, although the Clinton administration characterized the outcome as preservation of the law.[18]

Although the importance of advocacy groups is acknowledged, studies have not analyzed how the laws affect the groups themselves. Writers document how weak laws have made enforcement more difficult and less effective but do not consider systematically whether the laws have had positive or negative effects on the groups themselves. That is, do these policies foster strong advocacy efforts, or do they stunt groups' development, both of capacity and political strength? In other words, what are the political consequences of these two housing policies? This question is important not only for understanding the struggle for housing equality but also more generally. More and more frequently, if a national policy is to "work"—to affect social conditions—nongovernmental groups must actually carry it out.[19]

In this and the following chapters, I use the conceptual tools of policy design theory to analyze how fair housing and community reinvestment policies have shaped advocacy. This chapter's analysis first reviews the components of the two policy designs—their goals, target groups, and enforcement structures (their agents, rules, tools, and levels of discretion and funding).[20] I trace the evolution of each design, noting the key legislative or administrative actions that changed each one in significant ways for advocacy groups.

In the second part of the analysis, I consider the kinds of resources that each design offers to advocacy groups. Research on nonprofit-government links tends to emphasize the importance of funding,[21] but theories about policy design, policy tools, and institutions highlight the importance of nonmaterial resources in structuring action.[22] Thus, I distinguish between four kinds of resources: problem definitions, funding, tools and arenas, and information. Each policy's set of resources will require advocacy groups to have particular skills, will invite them into a particular institutional network, and will have particular implications for the groups' capacity.[23] A policy offers a particular set of ideas or approach to defining a problem that specifies who causes the problem and who suffers from it. Funding may be available directly from government (e.g., grants) or indirectly through procedures that a policy design establishes (e.g., winning damages through litigation). Policies offer arenas for group action and tools to use within them; they may explicitly offer groups a direct role in policy implementation. Policies may provide information that groups could use to influence local action. Once identified, we can consider how policy design resources are likely to shape advocacy at the local level. Policy designs have implications for at least four dimensions of group activity: the type of groups that participate, how they define discrimination, their actions, and their relations with government and industry.

THE EVOLUTION OF TWO POLICY DESIGNS

Before considering how fair housing and community reinvestment policy will influence advocacy groups, we need to describe and analyze the contents of the two policy designs. The Fair Housing Act and the Community Reinvestment Act constitute the national framework to address racial discrimination in housing. They address the problem with different strategies and at different scales. Fair housing is a people-based policy, while CRA is a place-based policy; fair housing is a race-based policy, while CRA is a class-based policy. Fair housing offers rights-based remedies, while CRA designates a responsibility toward potential victims. Since each law was enacted, amendments and adjustments have altered the original designs, although their broad approaches remain constant. Table 3.1 summarizes each design's features and key changes since enactment.

Evolution of Fair Housing Policy

The 1968 Fair Housing Act is a civil rights law seeking to eliminate instances of racial discrimination against individuals such that equal access to housing markets will occur. Real estate brokers are prohibited from treating clients of color differently (worse) than white clients. Examples of discrimination include lying about the availability of a housing unit, offering worse terms of purchase or rental such as higher rents or security deposits, or showing people of color different housing than white people solely because of ideas about where groups should live. Clients have the right to sue if they discover they have received such treatment. The U.S. Department of Housing and Urban Development (HUD), responsible for federal housing programs, implements the law. Since 1968, two laws have amended the original design in ways particularly significant for advocacy groups: the 1988 Fair Housing Amendments Act and the 1992 Housing and Community Development Act. National fair housing and civil rights organizations played key roles in securing these changes. The 1988 law strengthened

Table 3.1. The Fair Housing and Community Reinvestment Policy Designs

Design Features	Fair Housing	Community Reinvestment
Policy type	Civil Rights	Regulatory
Goals	To protect civil rights, to provide subsidized housing on a nondiscriminatory basis	To encourage banks to meet community credit needs (and to limit redlining)
Target Groups		
Benefits	Protected classes of people: race, national origin, religion 1988: People with Disabilities; Families with Children	Places: Low- and moderate-income neighborhoods
Burdens	Housing industry, most homeowners, federal government (HUD and participants in federal housing programs)	Federally regulated banks and savings and loan associations 1999: Advocacy groups subject to "sunshine" provisions
Enforcement structure		
Agents	Department of Housing and Urban Development, Department of Justice, state and local civil rights agencies (with substantially equivalent laws) 1987 and 1992: advocacy groups	Federal Home Loan Bank Board, Comptroller of the Currency, Federal Reserve Board, Federal Deposit Insurance Corporation
Rules	Prohibits specified discriminatory practices Covers most housing after three years Requires HUD to operate programs so as to "affirmatively further" fair housing	"Convenience and needs" means credit needs Lenders have "continuing, affirmative obligation to help meet the credit needs of local communities" 1999: Banks need "satisfactory" rating to merge/acquire nonbank affiliates
Tools	Complaint process, conciliation efforts (HUD) Work with housing industry (HUD) Private litigation (individuals) Pattern and practice suits (DOJ) 1988: HUD may initiate investigations Administrative law system created Cap on damages removed 1987 and 1992: Grants for nonprofit groups (Fair Housing Initiatives Program)	Community reinvestment examination (HMDA data available) Application review process 1989: Community reinvestment ratings and evaluations become public information (HMDA includes individual-level data) Descriptive ratings mandated 1995: Performance-based standards for community reinvestment examinations Exam schedule becomes public 1999: Exam cycle lengthened for some banks

Design Features	Fair Housing	Community Reinvestment
Discretion	Relatively low on Goal 1; high on Goal 2	High
Funding	Authorized, not guaranteed	None

Sources: Fair housing: P.L. 90-284, P.L. 95-128, P.L. 100-242, P.L. 102-550. Community rein-

HUD's enforcement powers and added to the protected classes people with disabilities and families with children. The 1992 law made permanent a grant program for nonprofit groups to enforce fair housing law.

Although the fair housing statute's stated goal is vague ("to provide for fair housing" throughout the United States), its content suggests two specific goals: to protect the civil rights of individual home seekers and to provide subsidized housing on a nondiscriminatory basis. The policy is most specific about the first goal while providing less guidance on the second. For example, the Fair Housing Act prohibited a series of discriminatory practices in housing transactions, including real estate sales, rental, and lending. But the only rule corresponding to the policy design's second goal is Section 808, which requires HUD to operate housing programs "in a manner to affirmatively further the purposes of this title."

Fair housing law grants enforcement authority primarily to HUD, with some jurisdiction for the Department of Justice (DOJ). The original fair housing law permitted HUD to add an assistant secretary to oversee fair housing implementation and directed the agency to convene with representatives of the housing industry to discuss implementation. HUD developed a national enforcement process to receive and investigate complaints, but when the agency determined that discrimination had occurred, it was able only to attempt conciliation. The law also mandated that HUD allow state and local agencies to handle complaints where a substantially equivalent state or local law exists. The 1988 fair housing amendments put "teeth" into fair housing law by authorizing HUD to initiate investigations rather than having to wait for claims to be brought. The agency was directed to establish an administrative law system to adjudicate claims. Since then, HUD has had the power to pursue remedies other than conciliation; administrative law judges may award actual damages, civil penalties to the government, injunctive relief, and attorney's fees.[24]

In selecting HUD, fair housing law assigned authority to a politically permeable agency; that is, its orientation and its resources regularly fluctuate with partisan changes in Congress and the presidency.[25] The agency's top tier of leadership is appointed by the president, subject to Senate confirmation. An assistant secretary for fair housing heads the agency's Office of Fair Housing and Equal Opportunity (FHEO). Its annual budget emerges from the congressional appropriations process, thus resulting from negotiations between the legislative and executive branches of government. With each budget cycle, a range of political actors has the chance to influence the funding level and direction of fair housing enforcement. And each presidential election brings the opportunity to alter the agency's top leadership.

In addition, HUD is often subject to budget cuts. Federal funds for urban programs began to decline in the late 1970s, and Republicans in Congress and the White House have frequently targeted the agency for cutbacks. From 1978 to 1994, HUD experienced the largest cuts of any cabinet-level department; its portion of the federal budget fell from 7.5 percent in 1978 to 1.3 percent in 1990.[26] The most drastic cuts occurred during the Reagan administration; under the Clinton administration, appropriations rose modestly. Nonetheless, after the 1994 midterm elections, HUD came under pressure again when the new majority of House Republicans called for the agency's elimination.

The original law empowered DOJ to initiate litigation where the agency found a "pattern and practice" of discriminatory behavior and to seek equitable relief and preventive relief such as temporary or permanent injunctions. The amendments enabled the department to seek monetary damages for individuals and civil penalties of up to $100,000 and to intervene in private cases deemed "of general public importance." Individual complainants may file suit rather than filing a complaint with HUD.[27] The amendments extended the statute of limitations and eliminated a cap on punitive damages.

Nonprofit fair housing groups became enforcement agents in 1992, when the Fair Housing Initiatives Program (FHIP) became permanent, enabling HUD to contract with them to enforce the law. This program funds private nonprofit fair housing organizations on a competitive basis to undertake enforcement activities. In the early 1980s, a two-year demonstration project had funded nine local fair housing groups.[28] FHIP was authorized in the 1987 Housing and Community Development Act as a demonstration project, becoming permanent in the 1992 version of the law.[29]

Evolution of Community Reinvestment Policy

As we have seen, the 1977 Community Reinvestment Act sought to reduce discrimination against neighborhoods (redlining) by stating that banks have an affirmative responsibility to serve their communities. CRA required bank regulators to review banks' lending rates to low-income neighborhoods. Regulators have the authority to withhold permission for a bank to merge with another on the basis of poor service to such neighborhoods. The 1989 Financial Institutions Reform, Recovery, and Enforcement Act (FIRREA), the 1995 overhaul of CRA regulations, and the 1999 Gramm-Leach-Bliley Financial Modernization Act altered certain aspects of the community reinvestment design.

CRA's stated purpose is to "encourage" financial institutions "to help meet the credit needs of the communities in which they are chartered." Chapter 2 showed that CRA was intended to limit lending institutions' practice of redlining, denying mortgage credit to individuals living in deteriorating urban neighborhoods. CRA defined its beneficiaries in terms of place and class, specifying that banks should service the low- and moderate-income neighborhoods in their markets. The Community Reinvestment Act stated that existing law already required federally chartered or insured financial institutions to demonstrate that they served "the convenience and needs" of their communities. CRA specified that "convenience and needs" included credit needs as well as deposit needs, and that financial institutions had "continuing and affirmative obligations to help meet the credit needs of the local communities in which they are chartered," including the low- and moderate-income neighborhoods in their service areas. It did not authorize or appropriate funding for implementation.

The law directed the four regulatory agencies that oversee banking to implement it. These include the Office of the Comptroller of the Currency (OCC), a bureau of the Treasury Department, which regulates national banks; the Office of Thrift Supervision (OTS) (formerly the Federal Home Loan Bank Board), also in the Treasury Department, which regulates savings and loans; the Federal Reserve Board, which governs bank holding companies and state-chartered banks that join the Reserve system; and the Federal Deposit Insurance Corporation (FDIC), which insures deposits and oversees state-chartered banks not part of the Federal Reserve system. The statute left these agencies a relatively high level of discretion; important terms (e.g., "community credit needs") and processes (e.g., assessment of an institution's community lending record) were not defined in the text.

The agencies charged with enforcing CRA have relatively low political permeability. All are self-funded agencies, generating their budgets from fees assessed on the banks they regulate; they do not rely on the congressional budgetary process. All have directors whose terms exceed four years, that is, they may remain in office longer than one presidential term. The Federal Reserve System is the most autonomous in this respect, as its directors are appointed by the president to fourteen-year terms. Other agency directors serve five-year terms. Although all agencies are subject to congressional oversight, two are housed within the Department of Treasury (OCC and OTS) and therefore fall somewhat more clearly under the purview of the sitting president. In my interviews with community reinvestment advocates and officials, respondents reported that, at least under the Clinton administration, the OCC and the OTS were more receptive to presidential priorities for CRA enforcement than the Federal Reserve Board and the FDIC.

This relative political autonomy gives the four agencies more control over the community reinvestment policy environment. Elected officials simply have fewer opportunities to influence the direction of these regulatory agencies. In addition, the perceived technical nature of banking issues invites deference from legislators who are not banking experts.[30] Sometimes an industry crisis creates an opportunity for legislative change, as the savings and loan debacle did in the late 1980s, leading to FIRREA.

The Community Reinvestment Act mobilized tools that regulators already used for other purposes. It directed bank supervisors to use bank examinations and application reviews to encourage banks to lend in low- and moderate-income neighborhoods. Agents were required to assess how well institutions were meeting community credit needs and to take this record into account when reviewing applications for insurance, mergers, relocations, and expansions/branches. Prior to CRA, regulators examined banks and considered applications primarily based on the fiscal "safety and soundness" of bank operations. It added another set of criteria for regulators to apply.

Changes to the law since 1977 focus on the community reinvestment examination, which now constitutes a separate process rather than one performed simultaneously with a "safety and soundness" exam. FIRREA altered the grading system and made regulators' evaluations public information. It mandated that community reinvestment evaluations and ratings, which regulators had kept confidential, be made public; ratings would move from a numeric to a descriptive system. Legislators supportive of FIRREA's public disclosure provision portrayed it as a necessary check on regulators who were tempted to be "friendly and favorable" toward banks.[31] Under the Clinton administration, agencies revised community reinvestment regulations to emphasize performance and to define more objective evaluation standards. As advocates requested, examiners now focus on a bank's lending, investment, and service record rather than its paper trail.[32] In 1999, legislation scaled back community reinvestment requirements and imposed burdens on advocacy groups. The 1999 Gramm-Leach-Bliley Financial Modernization Act reduced the frequency of community reinvestment exams for small banks and limited the compliance responsibilities of financial holding companies and their affiliates. It also required nonprofit groups to annually disclose information about loans, investments, and grants received through CRA agreements with banks.[33]

POLICY RESOURCES FOR ADVOCACY GROUPS

These policies vary in their goals, target groups, and enforcement structures. They also vary in the resources they offer to advocacy groups. Their evolution has generally expanded the resources available to groups, but in different ways and with key exceptions. Although the fair housing policy design has evolved to offer direct funding to advocacy groups, formally incorporating them into the enforcement process, community reinvestment policy has never done so. Instead, the community reinvestment policy design offers action channels and information to groups working to persuade local lenders to increase credit flow to low-income and minority neighborhoods and individuals. Yet for fair housing groups, HUD is not an ideal government partner. Over time, improvement in the information CRA provides to advocacy groups has strengthened their ability to monitor and intervene in the regulatory process. But community reinvestment advocacy groups have never enjoyed the legitimacy that fair housing groups hold

Table 3.2. Resources for Advocacy Groups

Resources	Fair Housing		Community Reinvestment
	Civil rights	Affordable Housing	
Problem Definition	Remove race from private-sector housing transactions	Nondiscriminatory provision of low-income housing	Redlining leads to deterioration of poor neighborhoods
Funding, direct	Fair Housing Initiatives Program (FHIP) Community Development Block Grant	None	None
Funding, indirect	Compensatory and punitive damages, attorney's fees	Compensatory and punitive damages, attorney's fees	Loans and grants from financial institutions
Tools and arenas	Federal and state courts Administrative law system	Federal and state courts Administrative law system	Bank examination process Application review process Public comment period
Information	FHIP conferences and technical assistance	None	HMDA data, neighborhood and individual Community reinvestment ratings

in policy enforcement, and their role has come under heightened scrutiny by opponents of the law. Table 3.2 summarizes the resource mix that the two policies offer nonprofit groups.

Fair Housing Policy Resources

The fair housing policy design offers two definitions of housing problems to advocates. The first, protection of individual civil rights, focuses on the process of housing transactions, with attention to how the real estate industry treats protected classes. The second, provision of affordable housing on a nondiscriminatory basis, concentrates on how government operates its housing programs.

Civil Rights Resources. The bulk of fair housing policy resources rests here. Funding, tools and arenas, and information are available to groups adopting an understanding of fair housing rooted in identifying and punishing discriminatory practices in housing transactions and in compensating victims. Three of FHIP's four initiatives offer funds to nonprofit advocacy groups: the private enforcement initiative, the fair housing organizations initiative (for start-up groups in underserved areas of the country), and education and outreach. (The fourth initiative is reserved for state and local government agencies.) Qualifying activities include receiving fair housing complaints and investigating them, conducting fair housing tests, and helping clients to file administrative complaints and navigate the administrative process that HUD operates regionally or that state civil rights agencies run with HUD subsidies. FHIP also funds education and outreach activities, though always at much lower levels. For example, 48 percent of FHIP funding from 1989 to 1996 went to the private enforcement initiative, and 18 percent went to the fair housing organizations initiative; both of these emphasize enforcement activities. In the same period, 24 percent of the grant money went to education and outreach activities.[34] Groups often receive grants under more than one initiative; amounts vary widely, from $10,000 to $1 million in 1996, with an average of $206,000. About 220 nonprofits received grants from 1989 to 1996.[35] With each notice of funding availability, HUD adjusts priorities for the program; thus, one year it may request that groups focus on mortgage lending discrimination, while the next year it emphasizes disability rights, and so on.

HUD holds annual conferences for FHIP grantees to promote information-sharing and to provide technical assistance. The agency's fair housing staffers attend national conferences of fair housing organizations to update them on HUD's latest programs and to learn about their activities. Data disclosed by financial institutions to comply with the Home Mortgage Disclosure Act also is sometimes used in fair lending cases.

Before FHIP existed, advocacy groups could sometimes secure special contracts from HUD to carry out fair housing activities such as audit studies or educational initiatives. Other than these irregular opportunities, HUD also offered small amounts of money to Community Housing Resource Boards (CHRBs). As part of the agency's mandated effort to cooperate with the housing industry, it signed a Voluntary Affirmative Marketing Agreement with the National Association of Realtors in the 1970s. HUD sponsored the creation of CHRBs made up of industry representatives and community members to monitor these agreements at the local level. Under the Reagan administration, the agency restricted CHRB activities and board membership, and it discontinued CHRBs altogether in 1992 when it signed a new partnership agreement with realtors.[36]

Another enforcement tool available to fair housing groups is litigation. The 1988 fair housing amendments removed caps on punitive damages and liberalized provisions for awarding attorneys' fees.[37] Both administrative law judges and trial judges or juries may award attorneys' fees and damages to fair housing groups.[38] The amendments also established an administrative law system to handle fair housing claims. The administrative route is less costly because legal fees either are not incurred or are lower than if litigation were pursued. Yet prospects for higher monetary judgments exist with litigation.[39]

Affordable Housing Resources. A second set of fair housing resources is rooted in an understanding of fair housing as the provision of affordable housing on a nondiscriminatory basis. Several tools are available, but not funding or information. FHIP dollars cannot be used to pursue claims against government. The Fair Housing Act requires HUD to integrate "fair housing" into its existing housing programs "in a manner to affirmatively further the purposes of this title" (Sec. 808). Thus, it directs attention to the operating procedures and outcomes of federal programs such as public housing, Section 8, and the Community Development Block Grant (CDBG). Groups may challenge HUD's, or any federal grantee's, practices as violating fair housing law.

Groups may file a fair housing lawsuit against HUD or a recipient of federal housing subsidies, such as a public housing authority or a local government, or both. Or groups may press for local policy changes by showing that local governments have not "affirmatively furthered" fair housing in their use of federal housing and urban development funds, as the Fair Housing Act requires of them. Sometimes groups can secure funds this way because local governments can claim compliance with the requirement by offering grants to fair housing groups. For groups pursuing nondiscrimination in subsidized housing, indirect funding resources constitute the extent of federal funding available through the policy design. These opportunities to intervene represent the primary resources that federal law offers.

HUD's orientation toward its mandate to "affirmatively further" fair housing influences the cost of using this resource—whether using these tools might result in decades of litigation or whether it might spur a settlement. The agency's broad discretion has resulted in variation over time in its approach to programs such as CDBG and public housing, though critics have long noted HUD's reluctance to aggressively root out discrimination in its ranks.[40] In the case of CDBG, the agency has long required state and local recipients to certify that they use the programs to further fair housing goals. But HUD's standards for such certification have fluctuated. Often, the certification process was pro forma—a matter of a grantee signing a statement as part of a request for funds. Sometimes local HUD officials suggested ways that a local government could meet the requirement, for example by participating in a Community Housing Resource Board. In 1995, the agency required local governments to undertake a fair housing planning process and to state how they would address fair housing problems in their communities. Some fair housing groups received contracts from local governments to produce documents analyzing local impediments to fair housing. But no follow-up monitoring of these planning processes occurred, and the requirement was later dropped.

In the case of public housing programs, HUD has varied in its efforts to desegregate public housing projects and to ensure that scattered site units and Section 8 vouchers do not reinforce segregated patterns. Often, the agency has been hostile toward claims of discrimination against it. When named as a defendant in a fair housing lawsuit, HUD typically has fought these charges, resulting in lengthy court battles with numerous appeals.[41] Under President Clinton and HUD secretaries

Cisneros and Cuomo, the agency began taking steps to desegregate some public and Section 8 housing and was willing to settle rather than to fight litigation.[42]

Community Reinvestment Policy Resources

The community reinvestment policy design defines housing inequality as redlining, disinvestment by private financial institutions from low-income urban neighborhoods. Advocates thus can use this policy to try to prompt local banks to "reinvest"—to make capital available—in poor neighborhoods. The policy design offers information that enables advocacy groups to assess whether banks have withheld capital from these neighborhoods. Banks submit data on lending activity to bank regulators, who make this information public. Groups can then analyze the number of loans made in particular locations, the loan applications denied, and the race and gender of the applicants. They can thus monitor the lending activity of banks in their cities and identify which are the poor performers.

Especially since 1989, CRA's informational resources have improved significantly. The Home Mortgage Disclosure Act of 1975 was the initial source of data that advocates used. It obligated banks to disclose home loan volume by census tract. In 1989, FIRREA amended HMDA to require disclosure of more data, such as the disposition of loan applications and the income level, race, and gender of applicants. Community reinvestment ratings and written evaluations also became public. In 1991, a CRA amendment required that regulators disclose the data they used to determine these ratings.[43] Regulations governing the exam process now provide quarterly advance notice of community reinvestment exams.[44] During the 1990s, much of these data became available on the Internet through the Web sites of regulatory agencies.

In general, groups now have access to a great deal of data on which to build a case for a CRA protest, an objection to a proposed merger. They can analyze an institution's loans and loan denials geographically and across racial and income groups. (Interpretation of these data remains controversial; groups argue that differential lending or denial rates constitute discrimination or redlining, while banks argue that the data are incomplete and cannot be interepreted as discrimination.)[45] Groups can review a regulator's examination of a particular bank and the data on which it was built. They can focus their research on banks whose exams are approaching and attempt to identify areas for improvement.

The policy design does not explicitly offer tools or procedures through which advocacy groups can become involved in enforcement. Rather, their opportunity to participate is embedded within regulatory processes predating the Community Reinvestment Act. These require regulators to hear public comments when reviewing applications from financial institutions and when conducting bank examinations.[46] The bank examination and the review period that occurs when a bank requests permission to merge with another thus constitute two moments when advocates can deploy CRA's informational resources in the regulatory arena.

When a lender requests permission from a regulatory agency to acquire or to merge with another bank, a review period occurs. Local advocacy groups may try to influence the institution's lending practices by filing a comment or protest during this time or by threatening to do so. Regulators rarely deny applications on community reinvestment grounds and only in limited cases have they approved mergers conditional on changes relating to community reinvestment practices.[47] Still, advocacy groups use the public comment period as a way to negotiate directly with banks about how to improve their services to poor communities, in what Fishbein calls an "informal dispute resolution mechanism."[48] While bank leaders may not think that regulators ultimately will deny their application to expand, they want to secure permission as quickly as possible. An advocacy group's CRA protest often threatens to slow down the process enough to motivate banks to negotiate. In addition, when groups use demonstrations to publicize their CRA protests, they draw negative attention to banks, also prompting bankers to negotiate.[49]

Besides acting during a review of merger requests, advocacy groups also can try to influence the regular bank examination process. Since community reinvestment ratings and evaluations became public information, groups have the opportunity to review the regulators' findings. National community reinvestment advocates advise local groups to study these carefully and submit any objections to the public record in case an institution later submits an application to merge. Otherwise, at the time of an application review, regulators could interpret advocates' silence on these publicly disclosed evaluations as a sign of agreement with them.[50] Besides submitting comments to the pertinent regulatory agency, they can request to meet with the examiner conducting a routine CRA compliance exam.[51] The extent to which examiners talk with community groups and local government agencies about the records of local lenders, and the influence that these conversations have on the ratings, varies by agency and by examiner.[52]

The community reinvestment policy design offers no direct funding to advocacy groups to engage in these activities. It does offer groups the prospect of securing grants or credit from financial institutions because federal regulators count a bank's support for local community organizations and community developers as evidence of compliance with the law. Thus when groups negotiate with lenders who have poor records of investing in low-income communities, they may strike an agreement for improved performance that includes grants or loans for local nonprofit groups. CRA agreements struck between banks and advocates may include commitments to provide loans for particular community development projects, to fund loan counseling programs operated by local community groups, or to fund competitive grant programs in which local groups may participate. Changes in 1999 to CRA include a "sunshine" provision obligating groups to annually disclose to regulators the funding they received through CRA agreements.

EXPECTATIONS FOR LOCAL ADVOCACY

In this chapter I have analyzed fair housing and community reinvestment policies in terms of basic design features and the sets of resources each offers to advocacy groups. The next step is to consider how groups would be expected to
respond. Deconstructing policy designs identifies the specific institutional
mechanisms that influence advocacy. When local advocacy groups choose to
take up the problem of housing discrimination, they confront these two policies,
each with distinct features and varying types and levels of resources. As they respond to policy, policy shapes them. It is useful to think about four aspects of
advocacy that policy designs can affect: the types of groups who engage in advocacy, how they define discrimination, their actions, and their relationships.
The dramatic differences between the fair housing and community reinvestment
policy designs should give rise to quite different local movements. Table 3.3
summarizes these propositions about local fair housing and community reinvestment advocacy.

Group Type

Advocacy groups active on fair housing are likely to be single-issue organizations, although groups with a broader civil rights agenda might become involved
from time to time. In contrast, advocacy groups active on community reinvestment are likely to be multi-issue organizations that incorporate these activities
into a wider mission. Differences in the resource mixes of the two policy designs
underpin these expectations. The fair housing design offers direct funding to advocacy groups engaged in fair housing enforcement. Damages and attorneys' fees
available through litigation attract the private bar and Legal Services to work on
fair housing cases. Community reinvestment policy offers no direct operational
support, so groups that pursue community reinvestment advocacy need other
sources of funds to support these activities. This means they are likely to engage
in other work for which funding is available. Although they can secure funding indirectly through community reinvestment advocacy by negotiating agreements
with banks, groups need an initial stock of operational support to engage in the research and organizing activity that could bring a bank to the negotiating table.

Problem Definition

Because the two policies define discrimination differently, advocacy groups
working with each of them are also likely to do so. Fair housing groups are likely
to define discrimination in terms of the housing process, to define "fair housing"
as one's right to participate in housing transactions on an equal basis with those
of the dominant racial group, those without disabilities, and those without children.[53] This right can be defended in court and remedied with monetary dam-

Table 3.3. Expectations for Fair Housing and Community Reinvestment Advocacy

Dimension of Advocacy	Fair Housing	Community Reinvestment
Group type	Specialists	Nonspecialists
Problem definition		
Discrimination	Individualized, rights-based, process-oriented	Place-based, uneven patterns, outcome-oriented
Goals	Civil rights (more activity), affordable housing (less activity)	Lending discrimination, other community needs
Target	Private sector housing (more), public sector housing (less), racial minorities	Banks, savings and loans, poor neighborhoods
Actions		
Tools	Enforcement activities	Research, mobilization of neighborhoods, public comments
Arenas	Court and administrative arenas	Regulatory arenas
Timing	Federal changes spark local changes; more activity post-1988, then stable level of activity	Irregular, sparked by bank actions and examination cycles; more activity post-1989
Relationships		
To government	Partnerships (civil rights) Adversarial (affordable housing)	Adversarial
To industry	Adversarial	Adversarial

ages. A definition of fair housing as a desired housing pattern, such as racial integration, should get less attention. Community reinvestment groups, on the other hand, should think of discrimination in terms of housing outcomes. For them, a neighborhood whose residents received fewer home loans than those in another neighborhood suffers from discrimination. These groups should understand community reinvestment as a matter of fairness rather than rights; while low-income neighborhoods may not have a legal right to home loans, bank redlining starves them of capital needed to maintain a decent quality of life.

Differences in the two policy designs promote these varying definitions of discrimination. Fair housing's target population includes individual members of protected classes, and its claim-driven enforcement process invites a focus on individual instances of discrimination. The statute's rules define discriminatory practices that occur in the process of securing housing. The focus on transactions

between individual home buyers and sellers suggests the causal theory that removing race (and other protected attributes) from the housing search process will
result in fair housing. The design does not specify whether a nondiscriminatory
market would be racially integrated; it stops short of offering rules or tools that
would promote integration.[54]

Community reinvestment policy targets places rather than individuals, as-
serting that banks should address the needs of all neighborhoods in their markets,
including low- and moderate-income areas. Its tools assess the degree to which
banks do so. Regulators consider a bank's overall level of lending, investment,
and service to low-income neighborhoods. HMDA data enable regulators and advocacy groups to examine aggregate lending patterns. Banks risk being faulted
not for denying a loan to an individual, but for denying loans at higher rates to
groups of people who live in low-income versus higher-income neighborhoods.

Actions: Tools and Arenas

Fair housing policy's features suggest that advocacy groups will develop the
legal and investigative expertise to work on fair housing case by case in their
cities. Most fair housing advocacy should consist of taking and investigating
claims, conducting fair housing tests, and using the court and administrative law
systems to advocate on behalf of complainants—racial minorities, people with
disabilities, and families with children. Fewer local efforts, especially among fair
housing specialist groups, should focus on public-sector, affordable housing. In
contrast, we would expect community reinvestment groups to work to ensure that
low-income neighborhoods receive their "fair share" of loans. But groups are
likely to demand more from banks, depending on how groups understand community needs. They are likely to conduct research on lending rates and to use the
bank regulatory process by filing comments on pending mergers and meeting
with bank examiners, hoping that the threat of sanctions or delays will encourage banks to change their practices. Advocates should be able to mobilize residents of particular neighborhoods around a common interest: improving the
neighborhood through better access to private capital.

The fair housing and community reinvestment designs promote these particular sets of activities. Fair housing's tools and arenas consist of opportunities
to use the courts and the administrative law system. Direct funding is available
to support this work, and statutory text delineates the enforcement process in detail. Groups working against public-sector discrimination cannot secure federal
funds, so these efforts should emerge only where local sources of support exist.
Community reinvestment's rules and tools direct activity toward the bank regulatory process and offer groups information to use when they intervene. Vague
statutory language mandating that banks meet "community credit needs" means
that advocacy groups can offer their own definitions of what constitutes CRA
compliance, based on their sense of a neighborhood's banking needs.

CRA's place-based set of beneficiaries and its focus on lenders invite a community organizing approach. Community reinvestment groups can use the law's focus on discrimination against neighborhoods to emphasize the common interests of neighborhood residents across racial and class lines. By targeting only one causal agent (banks), CRA offers advocates an "enemy" to galvanize neighborhood residents. By contrast, fair housing policy has no explicit spatial dimension, and its broad coverage of many sectors of the housing industry provides no single target to organize against. Community reinvestment groups can use lending data to show neighborhood residents how their area compares to other neighborhoods in rates of home loans. Redlining harms all of them, not only the residents whose loans were denied, because it contributes to physical deterioration and may harm property values throughout the neighborhood. Fair housing groups can use audit studies to show neighborhood residents that discriminatory treatment occurs where they live. This evidence points to violations of the principles of justice and fairness but not necessarily to material disadvantages for everyone.

Timing

National policy designs should also influence the timing of group action. Fair housing advocacy should occur more consistently than community reinvestment advocacy. Shifts in fair housing strategies should occur more often than shifts in community reinvestment strategies. And the major federal legislative changes in fair housing and community reinvestment policies should have prompted local shifts in advocacy.

The presence of direct funding for fair housing nonprofits since 1992 should result in a consistent level of local activity, at least from FHIP grantees. Advocacy groups that work on community reinvestment do not tap such funding that could enable consistent monitoring and action. Additionally, groups are most likely to influence banks when they merge, so local community reinvestment advocacy is likely to peak when local banks are involved in mergers, and to subside when they are not. The high political permeability of HUD compared with the greater autonomy of the federal banking regulators also should affect the timing of local action. The budgets and direction of HUD's fair housing programs shift with each budget cycle, and especially with each presidential administration. Local advocates will receive different levels of federal money, with different mandates attached to it, as these cycles play out. Because federal regulatory agencies are more autonomous, shifts in procedure cannot be anticipated as regularly. Local advocates are likely to face a more stable set of resources, prompting fewer shifts in their strategies.

Because of key shifts in the two laws, both community reinvestment and fair housing activity should have increased in the late 1980s. In the case of fair housing, the 1988 amendments increased resources for litigation, added protected classes, and in 1992, FHIP was established as a permanent program, all increasing incentives and constituencies for fair housing action. With community reinvestment, 1989 was a critical year, since FIRREA made community reinvestment ratings public and increased the information available through HMDA. Subsequent changes have continued to improve the quality of public information, and regulatory changes focus on performance-based measures of CRA compliance, meaning banks may have become more willing to change their practices. A consistent rise in community reinvestment advocacy since 1989 should be apparent to match this expansion in resources.

Relationships

Relationship to Government. Policy designs structure the relationships between government and advocacy groups. Although neither of the original statutes mentions nonprofit advocacy organizations, fair housing has evolved to incorporate them as legitimate partners in fair housing implementation and enforcement. Such an evolution has not occurred with community reinvestment policy. Consequently, we are likely to find partnerlike relationships between HUD and the fair housing nonprofits who pursue discrimination in private-sector housing, with the exception of groups bringing claims of discrimination in public housing. Here, relations are likely to be adversarial. The fair housing enforcement structure is driven by claims—to set fair housing enforcement in motion, someone must come forward with a claim of discrimination. Until 1988, HUD lacked the authority to initiate investigations. Staff in the agency's Office of Fair Housing and Equal Opportunity (FHEO) are likely to look upon nonprofits—or anyone who helps to generate claims—with favor. Indeed, HUD has come to rely on nonprofits to undertake certain enforcement activities it finds difficult, given its political vulnerability—namely, fair housing testing. Yet testing is critical to enforcement because minority home seekers often need to know how a housing professional treated clients of different races if they are to recognize discrimination in the post–Fair Housing Act era.

Nonetheless, fair housing's vulnerable position within HUD, the agency's political permeability, and its ties to the housing industry constrain its ability to be a strong ally to advocates. Within HUD, officials responsible for fair housing have had limited control and a weak position relative to other divisions of the agency. The department has a wide variety of programmatic responsibilities affecting a range of industries and constituencies; as one respondent described it, FHEO is "a little tail on a very big dog." Respondents noted that other HUD divisions, with larger budgets and staffs, see FHEO as meddling in their business when fair housing staff work to be sure that HUD programs comply with fair housing law. FHEO can require extra work for these divisions. More generally, tension arises from the fact that one division essentially is mandated with policing the others.[55] FHEO can be somewhat more autonomous in its administration of the private-sector enforcement process.

HUD's broad responsibility for implementing federal urban policies has made the housing industry one of its primary clients. The agency relies on the private sector to carry out many housing policies. HUD's political permeability means that industry can use its strong ties to Congress to influence fair housing enforcement. My interview data suggest, for example, that if the National Association of Realtors opposes FHEO practices, its lobbyists will threaten to take their complaints to Congress if HUD does not change them.

In the case of community reinvestment, advocacy groups' relationships with federal regulators are likely to vary more across contexts. Intervention risks branding them as troublemakers disrupting a process, but advocates also could be seen as legitimate sources of information about community needs. While fair housing advocates have the opportunity to build working relationships with local HUD officials, community reinvestment advocates have the more complex task of interacting with four sets of local or regional officials.

By accepting the organizational structure of banking regulation already in place, CRA introduced a complexity to implementation not matched by fair housing, where one agency has primary authority. Although the bank regulators are similar in some ways, they also have distinct management styles and procedures. Patterns of rating community reinvestment outcomes vary across agencies. For example, one study found that over time the OTS assigned 19 percent of examined banks a failing grade on CRA compliance, while the Federal Reserve Board found 9 percent of its banks to have failed.[56] The amount of time spent on community reinvestment exams and their frequency also vary across agencies, as do the quality of the written evaluations that agencies must publicly disclose.[57] Agencies vary in their willingness to meet with community groups about the records of local lenders and in the weight they give to local assessments in their exams.[58] Nonetheless, agencies to some extent have worked together on community reinvestment, issuing joint regulations and working through the Federal Financial Institutions Examinations Council.

Like FHEO's position within HUD, the divisions that handle CRA compliance have a subordinate status within regulatory agencies. Khademian describes the primacy of fiscal soundness in the attitudes of bank examiners across the agencies; consumer compliance issues such as community reinvestment seem less important at best, burdensome and troublesome at worst.[59] In 1980, a survey of the regulators found that managers and examiners considered consumer compliance the least important aspect of bank examinations and worried that examiners specializing in compliance had limited career opportunities.[60] When separate examiners conduct compliance exams, these employees are considered "stepchildren" or "second-class citizens";[61] when one examiner conducts both the commercial exam and the compliance exam, he or she is likely to view the latter as a distraction.[62]

Even if an individual examiner or community relations officer feels sympathetic toward community advocates, the general interests of regulatory agencies are allied with the banking industry. Although in theory regulators are intended to serve the public interest, in practice they tend to perceive financial institutions as their clients. Banks fund these agencies through fees and assessments. Agency leadership and staff often come from the ranks of the financial services industry.[63] The daily activities of these agencies—the examination and application reviews—create frequent interactions between regulators and bank staff. These sets of actors understand one another in that they share a familiarity with bank management practices, and, as noted above, they may view compliance issues with some disdain. As one compliance supervisor said, "Consumer compliance is burdensome. . . . And it's so annoying and insulting to bankers. To be mandated to disclose information to customers suggests you are not relating the information to customers in the first place; to demand community reinvestment suggests you are not reinvesting in the community in the first place."[64]

Relationship to Industry. Clearly, the issue of housing discrimination involves powerful industry groups—the real estate and banking industries—that enjoy systemic privileges in U.S. society. The dominance of free-market ideology and a history of public policies that bolster the positions of these industries in the name of preserving the economic health of the country give these players power in housing discrimination politics from the outset. Both fair housing and community reinvestment nonprofits should generally have adversarial relationships to industry, although each policy design offers some prospects for partnerships as well.

The fair housing policy design promotes an adversarial relationship between advocacy groups and housing providers because it enables these advocates to charge industry with wrongdoing using court or courtlike arenas that rely on adversarial processes to reach resolution. This result is especially the case since 1988, when HUD gained the ability to impose sanctions on industry. Prior to the 1988 amendments, the agency had to rely on conciliation, so it was more likely to promote partnerships between advocacy groups and industry.

The relationship that the community reinvestment policy design establishes between its target groups—banks and low-income neighborhoods—is somewhat unclear and open-ended in contrast to the adversarial relationship that the fair housing policy design explicitly established. The public comment period during an application review offers the possibility for adversarial relations between banks and community groups; if members of a low-income community believe they are being ill-served, they can communicate this deficiency to regulators. But the prospect also exists for a mutually beneficial relationship. Banks may find they profit from loans made in low-income neighborhoods, or at least they may believe that these loans will ensure smooth relations with regulators when they want to expand. On the other hand, bankers may believe they pay an opportunity cost if alternative investments would be more profitable than the loans made to comply with CRA. Negotiations with banks might inspire mutual respect and a feeling of partnership, or banks could feel as if they had been bribed.

At the national level, there is evidence that many of these scenarios have emerged. On the one hand, when advocacy groups challenge bank expansion applications, relations are explicitly adversarial. Bank responses to CRA indicate that they feel vulnerable to such charges: An "industry" of community reinvestment consultants advises lenders on how to comply, and trade associations clearly work to keep members up-to-date on regulatory requirements and provide models of community reinvestment strategies.[65] In political arenas, bankers and their trade associations consistently complain about the burdens imposed by the law, and supportive legislators consistently sponsor bills to limit them. The first Bush administration proposed creating "safe harbors" to protect banks with high community reinvestment ratings from challenges to expansion requests and to exclude small banks from community reinvestment obligations.[66] At the same time, some bankers publicly support CRA and offer testimony in Congress and in the media of the profitability and other benefits accruing from their community lending activities.[67]

CONCLUSION

The fair housing and community reinvestment policy designs both address problems of housing discrimination, but as this chapter has shown, they do so in quite different ways. In Chapter 2 I linked legislative processes to these policy designs. In this chapter I suggest that these policy designs are likely to influence local political mobilization and advocacy on fair housing and community reinvestment. Because advocacy groups are key implementers of policy, the effect that policy has on them ultimately influences whether the policies are effective at changing practices and patterns of housing discrimination. Although national policy designs generate expectations about local outcomes, the relationship between designs and action is not mechanistic; rather, local context should produce variation in how national policy structures local advocacy. Local contexts vary in their political, social, economic, and historical characteristics as well as in their housing markets. These differences are likely to result in varied mobilization around housing discrimination, even though groups across cities respond to the same national policies.

4

Advocacy for Housing Equality
in Minneapolis

Although African-American families lived only as far west as Third Avenue for much of Minneapolis's history, one family had succeeded in buying a house several blocks farther west, on Aldrich. Their neighbors were white. An African-American activist who began working for civil rights in the 1950s told Wendell Jones's story, which occurred during the 1960s. "The neighbors wanted to sell their house, but they were afraid that nobody would want to buy it if they knew there were blacks living next door." So they asked Mr. and Mrs. Jones not to sit on the front porch during their open houses and provided them with a schedule. "[Jones] said as a result of that, he made sure that somebody was on that porch on every one of those days."

Whether in the form of quiet resistance, as in this case, or angry protests, advocacy against housing discrimination has a long and dynamic history in Minneapolis. Housing was among the first civil rights issues to emerge in the city. In the late 1950s, African-American activists in civil rights groups and white activists based primarily in local churches and synagogues joined forces to work for state and city fair housing laws. At the neighborhood level, they tried to help the city's growing black population find housing and acceptance in white neighborhoods. In the 1970s and 1980s, these volunteers turned to other issues, and professionals—state and city civil rights agencies—stepped in to handle housing discrimination. In the 1990s, citizen-based grassroots fair housing activism reappeared, although these advocates brought a new understanding of housing problems and appropriate solutions. Now the dominant players in the fight for housing equality are legal activists and housing advocacy organizations. Although some activity aims to protect civil rights, the dominant thrust of fair housing action is to preserve the stock of affordable housing in Minneapolis and to increase its supply throughout the Twin Cities region. Most fair housing strategies focus on securing changes in the public sector—that is, state and local housing policies and the operation of subsidized housing projects. Advocates litigate, lobby the city council and state legislature, and use mobilization tactics to create a public dialogue about inclusive communities and to generate public demand for local policy change.

Advocacy for housing equality began to include community reinvestment efforts in the late 1980s. Community development corporations (CDCs) and city officials, along with the Association of Community Organizations for Reform Now (ACORN) and two faith-based organizing groups, drew attention to local banks' lending records and pressured some of them to improve their lending rate to low-income and minority neighborhoods and individuals. Today, a small set of advocates remain active, but the issue is marginalized within the larger housing advocacy community. Neither CDCs nor the city follow it closely. ACORN and one of the faith-based groups operate mortgage counseling programs in conjunction with several local banks.

In this chapter I recount the development of advocacy for housing equality in Minneapolis, drawing on field research conducted in 1998 and 1999. In addition to conducting forty-six in-person interviews, I consulted the archives of elected officials and voluntary organizations, back issues of the daily newspaper, and a range of published research reports and books. I also attended events related to housing advocacy that took place during my research trips.[1] After telling these stories, I consider them in relation to the two national policy designs. Did groups respond to these policies in ways we would expect? Did the movements take on features consistent with the resources that policies offer?

THE CITY OF MINNEAPOLIS

Minnesotans are the object of jokes and caricature, though in a good-natured spirit, by artists including Garrison Keillor and the Coen brothers, portrayed variously as complacent, provincial, reserved, wary of the unfamiliar, especially when the unfamiliar comes from the East or West Coasts. In Keillor's stories from Lake Wobegon, a character's friendly demeanor while serving up a hot dish at a church supper often masks harsh judgments kept inside or whispered to close friends. But certainly among urbanists, Minneapolis enjoys a good reputation. The city is praised for its relatively low unemployment rate, the high numbers of skilled workers who command high salaries, its general "livability," and the civic-mindedness and philanthropy of its business community.[2] Minnesotans in general are perceived, consistent with the "moralistic" political culture, to be civically active and interested in using government to advance the common good.[3] Minneapolis was an early leader in civil rights when in 1947 its young mayor Hubert Humphrey persuaded the city council to adopt the country's strongest municipal law protecting equal opportunity in employment.[4] Yet the socioeconomic status of people of color in Minneapolis has lagged persistently behind that of white people, mirroring national trends; these disparities in well-being are wider than they are in other cities.[5] Similar disparities exist statewide.[6] While racial and ethnic minorities constitute a small portion of the city's population compared to other U.S. cities, their persistent disadvantage makes a study of race policy and politics particularly important.

The city's history includes a legacy of racial and ethnic discrimination against black people and Jewish people. During the 1940s, Minneapolis was deemed "the capital of anti-Semitism in the United States."[7] At about 5 percent of the population, Jews (like blacks) faced discrimination in housing, employment, and public accommodations. One Jewish respondent remembered how anti-Semitism affected the details of her family's life during the 1950s, recounting that her parents could not obtain a credit card from the city's major department store and that her father used a pseudonym to make dinner reservations at restaurants.

Advocates for racial equality have grappled with the political consequences of the minority population's small size. In 1967, the president of the Urban League complained that "people tend to equate problems with numbers, . . . but [our] basic problems are the same as any city in the country."[8] A 1984 report on the status of minorities in Minneapolis was titled "The Unseen City."[9] My interviews uncovered a paradoxical dual narrative among racial minorities in the Twin Cities. Several African Americans described the region as holding vast opportunities and potential for them, greater than in other places. At the same time, they reported experiencing a high level of racism and discrimination in their daily lives, finding it especially offensive because of the broad sense among white residents that Minnesota is a liberal, progressive state where "these things" do not occur. Various series of articles in the daily *Star Tribune* have echoed these sentiments in 1978, 1990, and 1998. For example, one article from the 1990 series quoted a Latino director of a social service agency: "Minnesota was a very liberal place as long as there were only 10,000 minorities here."[10]

The city government in Minneapolis has a reputation for progressivism and liberal social policies. Its human services expenditures are comparatively high, and recent mayors have focused on social issues including family and child welfare.[11] The city's redevelopment policies have been fairly progressive in the 1990s, with an orientation to neighborhoods and an emphasis on citizen participation, thanks to the electoral successes of a strong neighborhood organizing movement that placed neighborhood activists on the city council.[12] But city officials have held back from explicitly requiring business "to pay for the opportunity to profit from use of city resources" through exactions or linkage policies.[13]

In 1994, Sharon Sayles Belton was elected mayor, making history as the first African-American woman to hold the office. In office while this research was conducted, Sayles Belton was reelected once but defeated in 2001. Although Minneapolis was an early leader on civil rights, the early legislative victories were highly contested, and the city's Civil Rights Department remains a source of controversy and susceptible to budget cuts. Department directors as well as commissioners on the Civil Rights Commission that reviews the department's cases have been the focus of protests. Directors have relatively high rates of turnover, with some accused of embezzling or mismanagement. They have had high-profile conflicts with city leadership over department initiatives, and the city council has publicly opposed agency decisions at times.[14]

Demographic and Housing Conditions

Table 4.1 presents demographic data for Minneapolis from 1970 to 2000.[15] Like many central cities, Minneapolis experienced declining population during the 1970s and 1980s while its suburbs grew. The largest decline occurred between 1970 and 1980, with a net loss of 63,000 people, or 15 percent of the population. From 1980 to 1990, the city's population remained stable, with a net loss of less than 1 percent; still, the suburban communities continued to grow. During this twenty-year period, the city's white population declined while the minority population grew, reaching 20 percent of the city's residents by 1990. The African-American and Asian populations grew the most. Accompanying these shifts has been a growing poverty rate. In 1970, only about 7 percent of Minneapolis families had incomes below the poverty line, whereas 14 percent did in 1990. Among individuals, about 19 percent had incomes below the poverty line in 1990, and 30 percent of children lived in poor households.

Census data from 2000 show a population increase of about 14,000 people, with continuing increases in the number of people of color. The portion of non-Hispanic whites dropped to about 62 percent of the population, while the African-American population increased to 18 percent, the Latino population tripled in size to nearly 8 percent, and the Asian population reached 6 percent. Together, these groups constitute about one-third of the city's population. Minneapolis has traditionally been a center for urban American Indians, but this group's share of the population dropped to 2 percent. Also during the 1990s, the family poverty rate fell to 12 percent.

From the earliest studies documenting housing conditions in Minneapolis, minorities have been found to suffer deteriorated and segregated conditions. In 1960, 90 percent of Minneapolis blacks lived in three neighborhoods, equal to one-tenth of the city's land area.[16] By 1969, the boundaries of these neighborhoods had expanded somewhat, but the general pattern persisted.[17] The League of Women Voters report noted that minorities, regardless of income, experienced poor housing conditions due to discrimination. American Indians suffered the most; 93 percent of them lived in substandard housing.[18] Overall, this report concluded that racial discrimination and a lack of affordable housing in the city "combine to permit the minority person with low income very little choice in where he lives."[19]

These original "pockets" remain the ghetto neighborhoods of the city, and current housing studies draw similar conclusions. In 1990, the segregation index for the entire metropolitan area (including thirteen counties) was 64, slightly less than the national average, although in Minneapolis, people of color continued to

Table 4.1. Minneapolis Demographic Data

	1970	1980	1990	2000
Total population	434,400	370,951	368,383	382,618
Percent white	93.7	87.7	77.5	62.5
Percent African American	4.4	7.7	12.9	17.9
Percent Asian	0.7	1.4	4.3	6.1
Percent American Indian	1.3	2.5	3.2	2.2
Percent Latino	0.9	1.3	2.0	7.6
Median family income	$9,958	$19,737	$32,998	$37,974
Poverty rate (families)	7.2	9.0	14.1	11.9

Notes: 1990 and 2000 racial percentages are based on non-Latino respondents; Latinos may be of any race; 2000 racial data are those reporting one race only.
Source: U.S. Department of Commerce, Bureau of the Census, 2000, 1990, 1980, 1970.

cluster in particular neighborhoods, especially those northwest and south of downtown.[20] Housing audits in selected neighborhoods documented that people of color received less favorable treatment in rental housing transactions, from 26 to 63 percent of the time,[21] and analysis of lending data found that Twin Cities blacks were turned down for home loans three times as often as whites.[22] Both middle-class and low-income minorities experienced segregation and neighborhood deterioration. Black households with incomes above the median lived predominantly in five neighborhoods; these were not "majority-minority" neighborhoods, but they were more "socially distressed" than the neighborhoods where whites with similar incomes lived.[23] In 1980, about one-quarter of Twin Cities blacks lived in ghetto neighborhoods; by 1990, nearly half of them did.[24] Forty percent of black people in Minneapolis had incomes below the poverty rate in 1990, a figure that dropped to 32 percent by 2000. The rate remained significantly higher than that for white people, which was 10 percent in 2000.[25] By 2000, the residential segregation index for blacks and whites in the Twin Cities metro area had declined to 57.8, just under the 60 threshold considered "high."[26] The segregation index for whites and Hispanics increased during the 1990s, to 46.6 from 35.6. Patterns of concentration within the city limits were still evident.[27]

As in many U.S. cities, waves of public and private redevelopment in Minneapolis have destroyed thousands of low-cost housing units from the 1960s forward. In the 1990s, trends converged to create a particularly acute shortage of affordable housing. One report estimated that downtown redevelopment demolished more than 3,500 low-cost housing units in downtown neighborhoods over thirty years.[28] Renters faced the most serious affordability problems. As rents have increased, renters' real incomes have dropped, and government assistance to poor families helped only 36 percent of those in need.[29] Vacancy rates for apartments had dwindled from 7 percent in the early 1990s to 1 percent by the end of 1998.[30] In 1999, more than 3,000 federally subsidized housing units in the metro area were at risk of conversion to market rate rents because of expiring federal mortgages. The Minneapolis Affordable Housing Task Force estimated that 20,000 additional units of affordable housing over the next fifteen years would be needed.[31]

FAIR HOUSING ADVOCACY IN MINNEAPOLIS

The development of fair housing advocacy in Minneapolis unfolded in three stages. In the late 1950s and 1960s, church-based and civil rights groups established state and local legal protections against discrimination in housing, trying to "open up" city neighborhoods to black families. During the 1970s and 1980s, government agencies and real estate industry actors became active on fair housing. The 1990s saw a resurgence of grassroots involvement, but these groups differed from their 1960s-era counterparts. Some specialized in fair housing, and many were affordable housing groups who took up the fair housing cause.

Advocacy in the Civil Rights Era

Housing discrimination was among the first civil rights issues to emerge in Minneapolis in the late 1950s. In this early peak of advocacy, civil rights and religious leaders worked together to promote adoption of state and city antidiscrimination laws. At the neighborhood level, these groups mobilized religious congregations to help the city's growing black population find housing in white neighborhoods. Archival material from this era lists numerous voluntary organizations that worked for housing equality; a partial list includes the Greater Minneapolis Council of Churches, the Unitarian Society, the Catholic Interracial Council, the NAACP, the Urban League, Unitarians for Equal Opportunity in Housing, and the Greater Minneapolis Interfaith Fair Housing Program. Accounts describe the racially segregated housing patterns in the city, mapping three to six "pockets" of the city where black people lived.[32] Custom and restrictive covenants maintained these segregated living patterns in the city, according to an elderly African-American civil rights activist. "African Americans in Minneapolis were permitted to live only in areas that had well-known boundaries. I learned as a child which streets I was not to cross."[33]

The Minnesota legislature passed a fair housing law in 1961 after the measure had failed in two previous sessions. The very modest law did not take effect until 1963 and exempted owner-occupied duplexes, owner-occupied rooming houses, and single-family homes not financed with federal funds. The law did not impose criminal penalties, and the State Commission against Discrimination was empowered to use only "conciliation and persuasion" to enforce it. In 1967, the legislature removed the exemption for conventionally financed single-family homes and prohibited blockbusting in 1968 . Religious and civil rights groups organized extensive lobbying campaigns to promote these changes. For example, a luncheon for legislators sponsored by the Catholic Interracial Council, the Minnesota Rabbinical Association, and the Minnesota Council of Churches brought three hundred advocates together to press for fair housing law in 1961.[34] During state Senate and House debates, hundreds of supporters and opponents turned out wearing buttons stating "I'm for Fair Housing" or "Defeat Forced Occupancy."[35] In 1967, the Minneapolis city council adopted a fair housing ordinance that extended open housing to owner-occupied duplexes; the council rejected an effort to extend coverage to owner-occupied rooming houses.[36]

In addition to pressing for legislation, fair housing advocates worked on the practical issue of finding homes for black families outside of overcrowded black neighborhoods and persuading white residents to accept them. The Greater Minneapolis Interfaith Fair Housing Program coordinated many of these efforts. The three-year pilot program, funded by the national headquarters of the United Church of Christ, intended to achieve racial integration of housing in the metro area primarily by mobilizing the local religious community. The group operated a housing bureau with listings of homes that were available for rent or sale to black people, organized conferences bringing together the many groups working on housing issues, and conducted workshops at individual churches. Churches set up "Interfaith Neighborhood Groups" to "prepare the district[s] for the coming of a Negro family" and urged members to sign "fair housing pledges" in which they committed to "speak and act for the inclusion of minority citizens in their neighborhood."[37] One pastor recalled setting up about a dozen neighborhood groups in southeast Minneapolis to discuss segregated housing and possible remedies: "It was an attempt to create a mood in a community that would say 'We're not going to settle for this kind of segregation.'"

The voluntary sector's participation in fair housing advocacy diminished in the late 1960s. Many of the church-based and civil rights activists became involved in the nationwide civil rights movement, raising money for groups working in the South and organizing lobbying campaigns to press for national civil rights legislation. Civil rights groups such as the NAACP pressed for advances in employment opportunities for black people and by the late 1960s were working against police brutality. Other groups such as the Urban League focused on providing social services in black neighborhoods. After riots along the main business district in the city's traditionally black North side, neighborhood issues came to the forefront, as advocates worked to organize residents and provide community services such as youth programs and job training. Groups raised city and federal War on Poverty funds and galvanized industry leaders to support these efforts. At the same time, some of the Minneapolis churches whose congregations had been active on fair housing were leaving the city, following their parishioners to the suburbs. The Greater Minneapolis Interfaith Fair Housing Program, the one group specializing in fair housing, was unable to secure local or national foundation funding after its pilot period, so it disbanded in 1964.

When these early activists left the fair housing arena, many of them believed that housing opportunities were opening up for black people, and they hoped that the legal framework they had helped to establish would continue to reduce racial discrimination and segregation. A Lutheran pastor active in these years shifted his focus after the legislative victories. While serving on the Minneapolis school board in the mid-1970s and grappling with school desegregation, he realized the fallacy of his earlier judgment, since racial segregation clearly persisted in housing patterns despite advocacy to promote integration and fair housing laws.

Professionalization of Civil Rights

During the 1970s and 1980s, advocacy on fair housing virtually disappeared. Voluntary groups disbanded or turned to other issues, and fair housing activity shifted to the government sector. The state and city civil rights agencies engaged in education campaigns and handled discrimination complaints. The local HUD office added fair housing staff once the national law was adopted. For twenty years, most fair housing activities took place in this community of professionals. But the state and city agencies for fair housing enforcement had limited capacity. The bulk of their casework consisted of employment discrimination claims, and the Minneapolis agency was responsible for implementing the city's contract compliance program for minority- and women-owned businesses. Still, this agency secured HUD funds to develop a media campaign about fair housing designed to inform citizens of their rights and how to report claims. The local HUD office's own capacity for fair housing enforcement has never been particularly high. Minneapolis claims were investigated from the regional Chicago office, and one Minneapolis staff member reviewed local federal housing programs for fair housing compliance.

The sole channel for community involvement during these decades was the HUD-sponsored Community Housing Resource Board (CHRB), dating from the early 1980s. The board consisted of real estate industry representatives, an African-American member, an Asian member, and officials from local governments in the metro area that received federal block grant funds. Its mission was to monitor the local real estate industry's fair housing efforts and practices, particularly its adherence to a voluntary agreement signed by HUD and the local board of realtors. The CHRB was not an enforcement body. HUD provided minimal and sporadic funding, which the board used to conduct a study of minorities in the local real estate industry and to develop a fair housing curriculum for elementary schools. The CHRB worked with the Minneapolis Board of Realtors to establish a scholarship fund for minority real estate agents and to persuade the state board of realtors to require continuing education in fair housing for licensing.

The Nonprofit Sector Returns to the Fair Housing Arena

In the 1990s, Minneapolis experienced a resurgence of nonprofit activity on fair housing issues. This resurgence took three forms: the founding of two nonprofits specializing in fair housing, the filing of two class-action lawsuits, and the entry of affordable housing advocates into the fair housing arena.

The effort to establish a nonprofit that would focus on fair housing originated among civil rights professionals within government and the city's legal aid organizations. In 1990, three lawyers, one each from the city's civil rights department, Community Action of Minneapolis, and the Legal Aid Society, organized a working group to discuss founding a nonprofit fair housing center. Their interest was prompted in part by Minneapolis's first fair housing audit study, funded by the city's Department of Civil Rights. The study of rental housing documented differential practices in the Phillips neighborhood, a low-income community south of downtown.[38] Activists were particularly distressed to find that in one of the city's most racially diverse neighborhoods, disparate treatment occurred at a high rate. The working group eventually split. One set of activists wanted to work on fair housing enforcement, taking claims and pursuing cases. This group became the Housing Discrimination Law Project (HDLP), based in the Legal Aid Society. Other activists wanted to mobilize community support for fair housing policies and to conduct policy-relevant research. They formed the Minnesota Fair Housing Center. HDLP has competed successfully since 1994 for federal Fair Housing Initiatives Program (FHIP) grants. The Minnesota Fair Housing Center has not won this money, most of which is earmarked for enforcement. Instead, it has received support from the city's Community Action Agency, from the state Department of Human Rights, and from local governments throughout the metro area.

The Minneapolis NAACP has become involved in two fair housing efforts. In 1992, the NAACP and the Legal Aid Society brought a class-action fair housing suit against HUD, the Minneapolis Public Housing Authority, the city, and the state for intentionally segregating African Americans in public housing in the near north side of the city. The lawsuit, *Hollman v. Cisneros,* resulted in a negotiated consent decree under which the 770 concentrated public housing units are being replaced with units scattered throughout the metro area, and a community planning process is guiding redevelopment of the north side public housing.[39] In 1995, the NAACP filed suit against the state charging that racial and class segregation result in inadequate education for Minneapolis children, violating the state constitution. Plaintiffs sought a metrowide housing integration policy as part of the relief. At the same time, the NAACP founded the Education and Housing Equity Project (EHEP), which worked to build public support for mediation of the lawsuit by organizing and facilitating "Community Circles" on schools, housing, and race.[40] Citizens formed neighborhood groups throughout the Twin Cities region to discuss patterns of racial and economic segregation and to develop ideas about solutions that their communities would support.

Finally, advocacy groups that specialize in affordable housing issues initiated fair housing efforts, which were linked to a broad agenda of preserving affordable housing and expanding its supply. Some efforts promoted dispersal of subsidized housing throughout the region, especially in the fast-growing south-west outer-ring suburbs. Several examples of these efforts include the Affordable Housing Preservation Project, a small group of activists and lawyers who developed a fair-housing litigation strategy to prevent Section 8 prepayment that threatened affordable units throughout the metro area (the units were at risk for conversion to market-rate housing because of the favorable economy). Another was the Metropolitan Interfaith Coalition on Affordable Housing (MICAH), which commissioned and produced a musical production about fair housing issues in the Twin Cities. Funded with an FHIP grant from HUD, MICAH took the play to religious congregations throughout the metro area and led discussions afterward about the problems and possible solutions. This group also helped a tenants' group in Brooklyn Park save 1,100 affordable housing units by supporting an organizing and litigation strategy. The Catholic Archdiocese Office of Social Justice coordinated a lobbying effort to increase state funding for affordable housing; "Metro Sabbath" distributed sample sermons and other materials designed to educate congregations about racial and income residential polarization and to generate political action.[41] Finally, state legislator Myron Orfield brought the regional concept of fair housing to the legislative agenda in 1993 when he sponsored a series of bills to reduce concentrated poverty in Minneapolis and St. Paul. Orfield termed his proposals "fair housing" efforts; though he talked about racial as well as class disparities, the legislation focused on encouraging suburbs to develop affordable housing.[42]

As actors from the affordable housing arena became more involved in fair housing politics, they challenged the traditional civil rights definition of discrimination that focuses on reforming the process of individual housing transactions. To them, the lack of an adequate supply of affordable housing constituted "unfair" housing. They believed that communities of color were disproportionately affected by this situation, and their preferred solution was to increase the supply of affordable housing. More specialized civil rights–oriented fair housing advocates in Minneapolis agreed that the lack of affordable housing was a problem for minorities but saw racial discrimination as a factor that would limit minorities' access to any new affordable housing units.

COMMUNITY REINVESTMENT ADVOCACY IN MINNEAPOLIS

The history of community reinvestment advocacy in Minneapolis is much briefer than that of fair housing activism. During nearly the first decade after passage of the 1977 Community Reinvestment Act, little activity occurred. Advocacy began in the late 1980s, as the city government joined with local community development corporations and used the CRA to persuade banks to participate in the city's development programs. In response to studies showing lending discrimination and possible redlining, grassroots advocacy organizations staged protests against local banks. Some banks responded to these actions, initiating new programs designed to address the credit needs of low-income people and agreeing to participate in city housing and economic development programs. By the late 1990s, community reinvestment advocacy consisted of program operation with some, though less, monitoring of bank performance. When national bank mergers affected the local scene, advocates reviewed performance of particular banks and testified at hearings.

City Government and CDC Involvement

A city government agency and a consortium of community development corporations (CDCs) were the first to become involved in community reinvestment advocacy. The Minneapolis Community Development Agency (MCDA) worked closely with the city's CDCs, which relied on MCDA commercial and housing subsidy programs for their neighborhood development projects. In 1987, MCDA and the Minneapolis Consortium of Community Developers, a coalition of the city's CDCs, realized that First Bank's participation in MCDA small business and housing programs had declined markedly since 1985. Participation fell from $10 million in 1985 to $1 million in 1987.[43] In St. Paul, the city's development agency and its CDCs had noticed a similar trend. Representatives from both cities and from the CDC coalitions began negotiations with First Bank, but these stalled after about a month.

At that point, representatives from Chicago's Woodstock Institute, a community reinvestment research and advocacy group, attended an event at the University of Minnesota. An MCDA staff member talked with Woodstock staff, who suggested that they use the CRA process to gain some leverage with First Bank. The bank was in the process of seeking to acquire a small bank in Bloomington, a Minneapolis suburb. The consortium of CDCs filed a petition with the Federal Reserve Board asking for an extension of the comment period on this merger. City officials also postponed designating First Bank as a city depository. One respondent reported that CDCs were uneasy taking a confrontational stance with banks, but that this petition seemed like a mild measure to them. Within days of the filing, CDCs, the cities, and First Bank reached a rough agreement for the bank's participation in city loan programs.[44] The final agreement committed First Bank to $47 million in St. Paul neighborhood lending and $42.5 million in Minneapolis neighborhood lending over five years. The agreement specified amounts for particular city programs, including low-income multifamily housing, single-room occupancy housing, economic development, and others.[45] The agreement also included a semiannual review by MCDA and the CDC consortium of the bank's community lending activities.

The city's depository designation program underpinned the CRA-related activity with First Bank. Since 1986 the city council had required applicants for depositories of city funds to submit reports to MCDA on their level of participation in the agency's programs. MCDA in consultation with the consortium of CDCs reviewed these reports, using the review as an opportunity to ask banks to increase their commitments to various programs. This process spurred the discovery of First Bank's cutbacks. Several years later, after corporate restructuring at First Bank, its participation declined once again. Negotiations with the consortium and the city's decision to place the bank on probation as a depository led to another round of commitments from the bank.[46]

Lending Studies and Bank Protests

Advocacy groups for low-income people in Minneapolis became involved in community reinvestment issues in 1990, when the first set of data was available under the amended Home Mortgage Disclosure Act (HMDA). Disclosure data now tracked loan decisions by individual application rather than only by census tract. This change was part of the 1989 Financial Institutions Reform, Recovery, and Enforcement Act (FIRREA) and the national division of the Association of Community Organizations for Reform Now (ACORN), an advocacy group for low-income people, had been part of the lobbying effort pressing for it. ACORN's studies showed disparate denial rates for minorities in Minneapolis; that same year, the Minneapolis newspaper, the *Star Tribune,* commissioned an analysis of older HMDA data from the University of Minnesota's Humphrey Institute for Public Affairs. The study compared lending activity in five predominantly white neighborhoods and five predominantly minority neighborhoods. It showed that from 1981 to 1988, residents of the white neighborhoods received from 1.4 to 3.0 times the level of conventional loans that residents of the black neighborhoods received.[47] The study indicated that minority neighborhoods had high levels of home sales, so demand for loans did not account for the difference.

These results prompted the Twin Cities branch of ACORN to organize a joint campaign protesting banks in Minneapolis and St. Paul. In coalition with two grassroots faith-based organizations, the St. Paul Ecumenical Action Committee (SPEAC) and the Minneapolis Joint Ministry Project, they staged pickets at banks they found to have the worst records. For example, in one action, about two hundred protesters tied a red ribbon around Twin Cities Federal Bank's Minneapolis headquarters; later, about fifty people went to the bank president's office and demanded to talk. ACORN and the Joint Ministry Project negotiated an agreement with Twin Cities Federal in which the bank pledged to earmark $65 million for low-income and minority borrowers.

Routinization

By the mid to late 1990s, the nature of community reinvestment advocacy in Minneapolis changed. Groups that had protested banking practices began to operate programs in conjunction with banks, and the city and CDCs pulled back from their efforts to shape community lending at local banks. The city's depository review process operated on a two-year cycle rather than annually and used lenders' community reinvestment ratings as a proxy for more detailed analysis of partici- pation in city programs. If lending institutions had a "satisfactory" rating (the sec- ond best, behind "outstanding"), they qualified as city depositories. (Nationally, 98 percent of banks receive at least a "satisfactory" rating.)[48] MCDA instituted these changes as the limitations of their former approach to community reinvestment ad- vocacy became more obvious to staff. The oversight process seemed to work more with some banks than others; negotiations with National City Bank, for example, never secured more than participation in a few projects per year.

Additionally, relationships between city, CDCs, and bank staff were difficult to maintain when bank employees changed. One respondent said, "I finally thought, there's just no point in beating up on First Bank anymore. The culture is not there at the top levels." As these limitations became apparent, a network of community banks emerged in Minneapolis, and these institutions participated heavily in city programs. The need for mainstream lenders thus declined. CDCs' attention to local lenders decreased in part because they relied more heavily on subsidy than on loan money as housing development costs rose, according to one consortium member. They focused their political activism on the state and city governments to try to raise more public funds for affordable housing.

As for the grassroots advocates who picketed banks in 1990, these groups op- erated homeownership counseling programs, working with prospective homebuy- ers to prequalify for mortgages and then channeling them to participating lenders. Nonprofit staff educated low-income people about the home buying process and worked with them to prepare their finances and applications, to deal with credit problems, and to incorporate nontraditional income and work histories into a mort- gage application. According to an ACORN staffer, "The biggest reason [banks] continue to work with us is not because they're afraid of protests, but because [the loan program] actually works." Not all lenders participated in these programs, but ACORN staff were pleased with the program nonetheless. Banks provided operat- ing expenses, and every year the group met with each participating bank to assess progress and discuss problems; for example, they might look at underwriting guide- lines that could be altered or loan officers who treated ACORN's clients poorly when they came to the bank. ACORN staff thought that bank program officers were committed to the group's counseling program and to increasing loans to low-in- come and minority borrowers, but they also wondered whether that commitment existed at the banks' top levels and believed that the existence of the Community Reinvestment Act kept banks cooperating with ACORN. More generally, within a year of the protests, most banks had community lending counselors,[49] and the city's largest banks had developed programs aimed at lending to low-income customers.[50]

The monitoring of lending outcomes that prompted the original protests per- sisted to some extent; one staff person at ACORN did it as part of his job, and University of Minnesota faculty also conducted studies, sometimes for local media. Such analyses continued to find disparate loan denial rates for whites versus minorities. For example, a 1993 study found that the loan approval rate for middle-income blacks in the Twin Cities was the lowest among Midwest metro areas and the eighth lowest in the nation.[51] Another study that same year found that 1992 loan denial rates in the state were 8 percent for whites but 21 percent for blacks, and that loans were more likely to be rejected when the homes were in minority and low-income neighborhoods.[52] It is unclear, however, whether such studies prompted public advocacy by the late 1990s.

When a shift in the banking landscape occurs, such as when a local bank wants to merge, there is some degree of heightened attention. Thus in 1998, the Federal Reserve Board held hearings in Minneapolis on the proposed merger of Norwest and Wells Fargo at the request of Minneapolis U.S. Representative Bruce Vento, Senator Paul Wellstone, and local community groups.[53] The summer before the hearing, ACORN staged a small protest against Norwest to criticize its bounced check fees and to state its opposition to the merger.[54] Sixty speakers from communities in which these banks operated testified; one-third of these were from Minneapolis, including representatives from ACORN and the CDC community. Of the Minneapolis-based witnesses, four speakers from ACORN, a representative from the state attorney general's office, a state legislator, and a representative from the state Public Interest Research Group urged the Federal Reserve not to approve the merger because of Norwest's relatively poor lending record to people of color and a range of practices that make banking services prohibitively expensive for low-income people.[55] ACORN representatives pointed out that Norwest refused to participate in its homeownership counseling programs. On the other hand, many affordable housing advocates and representatives from CDCs testified about Norwest's impressive record supporting their affordable housing projects in the Twin Cities.[56] The Federal Reserve Board approved the merger.

SOCIAL MOVEMENTS AND POLICY DESIGNS: CONSISTENCY AND DIVERGENCE

National policy designs establish a framework for action to address housing discrimination. The fair housing and community reinvestment policies, as outlined in Chapter 3, offer distinctive sets of resources to advocacy groups. It is likely that as groups use policy resources, they will come to "look like" the blueprint that policies embody; that is, they will adopt the particular ideas and strategies contained in the policy design. Yet policies do not compel a response, nor do they control action completely, as the stories of the fair housing and community reinvestment movements in Minneapolis demonstrate. On the one hand, aspects of both movements conform to policy design components. Yet in key ways, they also diverge from the policies' blueprints. Table 4.2 reviews the expectations for movement activity derived from analysis of the policy designs and summarizes the findings about the two movements in Minneapolis.

Table 4.2. Expectations and Outcomes for Fair Housing and Community Reinvestment Advocacy in Minneapolis

Dimension of Advocacy	Fair Housing	Community Reinvestment
Group type		
Expectations	Specialists	Non-specialists
Are expectations met?	*Mixed* Some specialists, more non-specialists	*Yes* Grassroots poor-people's groups, community development corporations
Problem definition		
Discrimination		
Expectations	Individualized, rights-based, process-oriented	Place-based, uneven patterns, outcome-oriented
Are expectations met?	*Mixed* Predominantly outcome-based, emphasis on class	*Mixed* Race added to definition
Goals		
Expectations	Civil rights (more activity), affordable housing (less activity)	Lending discrimination, other community needs
Are expectations met?	*No* Civil rights (less), affordable housing (more)	*Yes* Lending discrimination, participation in city programs, affordable housing development, low-cost banking services
Target		
Expectations	Private sector housing (more), public sector housing (less), racial minorities	Banks, savings and loans, poor neighborhoods
Are expectations met?	*No* Private housing (less), public housing (more), low-income racial minorities	*Mixed* Banks, savings and loans, poor people citywide
Actions		
Tools		
Expectations	Enforcement activities	Research, mobilization of neighborhoods, public comments
Are expectations met?	*Mixed* Enforcement, but also organizing and mobilization strategies	*Mixed* Citywide mobilization, program development, linkage of CRA to city housing programs
Arenas		
Expectations	Court and administrative arenas	Regulatory arenas
Are expectations met?	*Mixed* Court and administrative, but also legislative	*Yes*

Dimension of Advocacy	Fair Housing	Community Reinvestment
Timing		
Expectations	Federal changes spark local changes; more activity post-1988, then stable level of activity	Irregular, sparked by bank actions and examination cycles; more activity post-1989
Are expectations met?	*Yes*	*Mixed* Activity declined over time
Relationships		
To government		
Expectations	Partnerships (civil rights) Adversarial (affordable housing)	Adversarial
Are expectations met?	*Yes*	*Mixed* Adversarial with federal government, partnership with city government
To industry		
Expectations	Adversarial	Adversarial
Are expectations met?	*Yes*	*Mixed* Adversarial, then cooperative

Movements Mirror Policy Designs

The mix of resources in national fair housing policy, and the ideas about discrimination that it supports, led to expectations for a local movement dominated by specialist nonprofit groups who defined discrimination in terms of individual housing transactions. I expected local groups to spend most of their time working to protect these individual rights in private-sector housing, more so than to ensure that affordable housing was available on a nondiscriminatory basis. Groups were likely to engage in the enforcement activities that HUD's Fair Housing Initiatives Program (FHIP) supports and to use the administrative and judicial arenas to pursue claims. I expected local action to reflect federal shifts in priorities and more activity to be evident after 1988 (when amendments boosted incentives for litigation) and after establishment of FHIP.

The status and activities of the Housing Discrimination Law Project (HDLP) and the Minnesota Fair Housing Center conformed in many ways to these expectations. The former received significant funding from FHIP, the latter did not. The Housing Discrimination Law Project focused on fair housing enforcement in the private-housing sector. Staff attorneys advocated in court and used the administrative process on behalf of their clients. They contracted with the Fair Housing Center for tests to investigate particular complaints. Their claims included racial discrimination and discrimination based on family status. A separate agency within Legal Aid focused on issues related to people with disabilities, so HDLP did not pursue these fair housing issues. The timing of the project's founding coincides with HUD's expansion of FHIP. Finally, for HDLP, working toward the ideal of "fair housing" in Minneapolis means examining individual housing transactions for evidence of discriminatory practices and pursuing remedies for victims in specialized arenas.

Fair housing groups whose missions and strategies do not conform to HUD's FHIP priorities should have a harder time sustaining action. The Minnesota Fair Housing Center provides an example of such an organization. Its mission diverged enough from the national policy design that it had not won FHIP funds. It identified itself as a policy organization, interested in pursuing research and education about fair housing issues. The center's director was particularly interested in how public-sector practices supported segregated housing patterns. The center was smaller in budget and staff than HDLP, the enforcement organization and FHIP grantee. But the group raised funds indirectly from national policy resources. It contracted with HDLP to conduct fair housing tests based on complaints that the project was investigating. And it secured CDBG funds from several local governments that had to certify to HUD that they were "affirmatively" furthering fair housing. Some local governments hired the center to conduct the HUD-required "Analysis of Impediments to Fair Housing." The group also raised funds from Community Action and the state civil rights agency.

The contrast between these two organizations is what we would expect, given the resources available through national fair housing policy design. Nonprofit participation in the fair housing arena had declined in Minneapolis by the time that national fair housing law took effect in 1968. The return of nonprofit groups to the fair housing arena in Minneapolis coincides with the shift in federal policy toward incorporating nonprofit groups by offering direct funding and boosting the attorneys' fees and damages available through litigation.

In the case of community reinvestment, the types of groups that become involved, their wide-ranging goals, their strategies and the timing of their actions, and the arenas they used are all consistent with the resources available from national policy. As expected from the policy design's set of resources, there are no advocacy groups that specialize exclusively in community reinvestment. ACORN advocated generally on behalf of low-income people, working on a range of issues and supporting itself through membership dues, though banks finance the loan counseling program. CDCs sustain themselves with development fees and, to some extent, grants. These may derive indirectly from CRA, as banks participating in CDC projects claim such participation as evidence of compliance with the law. The city devoted part of a staff member's time to monitoring bank performance, using CRA to persuade banks to participate in city programs. As expected, neither CDCs nor ACORN had close relationships with federal regulators.

These groups stretched the definition of "community credit needs" to assert alternative visions of what constitutes bank compliance with the Community Reinvestment Act. The high discretion that the statute grants to government agents in assessing an institution's community reinvestment performance on meeting these needs also enabled community groups to propose their own definitions. Thus ACORN did call for the availability of loan products to low-income populations, but the group also demanded that other financial services be available, such as free checking accounts, reasonable fees for bank services, and reasonable penalties for items such as bounced checks. CDCs brought neighborhood development into the definition of community needs, pressing banks to comply with the law through participation in city programs that encouraged affordable housing and economic development.

Community reinvestment advocacy was sporadic in the Twin Cities, driven in part by the regulatory cycle and disclosure of data. Data disclosure in the late 1980s prompted ACORN's initial protest activities, resulting in establishment of the group's loan counseling program. First Bank's merger application offered CDCs and the city's community development agency a way to convince the bank to take their requests for program participation more seriously. Groups had not taken advantage of the chance to press banks for changes through commenting on community reinvestment ratings, although this activity is something that national community reinvestment activists have begun to recognize as a valuable point of entry for advocacy.

Movements Diverge from Policy Designs

The fair housing advocacy groups whose features and fates conformed to expectations made up only a portion of the larger fair housing movement in Minneapolis and the Twin Cities metro area. The balance of activity rested with groups and efforts that diverged in key ways from expectations grounded in policy design analysis. Most fair housing advocacy focused on public-sector housing, it targeted low-income people rather than racial minorities, and it articulated a definition of fair housing based on housing patterns rather than the process of securing housing. Some groups explicitly advocated racial integration. Relatively few advocacy groups secured national fair housing funding; instead they used the law's tools or did not use national resources at all.

For example, the NAACP's *Hollman* fair housing lawsuit sought to address segregation in public housing, thus focused on low-income minorities. The remedy relied on integration, both by class and race, through dispersal of subsidized housing units throughout the metro area. The Affordable Housing Preservation Project used fair housing resources to preserve affordable housing, receiving funding from a local housing foundation to develop strategies that included fair housing litigation. Some advocacy efforts ignored national policy resources. The educational equity lawsuit embraced racial integration as a policy goal and sought a remedy that required changes in housing policies to integrate the region, thus offering low-income and minority populations the chance for an equal education. This lawsuit challenged the state for violating its own constitution, not national fair housing law. Finally, state senator Orfield's legislative efforts aimed to achieve fair housing in the metro area through state-mandated regional dispersal of affordable housing. He has not engaged national policy resources in this effort.

Community reinvestment advocacy in Minneapolis diverged from expectations in its target groups and in the evolution of its strategies from adversarial to cooperative. Groups engaged in community reinvestment advocacy tended to work citywide rather than on behalf of specific neighborhoods, and they worked on behalf of low-income people generally but also low-income people of color. ACORN mobilized poor people citywide. Its loan program was available to residents of St. Paul and Minneapolis; the banks that participated defined their community, for CRA purposes, as the entire city. ACORN felt somewhat constrained by this boundary, since low-income people in the suburbs could potentially benefit from the program as well. Community development corporations are neighborhood-based in Minneapolis, but these groups did not mobilize constituents as part of their community reinvestment strategy.

ACORN and other groups also brought race into the target group definition, expanding the community reinvestment policy design beyond its stated target of low-income neighborhoods. For example, in testimony before the Federal Reserve Board in the public hearing about the Norwest merger, several ACORN speakers criticized the bank for having higher loan denial rates and lower rates of mortgage lending to Twin Cities minorities.[57] The local studies that sparked community reinvestment advocacy and protests compared lending rates to whites and minorities as well as across incomes.

Additionally, although advocacy began as adversarial, it evolved into cooperative strategies between nonprofit groups and banks. ACORN started out protesting banks and then became partners with four of the five major banks in the city. In testimony against the Norwest merger, the association took an adversarial position, noting that Norwest did not participate in its programs and that many requests made to discuss particular bank programs had been rebuffed. ACORN thus maintained an adversarial posture toward the bank that remained unresponsive. In the case of CDCs, the consortium initially took an adversarial position against First Bank, struck an agreement, and defended the agreement when the bank scaled back its commitments. The consortium did not follow CRA issues by 1999, nor did individual CDCs, though many of them had built individual relationships with local banks. In the Norwest hearings, many CDCs testified about the bank's outstanding commitment to community development in Minneapolis. They judged banks' responsiveness, their CRA compliance, differently than ACORN.

The policy design framework predicts that changes in local strategies would be prompted by changes in national policy resources. The Minneapolis story suggests that other factors also prompt change. In particular, when a group uses policy resources, it changes its orientation to those same resources and begins to use them differently. In addition, despite CRA's place-based targeting, the policy design has not inspired over the long term a collective interest or concern about community reinvestment generally. Rather, groups defined "compliance" differently, according to their specific agendas, and assessed a bank's performance differently, again often based on their individual experiences and relationships with banks. In Minneapolis, CRA divided the nonprofit organizations who used the law rather than bringing them together. Although groups such as grassroots poor people's advocates and CDCs each stood to benefit from banks that took CRA seriously, they did not collaborate and did not view collaboration as a valuable goal to pursue.

SUMMARY

Fair housing and community reinvestment advocacy have separate histories in Minneapolis, with different groups working on each issue over time and different trajectories of action. The policy design perspective suggests that the nature of these movements and their differences stem from features of the national policy designs that govern each issue. Although in some respects advocacy exhibits features expected from policy design analysis, in key ways it does not. Notably, the fair housing movement focuses on public-sector housing for low-income people, and the community reinvestment movement is fragmented and action has declined.

5

Advocacy for Housing Equality in Denver

"Are you guilty until proven innocent? What would a tester say if you asked: Are you a tester?" The questions were flying at a "Train the Trainers" workshop one summer morning at the Denver Board of Realtors headquarters. Real estate agents who worked as fair housing trainers, instructing new agents on the law, were attending a refresher course on fair housing policy and practices. The director of one of Denver's fair housing nonprofit groups was describing its testing program and trying to answer all of the questions. "What would lead you to believe someone was a tester?" she asked. "They would ask leading questions." "A tester wouldn't do that," the director said. The questions continued. "Your pool of testers—how do you get them? What training do they go through?" "Is it true that if you ask someone: Are you a tester, and they answer dishonestly, the test can't be used in court?" "No, that's not true," the director replied. "That's entrapment," an audience member declared.

Since at least the 1950s, advocates in Denver have been educating housing professionals and city residents about housing discrimination. The city stands out as an early leader on fair housing. And unlike the Minneapolis fair housing movement, where nonprofit advocacy disappeared for nearly twenty years, Denver advocates have held together some form of fair housing activity from the late 1950s forward. The city had one of the country's largest nonprofit fair housing centers well before the 1968 national law was enacted. The center's dissolution in the early 1970s was a low point for fair housing advocacy in the city, but a small cadre of advocates continued to work on the issue, keeping it alive in government and industry arenas and in a neighborhood organization. A new nonprofit center was established by 1987. Denver advocates have been particularly savvy about tapping federal funding resources, and their activities have ranged broadly across sectors of the housing industry, examining discriminatory practices in home rentals, sales, lending, and insurance. Denver advocates have consistently tried to link the issues of school and housing segregation, though without much success. Overall, Denver's fair housing advocacy displays an emphasis on partnerships with industry and government.

As in Minneapolis, advocacy on community reinvestment has been more limited. Little occurred during the act's first decade. In the early 1990s, a coalition of advocacy groups emerged and pressured local banks to improve performance on a range of indicators, from lending to low-income and minority customers, to hiring racial and ethnic minorities, to ensuring that services were available to people with disabilities. The Denver Community Reinvestment Alliance brought together a unique coalition of low-income, minority, labor union, and disability activists; it eventually faltered when disagreements emerged about advocacy strategies. Like in Minneapolis, the city government became briefly involved in community reinvestment efforts when it began to require "community responsiveness" from city depositories. But as the voice of community activists grew weaker, city attention to the issue wavered.

In this chapter I tell the stories of the struggles for housing equality in Denver—the movements for fair housing and for community reinvestment. During my field research in 1999, I conducted twenty-four interviews, attended a series of housing workshops and conferences offered by nonprofit groups, and consulted archival materials. I also volunteered for a fair housing organization, working as a tester.[1] After presenting the development of these movements, dating back to the 1950s, I analyze them in relation to national policy, considering how local groups responded to fair housing and community reinvestment laws. I ask whether groups reacted in ways consistent with national policy design features, or if movement characteristics diverged from national policy.

THE CITY OF DENVER

Accounts of Denver's history emphasize its transformation from a frontier backwater to a modern city, from "cowtown," "waterhole," or "mining center" to "global city," "world center," or "metropolis."[2] Boom and bust cycles have long characterized the city's economy. The energy boom of the 1970s gave way to recession in the 1980s, but the city rebounded during the 1990s, which local officials call "the Denver decade."[3] In the 1990s, the city's population grew 18 percent, and its economy diversified away from dependence on energy-related industry to include significant sectors in telecommunications, biomedicine, and computer-related firms. Business writers now rank Denver among the top cities for business. Unemployment rates have been low in recent years, the supply of skilled workers is high, and even low-skill work opportunities tend to have prospects for wage growth rather than to be "dead-end" jobs.

Denver has long been a multiracial city, which some historians call "fractured" because the black and Latino communities rarely collaborate on policy issues and tend to live in different parts of the city.[4] There is a history of racial conflict between whites and racial minorities. Denver was a bastion of western Ku Klux Klan activity in the 1920s, leading the *Denver Post* to call the group in 1925 "the largest and most efficiently organized political force in the state of Colorado."[5] A Klan sympathizer served as Denver's mayor and appointed Klan members to city jobs, including police chief; a Klansman served as governor as well, but the group's political power dwindled by the 1930s.[6] The city, under Mayor Quigg Newton, established a Human Relations Commission in 1947, instituted formal policies of nondiscrimination in city agencies and hospitals, and increased the rate of public housing construction.[7] Colorado was an early leader on fair housing, adopting a state law in 1959, the first to cover privately owned single-family homes. Yet despite formal policies, opportunities for minorities remained limited in employment, housing, public accommodations, and other areas.[8]

The 1960s and 1970s were marked by civil rights protests, meetings between local officials and leaders from the black and Latino communities, and litigation. African Americans and Latinos aimed to increase opportunities in employment, to achieve educational equality, and to address tensions with the police department. Denver also was home to the Chicano movement's nationalist group Crusade for Justice, led by Rodolfo "Corky" Gonzales. In 1973, a shootout between Crusade members and the police resulted in the death of a young Mexican-American activist and sparked a riot in which eleven police officers were wounded and dozens of Crusade members were arrested and beaten.[9] Also that year, the U.S. Supreme Court found Denver's school system guilty of segregating black children. A class of African-American families had filed suit in 1969. After years of appeals, the U.S. Supreme Court ruled in the plaintiffs' favor, and a busing plan to desegregate the schools began in 1974. The school system operated under the court order until 2000. Although they opposed busing, Latinos joined the litigation against the school system in 1984, demanding bilingual education. In 1971, the city engaged in redistricting to comply with the Voting Rights Act, with the goal of boosting minority representation on the city council.

There is evidence that Denver, especially since the 1980s, has politically incorporated blacks and Latinos relatively well.[10] Multiracial electoral coalitions have led to elections of minority mayors since 1983. Federico Peña was the first Latino mayor to be elected in a majority Anglo (non-Hispanic white) city; he served two terms and did not run for reelection in 1991. Wellington Webb, an African American elected in 1991, is serving his third term, which will end in 2003. Peña's administration marked a turning point in Denver politics, as minorities were appointed to more city boards and commissions and hired to high-profile city offices.[11] He expanded the city's minority contracting policy and shifted the community development agenda to incorporate neighborhood participation and concerns.[12] Mayor Webb, aiming to attract middle-class people back to the city, supported development of upscale downtown housing, though there were also efforts to address the needs of the working poor. He tapped federal funds for workforce development and youth-oriented programs, state funding for welfare programs with work components, creation of a range of city programs aimed to boost homeownership, new business startups, and training programs for low-income families.[13] Under Webb, Denver became the first city to establish a local earned income tax credit program.[14] Still, housing advocates often charged the mayor and city council with focusing too much on middle-class homeowners at the expense of the poor's housing needs.[15] Hero and Clarke observe that minority and equality issues still do not "receive equal footing" with economic development issues in city policy making.[16] The city's civil rights agency is relatively small and has functioned as an enforcement agency only since 1990, when Denver adopted a civil rights ordinance, predominantly due to advocacy from the gay community. Prior to 1990, the agency served in an advocacy and educational capacity only.

Demographic and Housing Conditions

Table 5.1 presents demographic data for Denver from 1970 to 2000. From the 1970s through the 1980s, Denver consistently lost population, averaging a net loss of 23,500 people per decade. But during the 1990s, the city gained population, reaching about 554,000 people by 2000. During the past thirty years, Anglos' share of the city's population dropped; in 1970, they made up 89 percent of the population, but by 2000 represented just over half, at 52 percent. The Latino community is primarily of Mexican origin in Denver, with only small populations of Puerto Rican, Cuban, and other groups. Most Colorado Latinos are U.S. citizens, and most were born here and can trace their heritage back several generations, although the numbers of new immigrants grew during the 1990s.[17] The Latino population grew from 17 percent in 1970 to 23 percent in 1990 and to 32 percent in 2000. African Americans made up 9 percent of the city's population in 1970, grew to 12 percent by 1980, and essentially remained at that level through the next decade, dipping to 11 percent by 2000. The portion of families under the poverty line grew from 9 percent in 1970 to 13 percent by 1990, dropping to 10 percent by 2000. In 2000, 14 percent of individuals had incomes below the poverty line, a decline of 3 percentage points since 1990.

Early studies documented the poor housing conditions of racial and ethnic minorities. A 1947 report found that 90 percent of Denver's blacks, 75 percent of its Latinos, and many Asians were "herded into an area where much of the property has been ruled unfit for human beings."[18] Most blacks lived in two of the city's census tracts, and nine of ten Latinos lived in substandard housing; their infant mortality rate was twice the city's average.[19] Although public housing was less segregated than private housing, several projects had concentrations of either African Americans or Latinos, and the Housing Authority reported reduced interest among Anglos in moving into them.[20] (By the 1980s, however, public housing projects were concentrated in minority neighborhoods.)[21] In 1957, the

Table 5.1. Denver Demographic Data

	1970	1980	1990	2000
Total population	514,678	492,686	467,610	554,636
Percent white	89.3	76.3	61.6	51.9
Percent African American	9.1	12.0	12.5	11.1
Percent Asian	0.7	1.8	2.1	2.8
Percent American Indian	NA	0.9	0.8	1.3
Percent Latino	16.8	18.7	22.8	31.7
Median family income	$9,650	$19,527	$32,038	$39,500
Poverty rate (families)	9.4	10.3	13.1	10.6

Notes: 1990 and 2000 racial percentages are based on non-Latino respondents; Latinos may be of any race; 2000 racial data are those reporting one race only.
Source: U.S. Department of Commerce, Bureau of the Census, 2000, 1990, 1980, 1970.

Commission on Human Relations reported the persistence of substantial discrimination against minorities. "Negroes (and to a lesser-degree, Spanish-speaking and Orientals) find it nearly impossible to obtain housing outside the 'ghetto' areas. A combination of real-estate and loaning institution practices creates this block to a free real-estate market for minority families."[22]

Racial minorities' housing options currently are not so restricted, yet these original minority neighborhoods remain the troubled ghetto neighborhoods in the city. Racial segregation levels were generally high in 2000, though not as high as rates in the older, industrial cities of the Northeast and Midwest.[23] The segregation index was 63 between blacks and whites and 57 between Latinos and whites, which represents a slight decline in black/white segregation but an increase in Latino/white segregation. (A score of 60 or above is considered high.) Blacks and Latinos were separated from one another at a rate of 62.3, a decline from 72.9 in 1990. Census data for city-designated neighborhoods show concentrations in residential patterns.[24] No neighborhood perfectly mirrors the racial and ethnic composition of the city. Three of the city's seventy-eight neighborhoods had a majority black population, while forty-one, or 53 percent, of neighborhoods had black populations under 5 percent. During the 1990s, some traditionally African-American neighborhoods saw growth in Latino populations. By 2000, eighteen city neighborhoods had majority Latino populations, while only eight neighborhoods had Latino populations under 5 percent. More than half of the city's neighborhoods had majority non-Latino white populations, and 20 percent had more than 80 percent non-Latino white residents.

Housing discrimination and housing disparities between whites and minorities have been found whenever studies were conducted. An audit study consisting of 253 tests in 1982 concluded that "discrimination remains a problem in Denver, for both Blacks and Hispanics. It is clear that overall, the quality and quantity of information given to Hispanics and Blacks involving availability is inferior to that provided Anglos."[25] For example, in their interactions with real estate agents, Hispanic and black auditors were told less about fewer homes and were shown fewer homes; agents were less likely to request their phone numbers so they could contact them later. In other words, agents seemed less eager to make a sale. Black auditors faced significant discrimination in the rental market as well. Audits in 1989 and 1991 also found patterns of discrimination against blacks and Latinos, though the 1991 study found that Latinos encountered lower rates of discrimination in Denver than in other cities.[26] In terms of lending, a 1993 study found that neighborhoods where minorities lived had one bank branch for every five in white neighborhoods.[27] Analyses in 1993 and 1997 found that, compared to whites, African Americans had lower approval rates and higher denial rates from mortgage lenders in the city, although the gaps decreased over the years.[28] A 1997 study found that property insurers provided home insurance "less readily" to African-American home buyers.[29]

During the 1990s, Latino neighborhoods in northwest Denver and black neighborhoods in northeast Denver came under gentrification pressure, and, more generally, evidence emerged of severe housing affordability problems, both for low-income and middle-class residents. Census 2000 showed that nearly 40 percent of renters were paying more than 30 percent of their income on housing. Vacancy rates were low, hovering around 4 percent.[30] Median home prices rose faster than wages during the 1990s, and average rents increased 72 percent from 1995 to 2000.[31]

FAIR HOUSING ADVOCACY IN DENVER

Denver was an early leader in fair housing advocacy, at least a decade ahead of national policy makers. A grassroots movement secured a state fair housing law and a metropolitan fair housing center well before passage of a national fair housing law. These early efforts molded a cadre of advocates who continue to pursue fair housing today, though in less public, specialized arenas. Although fair housing advocacy groups declined in the mid-1970s, they reemerged by the mid-1980s, representing a briefer valley in organized advocacy than Minneapolis experienced. In the late 1990s, fair housing advocacy was strongly linked to the real estate industry, with ties to the school system as well.

Park Hill and the Emergence of Fair Housing Advocacy

Fair housing advocacy began in Denver as a grassroots movement in one neighborhood, Park Hill. Branscombe and Branscombe[32] documented this movement in a series of articles for the Park Hill community newspaper. The following account draws heavily on their work as well as that of Woods.[33]

White residents of an east Denver neighborhood called Park Hill became concerned in the late 1950s when black families began to move from the two northeast neighborhoods where they were segregated, across a main boulevard, and into Park Hill. What distressed neighbors was the behavior of real estate agents, "panic peddlers," who approached white families, warned them that the neighborhood was changing, that their property values would decline, and that they should sell their homes while they still could. Several of Denver's large churches were located in Park Hill, and congregation members living nearby began to meet with clergy, arguing that the panic and prejudice that real estate agents were stirring up among white residents was not only immoral but also threatening to the churches' capital investments. A group of neighbors and local clergy formed an ad hoc committee and worked through local congregations to understand what was happening. They developed a vision of a stable, integrated neighborhood that could emerge if white homeowners would not succumb to racial fear and move away.

Part of the Park Hill group's agenda was legislative. These volunteers first supported one of their state representatives who sponsored the 1959 Colorado Fair Housing Act, then six years later, two other state legislators from the neighborhood who sponsored strengthening amendments to the law. As in Minneapolis, civil rights groups and coalitions of religious organizations campaigned for both laws. The 1965 state law was stronger than the national Fair Housing Act; it covered more housing and gave the state civil rights agency greater powers than the national law would give HUD three years later.

But the Park Hill Action Committee never believed that laws would be enough to achieve their goal of an integrated neighborhood. They developed strategies to intervene in the real estate process, working to persuade home buyers and sellers to consider the racial implications of their housing decisions and to make choices that fostered integrated housing patterns. To maintain a white presence in Park Hill, activists organized educational campaigns to reassure white homeowners that their property values would not decline as the area became integrated. To increase the supply of housing for black people, they visited churches in other white Denver neighborhoods to build networks of support for families of color. Park Hill activists tried to convince local real estate agents and black and white housing consumers to realize the ideal of stable integrated neighborhoods throughout the city rather than to make choices that would essentially resegregate the neighborhoods like theirs that bordered the ghettos. The group monitored the racial composition of blocks in the neighborhood and held social gatherings to build a sense of community and pride in their interracial neighborhood. Also during these years, the city's Human Relations Commission sponsored educational programs aimed to increase white residents' awareness of the housing problems that minorities faced. In 1957, for example, the commission's housing section sponsored bus tours of minority neighborhoods; it worked with churches in white neighborhoods, providing information for congregation members and materials for sermons focused on minorities and housing.[34]

Park Hill is the only Denver neighborhood to consistently strive for racial integration. It remains racially diverse, with about 56 percent black residents, 36 percent white residents, and 5 percent Latino residents; it is economically diverse, with 25 percent low-income, 48 percent middle-income, and 28 percent upper-income residents.[35] Activists have been vigilant over the years in monitoring what they perceived as external threats to this diversity. They were strong supporters of citywide school desegregation. They secured zoning changes to prevent single-family homes from being rented as multiple units. They were long a lone voice for dispersal of subsidized housing throughout the city and region. Longtime activists complained that their neighborhood had more than its "fair share" of subsidized housing because residents did not oppose such housing, as those in other neighborhoods did.

As time went by, however, newer neighborhood leaders began to question the emphasis on integration and placed priority on other issues, including crime, gangs, and environmental justice. They also noted that the neighborhood was internally segregated, with white families predominating in south Park Hill and minority families in the north. Some began to object to the quest for integration; to them, a desire to control the entry of people into the neighborhood seemed discriminatory regardless of its goal. Indeed, longtime activists acknowledged that black community leaders never fully embraced their strategies, although the Park Hill neighborhood group has always structured its board to ensure biracial representation. Such tensions echo those that have arisen in the handful of locations across the country where pro-integrative measures are instituted or considered.[36]

A History of Nonprofits

Park Hill activists took their cause beyond their neighborhood boundaries; they were key actors in the establishment of the early civil rights commissions in Denver and eventually convinced the mayor to establish a fair housing center. The Metro Denver Fair Housing Center began as a volunteer group in 1966. By 1973, it had become a government- and foundation-funded membership organization with a fifty-person staff, a two-story office building, seven field offices, and a $500,000 annual budget.[37] The federal Office of Economic Opportunity and the Ford Foundation were primary funders from 1967.

The center's work bridged fair housing and affordable housing issues. Many of Denver's early uses of federal housing programs happened through the center. A housing listing service combated real estate steering practices and worked to increase opportunities by helping individuals find housing throughout the city and its suburbs. Its affordable housing division used federal housing programs to build affordable housing with the intention of dispersing it throughout the metro area. Over time, the center's primary activities shifted to housing development; some observers were concerned that the housing listing service was merely helping people find housing rather than truly promoting desegregation, and they worried that there was not evidence of "an open fight against discrimination."[38] When federal War on Poverty money dropped, the state cut back its grant to the center. President Nixon's 1973 moratorium on federal urban spending was the final stroke, leaving the center without enough funding to remain open. Eventually, the state and city financed other agencies to take over the Fair Housing Center's housing development programs, and the fair housing promotion mission went to the state civil rights agency. Internal conflict among center staff also weakened the organization during this period.[39]

Denver was without a nonprofit fair housing center for about a decade, but former center employees moved into government jobs, including positions at the state civil rights and housing agencies and the city's community development agency. The state civil rights agency secured federal money fairly frequently for fair housing audits and supported a housing specialist who ran educational workshops for the housing industry. In 1979, Denver once again had a nonprofit group specializing in fair housing when advocates formed the Denver Community Housing Resource Board (CHRB) soon after the first agreement was signed between HUD and the National Association of Realtors. When HUD sponsored CHRBs, the Denver group received funding for its education and outreach activities, including production of informational brochures and sponsorship of a scholarship fund for minority real estate agents. The group had office space in one of the Colorado Civil Rights Division's (CCRD) neighborhood offices. In 1983, in response to HUD changes in the CHRB program under President Reagan, the board separated itself physically and operationally from the enforcement role played by CCRD and became a freestanding organization devoted exclusively to fair housing education and outreach.

When HUD discontinued the CHRB strategy in the early 1990s, the Denver group remained intact and in 2000 was one of only a handful of community housing resource boards still in existence. The group had one full-time salaried staff member and received funding from Denver's Community Development Block Grant (CDBG) program, the Colorado Association of Realtors, and the Denver Board of Realtors. The director was acting entrepreneurially and looking for other local funding sources as well as to market the CHRB's fair housing education services to the housing industry. Its board consisted primarily of housing industry members (real estate agents and brokers, representatives from the Apartment Association, mortgage brokers, and so on) and was chaired by the director of the state's real estate licensing agency, also a longtime resident of Park Hill. The CHRB had ties to Denver's public school system as well—a PTA member from northwest Denver and a school administrator served on the board.

The CHRB was always oriented to fair housing education and outreach rather than to enforcement. Most of its activities consisted of conducting continuing education training sessions for real estate brokers and other housing professionals. The group offered training programs for state-licensed fair housing trainers to update them on recent developments in fair housing regulations and implementation and to offer them fresh teaching methods to use in the courses required for licensure.

Development of a second nonprofit fair housing organization began in 1986, when activists took advantage of HUD's New Horizons program through which state and local governments could engage in a fair housing planning process. The mayor of Denver and the governor each appointed New Horizons task forces to make recommendations. Out of this process came a new metropolitan fair housing center called Housing for All. The group incorporated in 1987 just as the federal Fair Housing Initiatives Program began and has been funded primarily through this program ever since. In 2000, the center had four salaried staff members, and its board included several individuals from Park Hill. Board members also included real estate brokers, attorneys, a property manager, and until recently the director of the city's civil rights division. A panel of attorneys consulted with Housing for All on specific cases. The group took and investigated housing complaints and worked with complainants to prepare and file documents with the state civil rights agency or with HUD. Housing for All took part in a multicity national audit study in 1989. Since 1988, the group has devoted increasing attention to the fair housing rights of the disabled.

A second fair housing enforcement group was formed in 1999, also funded with FHIP funds. Home Inc. was housed in the offices of NEWSED, a community development corporation serving the primarily low-income Latino neighborhoods of northwest Denver. It conducted activities similar to Housing for All and held workshops for neighborhood residents on their rights as home seekers, tenants, and owners. In general, African Americans have been more involved in fair housing advocacy than Latinos. Home Inc. concentrated on the fair housing needs of the Latino community and found that new immigrants experienced different forms of discrimination and exploitation than longtime residents. When immigrants were undocumented, they were reticent to pursue complaints for fear of being deported, and the local legal community was reluctant to represent these individuals, even though fair housing law covers them.

Linking Schools and Housing

One distinctive aspect of Denver's nonprofit fair housing advocacy is a continuing effort to link the problems of segregated schools and segregated housing and to promote joint solutions. The group of fair housing activists who got their start in Park Hill and northwest Denver were always aware of the link between housing and school integration. When busing began in Denver in the early 1970s, they served as citizen monitors in newly desegregated schools. In 1981, Park Hill volunteers worked with the University of Colorado to sponsor a Community Schools/Community Housing conference to raise awareness about ways of achieving housing integration that could preclude the need for busing. Indeed, the court order to desegregate Denver's schools became increasingly unpopular; fair housing activists and elected officials perceived it as a key problem that was driving families out of the city and keeping newcomers from moving in. Release from the court order became a campaign issue in mayoral races. Fair housing activists tried to use this public dissatisfaction as an opportunity to promote housing integration measures in Denver. In 1992, the city sponsored Housing for All's demonstration project to promote pro-integrative real estate techniques and to show a route toward school desegregation other than busing. But such efforts were never able to amass enough support to take hold.

In 2000, advocates who attempted to link schools and housing did so with different goals in mind. Rather than achieving neighborhood integration, these advocates wanted to fight what they saw as an anticity attitude among Denver-area real estate agents. They reasoned that if agents knew more about Denver schools, they would be less likely to steer middle-class families away from the city. Thus the CHRB brings brokers into the schools through its "Yellow School Bus Tours"; the group ran eight tours in 1999, funded partly with CDBG dollars. Real estate brokers receive continuing education credit for the tours, which consist of riding a school bus to a particular Denver school (often a magnet school), touring the school and meeting the principal, and discussing fair housing issues with a CHRB member. A neighborhood tour is led by someone familiar with the history and landmarks in the area. During the fair housing discussion, brokers receive data emphasizing high achievement levels in Denver schools. The CHRB also runs a few programs in the schools each year designed to enhance students' pride in their neighborhoods.

COMMUNITY REINVESTMENT ADVOCACY IN DENVER

Like in Minneapolis, nonprofits became involved in community reinvestment issues in the early 1990s, as Home Mortgage Disclosure Act (HMDA) data became available and as local banks were being acquired. Groups formed a community reinvestment coalition to stage protests and to negotiate with banks, working with the city to integrate community reinvestment criteria into city contracts with banks. But the coalition broke apart within a few years. By 2000, local monitoring of bank practices did not occur, and the city had changed its oversight process to grant greater discretion to banks. A consortium of banks operated a home-ownership counseling and mortgage preapproval program with several community development corporations.

Grassroots Activism and Coalition Building

Community reinvestment advocacy began in Denver when the local Metropolitan Organization for People (MOP) held community meetings that identified vacant homes as a problem in several inner-city neighborhoods. Leaders of the group, a multi-issue grassroots organization that mobilizes church congregations, heard that people were having problems securing mortgage and home improvement loans in these neighborhoods. They conducted research on lending patterns and reviewed the community reinvestment plans that banks were supposed to keep publicly available. These local activists learned about CRA from the National Community Reinvestment Coalition and began to approach banks with requests for relaxed underwriting standards and for commitments to improve lending approval rates. They signed an agreement with Colorado National Bank in 1990, but the agreement did not include any specific lending goals. The following year, Norwest Bank in Minneapolis requested permission from the Federal Reserve Board to buy United Banks of Denver. MOP stated their intent to submit comments opposing the merger, and within several months the group signed an agreement with United committing to a multiyear lending goal of $80 million.

By 1991, MOP had shifted its attention to other local problems, and a staff member at the University of Colorado's Center for Community Development convened about twenty directors and staff members from Denver community development corporations, along with the director of the city's nonprofit fair housing enforcement group, to discuss the prospect of forming a coalition that would focus on community reinvestment issues in the city. In 1992 they formed the Denver Community Reinvestment Alliance (DCRA). One of the CDCs provided office space, the university center provided student interns and some staff time, and the group began to conduct research on local banks' lending records. They had begun discussions with Affiliated National Bank, but were not making much progress, when they learned that Colorado National was requesting permission to buy Central Bank. DCRA held a press conference to publicize their research on Central's lending disparities across race and income; they soon reached an agreement with the bank to lend $55 million in low-income and minority neighborhoods. In 1993, the Minneapolis-based First Bank Systems announced plans to acquire Colorado National, and the group's relationships with that bank, dating back three years, began to dissolve.

By this time, new groups and individuals had joined DCRA. No longer a coalition solely of CDCs, the alliance now included disability-rights activists and labor unions along with several individuals who had been involved in MOP's earlier campaign. A director of National People's Action, a national organization of neighborhood groups and an early leader in community reinvestment protests, visited Denver to talk with DCRA about advocacy strategies. Learning about their difficulties in eliciting a response from Colorado National Bank, he suggested they use some "people power." Labor union and disability-rights activists were comfortable with protest, and they staged several actions against the bank. They mobilized about one hundred people to picket the bank's downtown headquarters and attempted to visit the CEO's office. In another instance, they picketed in front of his home. But these actions elicited little response. In 1994, DCRA filed a complaint with the U.S. Department of Labor charging Colorado National Bank with employment discrimination; the charge was investigated and dismissed the following year.[40] The group then picketed the Federal Reserve Bank to protest its community reinvestment rating system.

Meanwhile, other banks proved more responsive to DCRA. Norwest agreed to work with the group to market more loans to people of color, people with disabilities, and low-income people; the bank contracted with the alliance to provide a sensitivity training course for its employees and placed a DCRA representative on a lending advisory board.[41] As part of the Washington, D.C.–based National Council of La Raza's Southwest Initiative, local CDCs worked with three banks to develop the Barrio Aztlan Homeownership Program. Banks created a loan pool and provided operating support to three CDCs to run the program. During this time, Denver advocates became involved in national community reinvestment efforts, attending conferences and serving on the board of the National Community Reinvestment Coalition.

City Depository Designation

In the early 1990s, while DCRA was forming and beginning to take action, the city adopted "community responsiveness" as a condition for banks to receive city business.[42] In an initiative from the mayor's office, the city created the Denver Community Reinvestment Partnership, a group of banks that received city accounts in exchange for lending commitments that would help the city meet its community development goals. At Mayor Wellington Webb's request, the city began a competitive bidding process for all city depositories, both existing and new accounts. In their bids, banks were asked to submit information on their services and prices and on their community involvement and reinvestment activities; Mayor Webb wanted city staff to give equal weight to these economic and community factors.

City staff reviewed the banks' proposals, assessing their community reinvestment ratings, their record of community lending and involvement, and what they proposed for the future. They negotiated with banks about how they could help meet the city's community development goals. Participating banks signed an agreement in 1993 committing them to three-year goals in four areas: small business loans, low- and moderate-income mortgage loans, minority-owned and women-owned business purchasing, and downtown historic preservation loans.[43] They agreed to try to make new loans equivalent to 2 percent of their Colorado assets. In return, the city divided its payroll and reserve deposits among the partnership banks for three years, with an option to extend for an additional two years.

According to a respondent who participated in setting up the partnership, banks at first were reluctant. While Mayor Webb wanted to try to gain some leverage with city accounts, certain characteristics of the accounts actually made them somewhat disadvantageous for banks. The city keeps low bank balances wherever possible, using the government bond market to maximize returns. The state requires banks to put up collateral for the accounts in order to protect the city in case of bank failure. Finally, the city charter requires special handling of the city's largest account, used for payroll, which limits the degree of automation that can be used, thus making the account more costly to operate. In addition to these issues, bank executives did not like the idea that the city was becoming another regulator who would require burdensome reporting. City staff were careful to clarify that they wanted only data required by federal and state regulators.

Some bank leaders were also unhappy that the mayor had appointed five DCRA activists to monitor the process. These advocates met with Mayor Webb to request community oversight of the partnership, so he formed a citizens' advisory committee, although it did not participate in the initial choice of banks. In the end, despite their reservations, banks joined the partnership because they did not want to appear hostile to the mayor, according to a city staffer. The agreement included annual reporting of progress and a public forum to present each annual review. After the first year, the city hired the Center for Community Development, which conducted analysis and training for DCRA, to conduct the first annual review. It showed that lenders had met their three-year goals in the first year, and four banks had increased their lending rates to low-income and minority borrowers. Nonetheless, disparities persisted in denial and lending rates to racial and ethnic minorities.[44]

Declining Advocacy, Retreating City

Attention to community reinvestment issues in Denver has declined since 1994. The DCRA disintegrated and the city's depository program fell behind in its annual reviews of partnership activity, then chose to take a less active role in shaping banks' community reinvestment strategies.

When the alliance turned to direct-action strategies, community development corporations left the coalition. CDCs need financial services in order to engage in affordable housing and economic development projects. Their staff became uncomfortable with the adversarial turn DCRA had taken, fearing that banks would become less cooperative with them on their development work. As one CDC director put it, "My energy has to go into being sure that I have a good relationship with the banks." Banks began to form community advisory committees as part of their CRA compliance strategies and invited CDC directors to take part. Some CDC staffers felt they could change banking practices this way, "from the inside." Even the CDC that had supported DCRA most directly pulled back; the director believed that the time for direct action had passed and that productive results could arise through partnerships.

The remaining DCRA coalition members chose to retain their adversarial stance and to remain independent of banks by not accepting operational support from them. But they had difficulty securing funding over the long term. The University Center for Community Development could sometimes provide part-time staff, and at one point the group secured a grant from a local foundation for a staff organizer. By 1998, the university staff member who had helped organize the coalition had moved away, and one of the principal leaders resigned. Three

DCRA members retained their seats on the city's Community Reinvestment Partnership advisory committee, but they served as individuals—their organization had disintegrated. The former members whose backgrounds are in grassroots organizing rather than community development are proud that DCRA got the attention of the banks and the city. Advocacy then shifted to an oversight role. These advocates were skeptical that community members could have a voice in bank practices and programs merely through serving on advisory committees. One former leader expressed doubt that the group could gather together enough people to stage a protest if one became necessary. Another observed that "DCRA's prospects are pretty bleak."

Local nonprofit capacity for monitoring banking conditions and performance declined. The city did not produce research reports from 1995 to 1997, and in 1998 hired the Washington, D.C.–based national community reinvestment advocacy group to conduct the Home Mortgage Disclosure Act analysis of partnership banks. In 1998, although one Denver CDC joined a national advocacy effort to secure public hearings on the Norwest–Wells Fargo merger, no Denver-based community reinvestment advocates testified.

The city's Community Reinvestment Partnership lagged as well. In 1996, Colorado National Bank, the institution DCRA felt had the worst record, quit the partnership, dissatisfied with results of a survey on small business lending that it believed did not fairly represent its practices.[45] The city extended its contracts by one year and in the fall of 1999 was preparing another request for proposals. The city committee altered the submission process, removing the city's goals and asking banks to report their own goals for community involvement and reinvestment. Banks would be able to specialize in areas of their choice, according to the community reinvestment plans they develop for federal regulators. One respondent observed that since the wave of bank mergers in the early 1990s, fewer bank leaders had personal connections with the mayor or city hall. On the other hand, this respondent felt that banks had come to terms with CRA and were more willing to make an effort to comply than they had been when the partnership was formed. He also noted that U.S. Bank, formerly Colorado National, would probably rejoin the partnership in the next round.

SOCIAL MOVEMENTS AND POLICY DESIGNS: CONSISTENCY AND DIVERGENCE

National policy designs offer a series of resources to advocacy groups interested in working to advance equality in housing. As previous chapters have suggested, it is reasonable to expect that these policies should influence local advocacy. In many ways, Denver's fair housing and community reinvestment movements "look like" the national policy designs that offer them ideas, tools, arenas, funds, and information. The strengths of Denver's fair housing and community rein-

vestment advocacy groups, and their challenges, often reflect the balance of resources present in the national policy design. Nonetheless, there are several ways
in which Denver's advocacy groups diverge from expectations. Table 5.2 reviews the expectations and summarizes the findings about the two movements in
Denver.

Movements Mirror Policy Designs

All of the advocacy groups active on fair housing in Denver in 2000 were specialists, and the activities they undertook reflected an understanding of fair housing as emerging from the process of housing transactions. Groups took individual
cases and advocated on their behalf, conducted tests to investigate how protected
classes were being treated, and conducted workshops for home seekers, inform-
ing them of their rights, and for real estate professionals, teaching them about the
law and how to abide by it.

This approach represents a shift from the 1960s when activists wanted to
achieve integrated housing patterns. Many fair housing advocates still supported
the idea of racial integration, but by 2000, no group pursued it directly. At key
moments, advocates tried to advance the goal of integration, usually linked to the
city schools, but none of these efforts resulted in any lasting program. Indeed, the
national policy design offers no resources to do so. Several of the older generation of activists were frustrated with the new generation's approaches, but others
acknowledged that integration does not seem to be an "idea in good currency"—
that a rationale for pursuing it would need to be developed for the contemporary
context and that some racial and ethnic minorities still see political disadvantages
to integrated housing patterns.

As expected, most fair housing activity focused on private-sector housing.
At various points, the Park Hill neighborhood group worked on affordable housing, attempting to persuade the housing authority not to concentrate subsidized
housing in Park Hill and nearby neighborhoods and promoting a strategy of regional dispersal. But these efforts pale when compared to the institutionalized
and multigroup efforts directed toward private-sector housing.

Denver's fair housing advocacy efforts have long been responsive to federal
initiatives. The first fair housing center flourished when federal dollars were available and declined when these funds were cut. Fair housing advocates who moved
to other agencies continued to access federal funds that became available. For example, at the Colorado Civil Rights Division, the housing specialist, also a Park
Hill fair housing activist, used federal money to conduct housing audits. When the
New Horizons program took effect, Denver advocates persuaded local leaders to
take part in this process that eventually resulted in a new nonprofit fair housing
center, Housing for All. This organization has relied on FHIP funds since its founding in 1987. As advocates pursued and secured federal dollars, they also adapted
their work to HUD's programmatic changes in federal fair housing implementa-

Table 5.2. Expectations and Outcomes for Fair Housing and Community Reinvestment Advocacy in Denver

Dimension of Advocacy	Fair Housing	Community Reinvestment
Group Type		
Expectations	Specialists	Nonspecialists
Are expectations met?	*Yes*	*Yes* Denver Community Reinvestment Alliance consisted of several types of groups, including grassroots poor-people's groups, community development corporations, disability activists, labor unions
Problem definition		
Discrimination		
Expectations	Individualized, rights-based, process-oriented	Place-based, uneven patterns, outcome-oriented
Are expectations met?	*Mixed* Park Hill activists remain committed to integration; some activists see the city as a victim of discrimination	*Mixed* Race and disability added to definition
Goals		
Expectations	Civil rights (more activity), affordable housing (less activity)	Lending discrimination, other community needs
Are expectations met?	*Yes*	*Yes* Besides lending, included participation in city programs, affordable housing development, low-cost banking services, disability access, bank employment practices
Target		
Expectations	Private sector housing (more), public sector housing (less), racial minorities	Banks, savings and loans, poor neighborhoods
Are expectations met?	*Yes*	*Mixed* Banks, savings and loans, poor people throughout the city
Actions		
Tools		
Expectations	Enforcement activities	Research, mobilization of neighborhoods, public comments
Are expectations met?	*Yes*	*Mixed* Besides research and public comments, mobilization occurred citywide; strategies included operating programs and linking CRA to city programs

Dimension of Advocacy	Fair Housing	Community Reinvestment
Arenas		
Expectations	Court and administrative arenas	Regulatory arenas
Are expectations met?	*Mixed* Little use of court arena	*Yes*
Timing		
Expectations	Federal changes spark local changes; more activity post-1988, then stable level of activity	Irregular, sparked by bank actions and examination cycles; more activity post-1989
Are expectations met?	*Yes*	*Mixed* Activity declined over time
Relationships		
To government		
Expectations	Partnerships (civil rights) Adversarial (affordable housing)	Adversarial
Are expectations met?	*Yes*	*Mixed* Adversarial with federal government, partnership with city government
To industry		
Expectations	Adversarial	Adversarial
Are expectations met?	*No* Cooperative	*Mixed* Initially adversarial, then cooperative

tion. When HUD began to examine practices in a broader range of housing-related industries, Denver groups secured agency funds to study mortgage lending discrimination, to conduct fair housing audit studies, and to study insurance redlining. When HUD began working to advance the housing rights of people with disabilities, so did local groups. And when HUD developed and supported Community Housing Resource Boards (CHRBs) to focus on fair housing education and monitoring, Denver's group competed successfully for the limited grant funds.

The community reinvestment movement in Denver also mirrored the community reinvestment policy design in a number of ways. The advocacy groups working on community reinvestment were multi-issue groups, including grassroots poor people's organizations, community development corporations, and eventually disability rights advocates and labor unions. They formed a coalition aimed at addressing community reinvestment issues in the city. But without funding available from the policy for the work of advocacy and with its commitment to maintaining an adversarial stance toward banks, this coalition disintegrated, leaving Denver without the capacity to monitor or to improve upon its community reinvestment successes.

The broad discretion on the definition of community reinvestment within the policy design invites advocacy groups to promote their own understandings, based on their sense of community needs. Denver's community reinvestment advocates did evaluate how well banks were serving the needs of low-income neighborhoods, but their definition of the issue eventually included much more than that. MOP's initial activity grew from neighborhood concerns about vacant houses, and from the start, there was a clear concern about racial disparities in lending in addition to low-income issues. DCRA eventually also looked at the hiring practices of banks and was critical of the lack of minorities in key decision-making roles. Their CRA agreement with Norwest included sensitivity training for loan officers.

Advocates brought concerns about people with disabilities and labor relations into the definition of community reinvestment, both unusual among nationwide community reinvestment efforts. They pressed banks to be sure their buildings were accessible to the handicapped and articulated the sense that people with disabilities were not receiving financing as readily. Unions were concerned that banks' contracts for services supported companies with exploitative labor practices. CDCs were interested in funding for affordable housing and neighborhood economic development. Finally, with the city's involvement in attempting to shape community reinvestment through its depository designation process, the issue was defined to include economic development (small business loans), historic preservation, and contracts with minority- and women-owned businesses.

Merger activity appeared to drive advocacy, at least during the initial phase of community reinvestment activity. Although MOP had begun to research lending practices, the pending acquisition of United pushed them into a position of more leverage, and they secured an agreement. DCRA's advocacy also peaked when First Bank's acquisition of Colorado National was pending.

Movements Diverge from Policy Designs

Analysis of the two national policy designs did not anticipate several key aspects of Denver's fair housing and community reinvestment movements. With regard to fair housing, Denver's advocacy groups generally did not use the tool of litigation, even though the national fair housing movement tends to view litigation as the most powerful of the policy design's resources. The court system thus goes virtually unused in favor of the administrative law arena. Groups pursue administrative enforcement in the state civil rights division or at HUD, or they work on preventing discrimination through educational programs. Denver advocates by and large favored partnerships. Those who would like to pursue litigation more aggressively were in the minority. In fact, differences in opinion about how adversarial a stance to take toward the state civil rights agency and city government contributed to internal conflict at Housing for All that resulted in staff turnover.

Some thought that a director who adopted an adversarial position harmed fair housing advocacy generally, and the group's relationship with the city and state governments in particular. Nonetheless, a small minority of advocates believed successful litigation with high damages would send a strong message to industry and would be worth the risk of rocky relationships with government.

Another unanticipated aspect of Denver's fair housing movement was that its CHRB survived federal cuts and remained active. When HUD abandoned the CHRB program, Denver's group held together, existing informally for several years and then succeeding in securing local sources of funding from the real estate industry and government. Denver advocates' continuing efforts to link fair housing to school desegregation also were not anticipated, although the struggle that they had in achieving results does highlight the challenge groups face when they undertake fair housing activities that are not supported by national policy resources. One advocate thought that the city and the school district should conduct audit studies of the real estate industry to document the steering of families away from the city. Separation of government agencies responsible for schools and for housing makes connecting the two domains even more difficult, and the national policy design provides no resources to help bridge this divide. In any case, the city did not fund fair housing testing, preferring to encourage fair housing practices through the educational approaches of the CHRB, and through housing counseling services that help individuals find housing and learn how to become homeowners.

As for the community reinvestment movement, the decline of advocacy was unexpected. As groups joined the community reinvestment coalition with their own definitions of "community credit needs," and as banks responded unevenly to coalition members, pressures on the coalition emerged. CDCs eventually became incorporated into the banks' community advisory committees, but banks did not respond to union or disability advocates. With the disintegration of DCRA, their concerns were no longer voiced. The city secured commitments on its definition of reinvestment for the initial three-year period but then decided to defer to banks' definition of community reinvestment in future reviews for depository status. Also apparent is the fact that merger activity does not automatically inspire action. Although mergers sparked advocacy early in the movement's history, the more recent Norwest–Wells Fargo merger attracted little attention in Denver. The tensions that emerged within the community reinvestment coalition between CDCs and grassroots organizing and consumer-oriented groups contributed to the decline in advocacy.

SUMMARY

Fair housing and community reinvestment advocacy have separate histories in Denver, with different groups working on each issue over time and different trajectories of action. Denver's fair housing movement conforms relatively closely to expectations of the policy design analysis, more so than its Minneapolis counterpart. It consisted of specialized fair housing groups that emphasized enforcement and education in the private housing sector. Unsupported by national policy design, efforts to maintain a focus on integration remained weak, as did efforts to link housing and schools. Nonetheless, the presence of these efforts is notable. Denver's community reinvestment movement displayed the challenges of supporting a specialized community reinvestment organization without direct funding available from national policy. Advocacy peaked when bank mergers occurred, but the breakdown of consensus among coalition members contributed to a decline in local capacity for monitoring CRA complicance. Recent bank mergers prompted limited response.

6

A Comparative Analysis of Fair Housing and Community Reinvestment Movements: National and Local Impacts on Advocacy

"I couldn't get fifteen people out here to demonstrate for fair housing," said a Denver city official in the summer of 1999, citing a lack of visible public demand and activity as one reason why the city devotes few resources to the issue. Yet just the week before, one of Denver's nonprofit fair housing organizations, Housing for All, won a "Best Practices" award from HUD for its innovative Residential Insurance Council, a partnership with insurance companies to improve fair practices in homeowners' insurance provision. The council launched a loss-mitigation project in Denver's low-income neighborhoods. In Minneapolis, by contrast, city officials are well aware of local fair housing activities because an advocacy group sued the city in 1992 for racially segregating public housing on the city's north side. The mayor and city council participate in the resulting court settlement's implementation. In another recent action, a tenant group in an inner-ring suburb of Minneapolis joined with a regional affordable housing advocacy organization and the Legal Aid Society to organize residents of an apartment complex threatened with demolition; nearly 60 percent of the residents were people of color. The city had declared the site blighted to qualify its redevelopment for tax increment financing. Advocates testified at city hearings, wrote letters to government officials and newspapers, held community meetings, placed flyers on car windshields, and eventually threatened a fair housing lawsuit. The result was preservation of 1,100 units of affordable housing.

These examples epitomize the different orientations of fair housing movements in Denver and Minneapolis. Faced with the same national fair housing policy, Denver groups forge quiet partnerships with private industry, whereas Minneapolis groups confront and oppose government practices. When it came to community reinvestment, however, faced with the same national policy, Minneapolis and Denver groups used similar tactics and experienced similar trajectories. For example, in the early 1990s, the Denver Community Reinvestment

Alliance (DCRA) staged a series of protests drawing attention to Colorado National Bank's poor record of lending to low-income people and to minorities. In one action, the group picketed the CEO's home. "Strangely enough, red tape ended up in his trees," one activist recalled. Yet in the spring of 2000, she said, "If we heard that a bank was doing poorly, would I be able to gather up the individuals like we did before? Honest to God, my guess is no." Indeed, the organization has virtually disappeared. Two former members serve on a mayor's task force that oversees the city's choice of depositories.

In Minneapolis, as part of a campaign by the Association of Community Organizations for Reform Now (ACORN) against TCF Bank in the late 1980s, two hundred protesters tied a red ribbon around the bank's downtown headquarters. In another action, about fifty people went to the bank president's office and demanded to talk. Today ACORN operates a loan counseling service for four local banks, including TCF. According to an ACORN staffer, "The biggest reason they continue to work with us is not because they're afraid of protests, but because [the loan program] actually works." In both Denver and Minneapolis, groups constituting the community reinvestment movement replaced protest strategies with partnerships, and their overall level of activity declined.

In Chapters 4 and 5, I presented detailed case studies of the fair housing and community reinvestment movements in Minneapolis and Denver in order to assess whether, and how, local movements responded to national policies against housing discrimination. Here I take stock of these stories, tracing variation and uniformity across movements and across cities. On the one hand, as I suggested in Chapter 3, there is good reason to expect uniformity across fair housing movements and across community reinvestment movements. Fair housing groups and community reinvestment groups respond to different national policy designs, each with a distinct set of resources, so despite any common interest among them in reducing housing discrimination, they should take rather different paths. In cities across the United States, we would expect fair housing groups to resemble one another and community reinvestment groups to resemble one another because everywhere these groups face the same national policy designs.

The anecdotes opening this chapter, however, show that this pattern does not emerge neatly or clearly. Although the fair housing and community reinvestment movements differ substantially from one another in both cities, the movements for fair housing in Denver and Minneapolis also differ substantially. And what do we make of the decline of community reinvestment movements across cities? Theory about policy designs offered no predictions about whether movements would grow or decline. In Minneapolis and Denver, the fair housing movements were stable or growing, but community reinvestment movements were fragmented and weak.

In this chapter, I examine each of these outcomes. First I distinguish between community reinvestment and fair housing advocacy, reviewing evidence from the case studies and linking these differences to the national policy designs. Second, I examine each movement in turn. I show that the national policy design had a consistent effect on community reinvestment advocacy, shaping two similar movements in the two cities. In contrast, one national policy design gave rise to quite different fair housing movements across cities. Although policy design theory does not anticipate these differences, I show that key contrasts in the local contexts of Denver and Minneapolis explain why advocacy groups responded so differently to fair housing law. In the chapter's final section, I consider the question of movement trajectories and argue that differences in the resources that national policy designs offer to local groups account for the unanticipated decline of community reinvestment advocacy and the relative health of fair housing efforts in each city.

TWO POLICY DESIGNS, TWO SOCIAL MOVEMENTS

The first question to ask of these case studies is whether the boundaries of national policy and local movements were the same. That is, did advocacy groups in Minneapolis and Denver choose national resources from one policy design or from the other? Or, since the two national policies both address the problem of discrimination, did advocacy groups knit together resources from both of them into a seamless package? In other words, are there two distinct local movements, mirroring two distinct national policy designs? The answer is yes. In both cities, groups chose one set of ideas and one set of tools, putting them to use in separate arenas, thereby cultivating two movements for housing equality: one focused on fair housing, the other on community reinvestment. Table 6.1 presents the expectations for advocacy derived from the policy designs in Chapter 3 with the movement characteristics found in each city. It summarizes the discussion that follows by showing that movement dimensions were generally consistent with policy designs and resources.

In both cities, fair housing advocates included legal activists who could navigate the court system and nonprofit groups supported through FHIP who specialized in fair housing enforcement. In contrast, community reinvestment advocates in both cities were grassroots community groups and community development corporations. Fair housing advocates in both cities pursued enforcement activities such as taking and investigating claims from individuals, while community reinvestment advocates worked to pressure banks to improve their lending records to low-income communities and to racial minorities. Fair housing advocates such as Denver's Housing for All and Minneapolis's Housing Discrimination Law Project used the courts and HUD's administrative process to pursue remedies for individuals who came to them with claims of discrimination. In contrast, changes in the local banking landscape prompted community reinvestment advocates into action. Thus, the Denver Community Reinvestment Alliance picketed Colorado National Bank when it was being acquired by First

Table 6.1. A Comparison of Expectations and Outcomes for Fair Housing and Community Reinvestment Advocacy in Minneapolis and Denver

Dimension of Advocacy	Fair Housing	Community Reinvestment
Group type	Specialists	Nonspecialists
M	*Mixed*	*Yes*
D	*Yes*	*Yes*
Problem definition		
Discrimination	Individualized, rights-based, process-oriented	Place-based, uneven patterns, outcome-oriented
M	*Mixed*	*Mixed*
D	*Mixed*	*Mixed*
Goals	Civil rights (more activity), Affordable housing (less activity)	Lending discrimination, other community needs
M	*No*	*Yes*
D	*Yes*	*Yes*
Target	Private-sector housing (more), Public-sector housing (less), racial minorities	Banks, savings and loans poor neighborhoods
M	*No*	*Mixed*
D	*Yes*	*Mixed*
Actions		
Tools	Enforcement activities	Research, mobilization of neighborhoods, public comments
M	*Mixed*	*Mixed*
D	*Yes*	*Mixed*
Arenas	Court and administrative arenas	Regulatory arenas
M	*Mixed*	*Yes*
D	*Mixed*	*Yes*
Timing	Federal changes spark local changes; more activity post-1988, then stable level of activity	Irregular, sparked by bank actions and examination cycles; more activity post-1989
M	*Yes*	*Mixed*
D	*Yes*	*Mixed*
Relationships		
To government	Partnerships (civil rights) Adversarial (affordable housing)	Adversarial
M	*Yes*	*Mixed*
D	*Yes*	*Mixed*
To industry	Adversarial	Adversarial
M	*Yes*	*Mixed*
D	*No*	*Mixed*

Note: M = Minneapolis, D = Denver.

Bank. A coalition of Minneapolis community development corporations negotiated an agreement with First Bank when it was buying a nearby suburban bank.
With a few exceptions, local fair housing and community reinvestment groups
generally did not cross paths. Although some recognition of common ground was
apparent during my interviews with advocates, little interaction among fair housing and community reinvestment advocates occurred.

Thinking theoretically, the case study evidence supports the notion that each
policy design fostered a distinct movement for housing equality. Although both
designs address housing discrimination, they do so with different approaches —
different goals, target groups, and enforcement structures. Thus, even when advocacy groups share an interest in reducing discrimination, by choosing one set
of resources over another, they set themselves on different paths. Policy designs,
as institutional structures, channel social movements in different directions.

NATIONAL POLICY'S IMPACT: VARIABLE OR UNIFORM?

A second question to ask of the case studies is whether the movements linked to
each policy design were similar across cities. Theoretical literature supports conflicting expectations. On the one hand, the policy design perspective does not explicitly theorize about how federalism could mediate the effects of national
policy on local action. Articulations of the theory suggest the expectation that
one policy design would uniformly impact advocacy across government scales.[1]
That is, fair housing movements across cities should resemble one another, as
should community reinvestment movements. But theory and empirical work on
federalism and urban politics suggest otherwise. Although these studies focus on
decision making by government officials rather than by advocacy groups, they
find variation in the local implementation of federal policies. Local officials
adapt national policies to their political and social needs, sometimes subverting
national policy goals in the process.[2] Empirical work on local economic development and housing policies finds that local configurations of interests are likely
to lead to distinctive policy choices across cities despite common economic pressures or federal programs.[3] The case studies offer support for each of these perspectives. Community reinvestment advocacy conforms to expectations of
policy design theorists, whereas fair housing advocacy supports theories of federalism and urban variation.

Community Reinvestment Advocacy in Two Cities

The national community reinvestment policy design prompted similar responses
from groups in Minneapolis and Denver. Advocacy peaked in the early 1990s
and declined within the decade. Table 6.2 summarizes the pattern of community
reinvestment activism.

Table 6.2. Community Reinvestment Activism in Denver and Minneapolis

Dimension of Advocacy	Phase 1	Phase 2
Group type	CRA Coalitions Multi-issue groups CDCs	Multi-issue groups CDCs
Problem definition		
Discrimination	Patterns/outcomes	Varies by group type
Goals	Change lending patterns to low-income, minority neighborhoods and individuals	Varies by group type
Target	Selected lending institutions City Hall	Selected lending institutions
Actions		
Strategies	Protest Negotiation	Cooperate with banks Operate programs
Arenas	Public arenas High visibility	Private, specialized arenas Low visibility
Timing	Activity begins post-1989 Bank merger activity occurs	Bank merger activity occurs
Relationships		
To government	Adversarial	Limited
To industry	Adversarial	Partnership

Phase 1: Research and Mobilization. Advocacy did not begin in either city until the early 1990s. Groups conducted research using HMDA data to identify banks with poor lending records to low-income people and people of color. They approached banks about addressing these problems, but banks initially were not responsive. In both cities, advocates turned to protest strategies. They drew on symbols of redlining: in Minneapolis, groups tied red ribbons around downtown bank headquarters; in Denver, advocates hung red tape from the trees in a bank CEO's yard. These efforts occurred in public arenas and received media attention.

The groups who engaged in these activities generally formed loose coalitions of grassroots advocates for the poor (such as ACORN), faith-based groups (such as Metropolitan Organization for People), and community development corporations. In Denver, disability-rights and union activists also took part. Coalitions received help from local university professors in analyzing the HMDA data and from national nonprofit organizations who track community reinvestment issues and provide technical assistance on data analysis and the intervention process. In both cities, advocacy groups also worked with local government officials to inject community lending into the city's set of criteria for choosing its depositories. On the whole, these advocacy efforts were moderately successful. In each city, groups secured a few CRA agreements with local banks.

Phase 2: Fragmentation and Decline. In neither city were advocacy groups able to sustain a high level of activity on community reinvestment issues. By the late 1990s, they continued to monitor lending activity only to a limited degree. Coalitions disintegrated, and groups either had abandoned protest strategies in favor of partnerships with banks or simply had moved on to other issues. In both cities, some banks supported nonprofit groups who operated homeownership counseling and mortgage preapproval programs. Some banks invited CDC directors to serve on advisory committees. Other CDCs received loans or grants for community development projects. In both cities, local government officials scaled back their community reinvestment requirements for city depositories. The community reinvestment advocacy that did occur tended to happen in private arenas. In Denver, advocates doubted they could mobilize constituencies if a new opportunity for intervention, such as a merger, arose.

Fair Housing Advocacy in Two Cities

Although the community reinvestment movements in Denver and Minneapolis seemed similarly shaped by national policy, the fair housing movements in the two cities differed. In effect, I found two models of fair housing advocacy: (1) protecting civil rights through partnerships and education (Denver) and (2) providing affordable housing through mobilization and confrontation (Minneapolis). Table 6.3 summarizes these differences.

In Denver, fair housing advocacy had become the province of specialists. Three nonprofit organizations focused exclusively on fair housing: Housing for All, the Community Housing Resource Board, and Home Inc.@Newsed. In Minneapolis, a wider range of nonprofits was active on fair housing. Two groups specialized in the issue, but they were joined by several affordable housing and multi-issue groups that had taken up affordable housing. These included the Metropolitan Interfaith Coalition for Affordable Housing (MICAH) and the Catholic Archdiocese Office for Social Justice. The NAACP and its legal advocates also engaged in fair housing advocacy.

Dominant definitions of discrimination varied across the cities. Denver groups worked against discrimination in the process of housing transactions, mostly on behalf of individuals. Most Minneapolis groups, on the other hand, were working to change housing patterns they believed were discriminatory. Group action in the two cities also varied. In Denver, educational strategies and partnerships with the housing industry characterized fair housing activity, which occurred out of the public eye. In Minneapolis, confrontation was common, and activists attempted to mobilize the public to press elected officials for policy change. Action in Denver spanned the protected classes and sectors of the private housing industry, whereas in Minneapolis fair housing activity targeted low-income minorities and aimed to change government practices that create barriers to affordable housing. Denver fair housing advocates sought a cooperative rela-

Table 6.3. Two Models of Fair Housing Advocacy

Dimension of Advocacy	Denver	Minneapolis
Group type	Fair housing groups	Fair housing groups Affordable housing groups Civil rights groups
Problem definition		
Discrimination	Individuals, process	Patterns, outcomes
Goals	Civil rights	Affordable housing
Target	Private-sector practices	Public-sector practices
Actions		
Strategies	Partnerships with private sector Education of private sector Enforcement activities	Litigation Mobilization Enforcement activities
Arenas	Behind-the-scenes, specialized Administrative arena Low visibility	Courts Legislature (state and city) High visibility
Timing	Responsive to federal changes Consistent activity	Responsive to federal changes Inconsistent activity
Relationships		
To government	Partnership	Adversarial
To industry	Partnership	Adversarial

tionship with government and the housing industry, whereas Minneapolis advocates directly challenged these actors.

A good example of Denver's orientation to partnerships was its Residents' Insurance Council. Housing for All won federal FHIP funding to conduct an audit study of local insurance companies. Rather than using the findings to file claims of discrimination against insurance companies, the groups used the results to convene a working group on insurance discrimination, consisting of representatives from the insurance companies, state and local government officials, and fair housing advocates. The Residents' Insurance Council won a grant from the Ford Foundation to undertake a loss-mitigation program in the neighborhoods that Housing for All found to be suffering from redlining.

A contrasting example of the Minneapolis orientation to mobilization was the effort to save Huntington Point and Huntington Place in Brooklyn Park, a suburb bordering Minneapolis.[4] In 1998, tenants in these apartment complexes worked with MICAH, an affordable housing advocacy organization, and the Legal Aid Society to prevent demolition of their homes. City officials and the development's owners wanted to redevelop the housing complex using tax increment financing. The city had to declare the site blighted to qualify for this subsidy. More than half of Huntington Point and Place residents were people of color, thus advocates argued that destroying their homes violated fair housing law while also depleting the region's supply of affordable units. Advocates testi-

Table 6.4. Local Context, Minneapolis and Denver

	Minneapolis	Denver
Rate of change: racial diversity and poverty	High	Low
State political context	Liberal	Conservative
Historical networks	Absent	Present

fied at city hearings, distributed flyers at the apartment complex, and threatened to sue under fair housing law. These actions halted demolition, preserving 1,100 affordable homes.

The Influence of Local Context

In Minneapolis and Denver, groups facing the same set of policy resources and incentives chose very different courses of action. This result highlights the insufficiency of the policy design approach for predicting local outcomes, and supports urban scholarship positing the importance of local context in shaping local outcomes. Three local factors seemed to condition fair housing advocacy groups' responses to the national policy design: the rate of change in racial diversity and poverty, the state political context, and the presence and nature of historical organizational networks. Table 6.4 summarizes these differences.

Changing Racial Diversity and Poverty. Differences in the rate of demographic change help explain why fair housing activism in Minneapolis focused on low-income minorities, and why activism was more visible to the public in that city than in Denver.[5] Although in both cities a majority of residents are white, Denver is a historically multiethnic city with a sizable Latino population and somewhat smaller black population. The proportion of Denver residents who are black remained essentially the same from 1980 to 1990, then dropped by 1 percent to 11 percent in 2000; in the same period, the proportion of Latinos grew from 19 to 23 percent, a 23 percent increase. Latinos made up 34 percent of the population by 2000, a 40 percent increase. They have not been as active on fair housing issues as whites and blacks in Denver.

Minneapolis, on the other hand, experienced during the 1980s and 1990s much more rapid and dramatic shifts in the racial composition of its population. The minority population grew by 32,000 people during the 1980s, a 69 percent increase, and has continued to increase, in numbers and diversity, in the 1990s.[6] Census 2000 showed that minorities and immigrants accounted for all of the city's 3.6 percent population growth. The nonwhite population grew by 54,000 people, or 68 percent. The city has the largest black, American Indian, and Hispanic populations in the state and the second largest Asian population.[7] Not surprisingly, education data showed increases since 1990 in the numbers of school-age students speaking Southeast Asian or African languages or Spanish.[8]

In addition, the minority population in Minneapolis became more impoverished during the 1980s, although there is evidence that the 1990s brought some improvement in their status. One study concluded that "when compared to the nation as a whole, minority races in Minnesota are experiencing more poverty at a faster rate of growth, while their White counterparts are generally better off in Minnesota than across the country."[9] Whereas poverty declined slightly among blacks nationwide during the 1980s, in Minnesota it grew from about 24 percent in 1980 to about 36 percent in 1990.[10] Indeed, black poverty rates in the Twin Cities have been among the highest in the nation.[11] In 1980, about one-quarter of Twin Cities blacks lived in ghetto neighborhoods; by 1990, nearly half of them did.[12] The poverty rate for blacks in Minneapolis grew from 30 percent in 1980 to 41 percent in 1990. By 2000, the rate had dropped to 32 percent, still significantly higher than the rate of 10 percent for whites.[13] In Denver, the black poverty rate changed from 21 percent in 1980 to 27 percent in 1990; for Latinos, the rate changed from 24 percent to 31 percent.[14] By 2000, both of these rates had dropped; 19 percent of blacks and 23 percent of Latinos were poor, lagging behind the white rate of 11 percent.

These differences in the rate of racial change and the relative impoverishment of minorities have two implications for fair housing action. First, they drive the convergence of fair housing and affordable housing issues in Minneapolis. Affordable housing advocates (primarily white) have realized that their constituents, at least in the central city, now are often people of color. Fair housing becomes a tool to achieve their affordable housing goals. For example, threats to demolish affordable housing can be framed as racially discriminatory, or at least as having a disparate impact on racial minorities. Thus, affordable housing advocates in the 1990s became interested in, and open to, the incentives to participation that fair housing policy design offers.

Second, the novelty of diversity means that race is news in Minneapolis, so the media focus on racial issues. For activists, this attention both helps and hurts their cause. To some extent, media images of minorities are associated with crime and welfare and thus fuel negative stereotypes, making advocacy more challenging.[15] On the other hand, the publicity gives race and housing issues agenda status in a way not experienced by activists in Denver. Most activists interviewed, however, felt that media coverage of race hurt more than helped their advocacy efforts, and they therefore tried to frame housing issues in terms of class—for example, when trying to persuade suburban jurisdictions to build affordable housing. Ironically, the increasing salience of race in Minneapolis has prompted many advocates to keep it out of their public rhetoric on housing issues.

State Political Context. Different political contexts in the two states help account for the focus on private-sector practices in Denver and public-sector policies in

Minneapolis; this difference also influences the visibility of fair housing issues. Although the cities both have histories of liberal, progressive leadership, the state contexts differ. Colorado is a generally conservative and Republican state compared to liberal Minnesota, where even Republicans have a tradition of progressivism.[16] Republicans controlled both houses of the Colorado legislature from 1976 to 2000, when Democrats gained a one-seat lead in the Senate.[17] In Minnesota, Democrats have controlled the state senate for twenty-nine years and the house for a decade until the 1998 elections.[18] In Minneapolis, affordable and fair housing activists turn to the state, both for policy changes and funds, but Colorado fair housing activists did not see the state as a viable source of support, either in terms of programs or funding opportunities.

In Denver, where fair housing activism is oriented toward protecting civil rights, activists and government-agency staff reported that they purposely tried to keep a low profile. Higher visibility of fair housing activities could attract negative attention. Nonprofit fair housing enforcement groups were funded through HUD so did not depend on the state for material support, but they relied on the state civil rights agency to enforce both state and federal fair housing laws. (The Colorado Civil Rights Division was known among housing activists as being conservative in findings of cause on housing discrimination cases.) In this context, it is perhaps not surprising that fair housing groups tried to partner with industry and to keep adversarial relations to a minimum, confined to specific allegations and investigations of discrimination. The state civil rights agency persuaded the legislature to make changes in state fair housing law (so it conforms to national law and thus qualifies the agency for federal funding) by framing the issue in terms of how changes would benefit the housing industry—for example, reducing uncertainty for industry and providing a viable state adjudication process rather than relying solely on the lengthy federal process. The agency employed a fair housing specialist who did education and outreach, often to housing professionals. In a recent budgeting cycle, her position was preserved essentially because the housing industry supported her; she helps them navigate the complex regulations of federal fair housing law.

The state context constrains a regional affordable housing/fair housing agenda in Colorado. Denver activists did not see fair share legislation, for example, which succeeded in the Minnesota legislature (albeit in a weak form) as even in the realm of possibility in Colorado. In Minnesota, with a stronger tradition of using redistributive policy,[19] activists viewed the state as the locus of government with most resources to contribute to affordable housing. The 1998 elections brought a Republican majority to the state House of Representatives. Newly elected Governor Ventura left advocates wondering what to expect, but during his first year in office, the legislature appropriated the highest level of funding for affordable housing in Minnesota history.[20] The state thus represents a viable resource and instrument for Minnesota advocates. The Minnesota Fair Housing Center, though denied HUD funds, secured research grants from the state Social

Services Department to study the link between homelessness and fair housing and helped secure a special appropriation for the Human Rights Department for fair housing testing.

Organizational Networks. Fair housing advocacy in these cities is embedded in different historical networks, with implications for contemporary movement orientations. Fair housing activism in Denver is rooted in a civil rights tradition, whereas in Minneapolis, the current fair housing efforts largely consist of activists from other spheres adapting to new circumstances by engaging fair housing policy tools. In Denver, current fair housing activity is part of a long and continuous history of fair housing activism, which first emerged in the late 1950s in the city's Park Hill neighborhood.[21] Residents of this neighborhood mobilized to fight blockbusting and racial turnover and to promote stable integration. Their efforts led to passage of the state fair housing law in 1959, preceding national law by nine years and the first in the nation to cover private housing. Activists who got their start in these early fair housing battles still lived in Park Hill, and many had made careers of fair housing, community development, civil rights, and related pursuits in government and nonprofit settings. Former employees of Denver's original fair housing center, which had fifty employees before the national law ever existed, were scattered throughout state and city government and the housing industry— in Denver's Community Development Agency, heading the Colorado Housing Finance Authority, working as real estate agents in the city, active on industry fair housing training, and serving as board members of Housing for All and the CHRB. With such a network, it is not surprising that Denver groups took advantage of most funding opportunities from HUD since 1968, whether special demonstration projects, nationwide housing audits, fair housing planning projects, and finally the Fair Housing Initiatives Program, securing grants year after year to support the local fair housing center. Fair housing activists in Denver adapted their strategies to incorporate changes in national law, such as the addition of people with disabilities and families with children to the protected classes; as the national fair housing movement and HUD turned attention to discrimination in mortgage lending and insurance, Denver activists also explored these issues.

Minneapolis had nothing like this continuity of activism and expertise on fair housing. Rather, the current movement drew on the network of affordable housing activists that developed and gained strength during the 1970s and 1980s. Although a local fair housing movement in the late 1950s and early 1960s secured passage of state and city fair housing laws, these activists moved on to other causes. Many became involved in the national civil rights movement. Some, including churches, became involved in housing development. Civil rights groups turned to employment issues, policy brutality, and neighborhood revitalization. Many of the federal fair housing resources that Denver activists took advantage of were untapped in Minneapolis. But in the 1990s, as demographic changes converged with a shortage of affordable housing, affordable housing advocates and advocates for the poor became fair housing activists as well, adapting fair housing tools to their purposes. These activists are politically skilled, comfortable with public engagement, and oriented toward mobilization strategies that have worked for them on affordable housing issues, and they brought these orientations to the fair housing issue.

POLICY DESIGN RESOURCES: UNIFORMITY, VARIATION, AND THE EVOLUTION OF ADVOCACY

The patterns just described prompt several questions. Why do the community reinvestment movements look the same across cities, but the fair housing movements differ? Why, during the 1990s, did the community reinvestment movements decline, while the fair housing movements remained stable (as in Denver) or grew (as in Minneapolis)? A closer and comparative look at the types of resources contained within each policy design sheds light on these questions. In answer to the first question, I suggest that the fair housing policy design offers a wider array of resources that groups more easily can adapt to local circumstances, whereas the community reinvestment policy offers a more limited set of resources, constraining local adaptability. This difference means that local community reinvestment movements are likely to look more similar across cities than fair housing movements are. In answer to the second question, I suggest that the resources within community reinvestment policy have a demobilizing effect on local movements over time. Using the Community Reinvestment Act can jump-start a movement, but then it also can stab it in the back. More generally, some policy resources foster the strength of advocacy groups, while others strip them of it.

Key differences in the types of resources contained in fair housing and community reinvestment policy thus have important consequences for the political strength, organizational capacity, and survival of these two movements. Each type of resource—problem definition, funding, tools and arenas, and information—has a unique set of advantages and disadvantages for groups. For example, funding offers advocacy groups the chance to build capacity but may reduce their autonomy.[22] Some policy tools may require a degree of autonomy before a group can use them. Thus, advocacy groups need funds and expertise to file a lawsuit. Considering the evidence from the case studies of group activities and trajectories in conjunction with comparative analysis of policy design resources identifies key dilemmas that fair housing and community reinvestment groups generally face. Table 3.2 in Chapter 3 summarizes the differences in policy design resources.

Policy Design Impacts on Group Adaptability

The case studies suggest that each design hampers a group's ability to adapt national resources to local context, but the community reinvestment design does so to a greater degree. This difference contributed to the uniformity of the community reinvestment movements across the two cities and the variation in fair housing approaches.

Community Reinvestment. The community reinvestment policy design seems to limit the ability of advocacy groups to respond to changing conditions in the local banking industry and to incorporate other constituencies who may suffer from limited access to credit besides low-income people and racial minorities. Although the design's resource mix enables nonprofits to generate funding from the local lending community, this success may limit groups' capacity to use the same resources later. That is, using the law erodes the capacity for continuing to tap its resources. For example, a common outcome of community reinvestment negotiations is that lenders begin to fund community groups to operate home-ownership counseling programs. Groups work with prospective homeowners to overcome credit problems, to assemble the necessary downpayment and closing costs, to navigate the mortgage application process, and to learn about home maintenance and repair. This type of program certainly benefits members of low-income communities, but it also diverts time and staff from a group's CRA monitoring function—analyzing data, reviewing institutions' CRA evaluations and programs, and so on. In effect, this diversion limits the capacity to continue to monitor local lending activity and to demand further change. And as groups build partnerships with lenders, they may become less willing to take on an adversarial role.

A similar dilemma arises for CDCs, whose primary goal is to engage in development, not to monitor lending performance. These outcomes—CRA "successes"—have emerged in both Denver and Minneapolis and certainly help poor and minority neighborhoods. Especially if this capital flow becomes institutionalized into a formal CRA agreement, it may represent a long-term benefit. In part, banks, in their effort to comply with the law, may come to appreciate the resources that nonprofit groups bring them. CDCs offer their access to federal, state, and local housing program dollars as well as their ability to knit together the financing packages that affordable housing projects require. Poor people's groups offer knowledge of their constituency to banks and can help low-income people become bank customers.

Although groups can thus secure funding for counseling programs or affordable housing development, they rarely receive funds to analyze lending data and to monitor CRA compliance. Community reinvestment policy offers no funding from government either, thus these functions may decline. The danger is that if a lender scales back its community reinvestment commitments, advocacy groups find that the technical expertise, the political courage, and the coalitions may have eroded. Indeed, in the case cities, CRA agreements were outdated and had not been renewed, local governments had scaled back community lending requirements for banks serving as city depositories, and public comment periods on bank mergers had occurred—all without significant involvement or protest from advocacy groups.

The community reinvestment policy design offers a limited range of tools, a limited set of financial institutions required to comply with the law, and a limited range of burdens that regulators impose to punish inadequate compliance. These limitations constrain advocacy groups' ability to respond to specific features of a local context. In both case cities, groups were successful in challenging lending practices of some lenders but not others. In each city, one lender persistently resisted group challenges and invitations to negotiate. Eventually, having no further means to prompt change, groups ceased these protests, focusing instead on the lenders who responded. Similarly, some regulatory agencies emphasized the importance of CRA compliance more than others; thus advocacy groups, regardless of their internal characteristics and capacity, are likely to find themselves differentially effective in influencing the practices of local lenders.

Finally, some community reinvestment coalitions may try to adapt the definition of community reinvestment to reflect local needs or constituencies. In Denver, disability rights advocates and union members took part in an initial phase of community reinvestment organizing and protest, arguing that Denver banks should ensure accessibility in their offices for the disabled and should hire union workers. Claims supporting these alternative target groups, which are not part of CRA's problem definition, did not succeed.

Fair Housing. The fair housing policy design offers advocacy groups a wider range of resources than the community reinvestment design offers. This diverse set of direct and indirect funding and an array of tools has mixed implications for group capacity and survival. The fair housing policy design seems to enable advocacy groups to integrate fair housing into their local context, but doing so results in a partial approach to solving fair housing problems.

The case studies showed two patterns of fair housing activity at the local level, reflecting two sets of group choices about which policy resources to use. In Denver, local fair housing groups generally used national policy resources to pursue the protection of civil rights in private sector housing. In Minneapolis, a wider range of groups has focused on opportunities for intervening in the public housing sector to secure affordable housing throughout the metro area. While Denver groups rely heavily on federal funds, fewer Minneapolis groups do so.

Groups can use fair housing policy resources to compensate for local deficiencies, or they can bolster weak national resources with strong local ones to address particular local needs. Thus in Denver, with a conservative political context and a local network of advocates less inclined to adversarial strategies, fair housing organizations used federal funds to carry out fair housing enforcement activities. They tapped local funds for cooperative and educational efforts. In Minneapolis, where local resources existed for major lawsuits and a network of advocates concerned about regional disparities dominated housing issues, groups could use fair housing's litigation tool to pursue reform of federal, state, and local government practices.

Sometimes local resource strengths protect advocacy groups from federal retrenchment. In Denver, the Community Housing Resource Board, with its educational focus, sustained the withdrawal of federal funding (due to program shifts at HUD) by gaining access to local resources, in part because Denver's embedded network of housing professionals supports fair housing education. Organizations dedicated to the affordable housing mission of fair housing policy emerged only in Minneapolis, where a local resource base existed. The same is true for groups pursuing discrimination complaints with litigation rather than through the administrative process—there is a need for an initial stock of resources to support a lawsuit, which, only if successful, will bring financial resources (damages) to the group. One reason Denver's fair housing group pursued a partnership strategy with insurance companies was that it could not afford to mount a major class-action lawsuit. Minneapolis had this capacity in a sophisticated network of affordable housing and legal advocates, including local foundations and agencies such as Legal Services. Groups could file two major class-action lawsuits and fund a nonprofit to organize support for one of them.

The case studies highlight how the fair housing policy design's resource structure influences group strategies. The design offers more resources to support a process-oriented definition of discrimination, focused on reducing differential treatment in individual housing transactions. Denver groups, heavily reliant on federal resources, emphasized this goal. They worked behind the scenes in specialized arenas. Although they did maintain activity, they lacked a broad political constituency in the city. Denver's necessary reliance on federal funds for fair housing enforcement leaves these groups vulnerable to federal budget cuts, requiring that they adapt their mix of activities to HUD's changing programmatic requirements and refrain from overtly political activity such as lobbying.

Minneapolis fair housing advocates articulated an outcome-based understanding of discrimination, focusing on overall housing patterns rather than the process of acquiring housing. Federal policy resources do not support this definition of fair housing as strongly; tools are available (opportunities to file lawsuit), but no money or informational resources. Yet building on the strengths of local resources, such as the skills of local affordable housing networks, Minneapolis groups were able to mobilize a constituency and to generate a sense of collective interest in racially (to some extent) and economically diverse communities.

When local conditions strongly shape group choices about which national resources to use, the inevitable result is a partial approach to addressing housing discrimination. In Denver the movement faced the danger of industry co-optation. Partnership was preferred by the majority of advocates, litigation was frowned upon. Indeed, groups generally could not raise funds to pursue major lawsuits, thus a major national policy resource remained virtually untapped. Additionally, public-sector policies that perpetuate segregation, such as public housing siting and zoning laws, remained unchallenged. In Minneapolis, the focus on the public sector leaves the private-sector housing industry basically untouched and not held accountable for housing patterns in the region. The strongest advocacy groups in the Twin Cities defined fair housing in terms of class, with a focus on affordable housing, so that middle-class minorities were less likely to be protected against discrimination.

Policy Design Impacts on Group Legitimacy

If advocacy groups are to become or remain strong players in a particular policy arena, they must be viewed as legitimate participants within it. Fair housing policy resources foster legitimacy for the work of advocacy groups in fair housing enforcement. But community reinvestment policy resources undermine group efforts to gain legitimacy. This difference helps explain the decline of community reinvestment movements in Minneapolis and Denver and suggests that groups in other cities may also face this challenge of legitimacy.

Fair Housing Advocacy. The fair housing policy design's tools and funding serve to legitimize fair housing nonprofits as partners with government, coproducers of fair housing enforcement. Fair housing enforcement is claims-driven; to set enforcement in motion, individuals must come forward and file a claim of discrimination. Advocacy groups help to generate these claims, which are critical to HUD's ability to do its fair housing work. Government thus relies on nonprofits to fulfill its obligation to enforce fair housing. HUD fosters this partnership through the Fair Housing Initiatives Program (FHIP), which funds nonprofits to undertake enforcement activities. The agency helps nonprofits develop skills through annual technical assistance conferences and dissemination of best practices. HUD staff attend fair housing association conferences and work with nonprofits to solve problems with the FHIP contracting process.

A partnerlike professional relationship between fair housing advocates and government officials was evident in both case cities. In Denver, the staff member handling fair housing for the state's civil rights agency, the fair housing director of the regional HUD office, and the directors of both nonprofit fair housing enforcement groups knew one another and interacted fairly often. The same was true in Minneapolis. Advocates were not always happy with officials' decisions, and officials were not always happy with advocates' work on individual cases, but these sorts of differences are inevitable. More important was the professional working relationship that existed among them.

My field research also suggested that HUD fair housing staff viewed FHIP-funded agencies as critical to their mandate under the Clinton administration, especially under HUD Secretary Andrew Cuomo, to generate more fair housing claims. The fair housing director of Denver's HUD office was pleased to have two FHIP agencies, likening it to having more cops on the streets to catch speeders. Denver staff members of one FHIP agency felt increased pressure to file claims because applications for funding were increasingly emphasizing the numbers of claims produced. At the national meetings of fair housing advocates that I attended during my field research, HUD staff were present to report on fair housing activities, to hear advocates' views on FHIP, and to answer questions.

Another aspect of their legitimacy is that fair housing advocates have legal standing to file fair housing lawsuits. In doing so, whether a judge decides a case or a settlement is negotiated, advocacy groups play an active role in depicting the violation of law and shaping the remedy. Legal Services in Minneapolis, representing the NAACP and a class of plaintiffs in the *Hollman* public housing case, had representation on the committee overseeing implementation of the settlement mandating redevelopment of segregated public housing and construction of dispersed units throughout the metro area. Likewise Housing for All in Denver, along with a class of tenants, successfully litigated against a developer who violated the Fair Housing Act's provisions on accommodating the needs of people with disabilities.

Advocacy groups' legitimacy as participants in fair housing enforcement is not absolute; the resources that contribute to it have weaknesses. Indeed, the policy design's enforcement structure—its assignment of HUD as enforcement agent and the procedural resource of litigation—temper advocates' legitimacy as fair housing actors. Defendants in court routinely challenge the legal standing of fair housing groups, and not every judge or jury will award them damages, even if their client wins a judgment. Also, HUD represents a weak government partner, and its weakness undermines the political position of fair housing groups. As noted in Chapter 3, the agency depends on annual appropriations from Congress, and it relies on the private real estate and development industry to carry out many of its housing programs. The industry lobby routinely tries to influence Congress to restrict fair housing appropriations and to limit the activities that the Fair Housing Initiatives Program permits nonprofits to undertake. Officials responsible for fair housing have a weak position relative to other divisions of HUD. Finally, fluctuating levels of FHIP funds and changes in the program's goals and priorities from year to year as the political winds shift create a certain degree of instability for fair housing nonprofits.

While conducting my field research at the local and national levels, I talked with many advocates who worried about whether they would continue to win FHIP funding, who reported financial difficulties after not receiving a grant, or who worried about whether their mission, tailored to a particular local community, would work against them if HUD's priorities for that year differed too much from their local expertise. Stories circulated about grants taking so long to arrive that groups laid off staff or of long-standing groups considered experts by their peers that had lost funding because their focus did not match HUD's.

Community Reinvestment Advocacy. Despite the ways in which the fair housing policy design tempers the legitimacy of advocacy groups, it contrasts favorably with the community reinvestment design, in which these groups enjoy no explicit enforcement role. The tools available to advocacy groups are embedded in the process of banking regulation and examination, which allows for public comment on regulatory actions. Banking regulators, in contrast to HUD, do not view advocacy groups as enforcement partners. Rather, they traditionally are closely allied to the banking industry. Although in theory regulators are intended to serve the public interest, in practice they tend to perceive financial institutions as their clients. As noted in Chapter 3, banks fund these agencies through fees and assessments, and agency leadership and staff often come from the ranks of the financial services industry.[23] Their daily activities create frequent interactions between regulators and bank staff. These sets of actors understand one another. They share a familiarity with bank management practices, and they may view consumer compliance issues with some disdain. As one informant described it, the concerns and perspectives of advocacy groups are not likely to be "in the heads" of the regulators like the perspectives of bankers are.

My field research revealed little evidence of working relationships between advocates and regulators locally, although members of national community reinvestment advocacy groups had ties with community outreach representatives at the regulatory agencies. At the local level, working relationships were present in some cases between bank staff and advocates from groups that operated bank-funded programs, such as homeownership counseling. Another sign of the difficulty that advocacy groups have in penetrating the regulatory process is the role of national advocacy groups in advising local groups about how and when to file comments. These national groups help local advocates submit comments about banks during regular bank examinations so that in the case of a merger, they will have established a record of participating, thus bolstering their chance of being heard. This type of groundwork is not needed to the same extent in the world of fair housing.

These characteristics of the government agents who enforce the Community Reinvestment Act and the lack of an explicit enforcement role for advocacy groups mean that when groups use CRA resources—the public comment process and lending disclosure data—bankers and regulators often cast them as troublemakers, disrupting a process rather than legitimately participating in it. The protest strategies that groups use to generate public attention only exacerbate this image. Because regulators have wide discretion in how to respond to public comments, groups often turn to the media to attempt to gain leverage and influence in the regulatory process. Banks may respond to these strategies and negotiate with advocates to prevent public relations problems or to speed up the pending merger or acquisition.

When fair housing groups bring a claim of discrimination to court, they face nothing like this shadow of illegitimacy. By offering advocacy groups only one particular avenue for participation, the community reinvestment policy design contributes to the challenge of legitimacy that these groups face. Indeed, oppo-

nents can more easily question their right to participate. Such questioning occurred during the process leading to the 1999 Financial Modernization Act,
which imposed "sunshine" regulations on community groups and scaled back
some aspects of the Community Reinvestment Act. The chairman of the Senate
Banking Committee, Senator Phil Gramm, referred to the nonprofits active in
community reinvestment as extortionists engaging in "legalized bribery." The
gains of advocacy groups are cast as illegitimate in a way that legal damages paid
to fair housing groups are not.

Policy Design Impacts on Forging Alliances

The ability to forge alliances is critical to movement survival and strength; policy resources can foster or constrain groups' ability to find supporters and to hold
coalitions together. Both policy designs work to constrain rather than to foster alliances, helping to explain why community reinvestment movements fell apart in
both cities. The CRA design seems to spark coalition building when groups first
become active, but over time, their incentives for collaboration erode. As for fair
housing groups, the skills that policy resources encourage them to develop, and
the activities they undertake, do not lend themselves to generating public attention, making it hard to build alliances. This finding also helps to explain, along
with local contextual factors noted above, the relatively isolated position of Denver's fair housing movement compared to that in Minneapolis. Minneapolis
groups rely less heavily on federal resources, having a stock of local resources
upon which to draw, and have less difficulty finding and keeping supporters, at
least in this present phase of the movement.

Community Reinvestment. The community reinvestment policy design's mix of
resources catalyzes the formation of community reinvestment coalitions at the
local level but then may erode them by dividing the collective and self-interests
of such constituencies. Whereas the fair housing policy design prompts nonprofit
groups to specialize in fair housing enforcement by directly funding them, CRA
offers no comparable funding for its enforcement. The prospect of securing financial support from lending institutions—either credit or grants—provides an
incentive for diverse groups to support local community reinvestment advocacy.
In this way, a community's collective interest in increasing access to private capital coincides with the self-interests of individual advocacy groups that seek
funding to carry out their development or other community-building activities.

The case studies show three types of groups becoming involved: multi-issue
groups such as the Association of Community Organizations for Reform Now
(ACORN), a poor people's advocacy group that works on many issues at once;
neighborhood organizations; and community development corporations (CDCs)
that develop affordable housing in poor neighborhoods. These groups come together to work on community reinvestment for different reasons: to assure low-

income constituents access to banking services (e.g., ACORN), to secure investment in a neighborhood deteriorating due to redlining (e.g., a neighborhood organization), or to gain access to loans and grants for affordable housing and
economic development (e.g., CDCs). This range of advocacy groups pursuing
their distinct missions and serving their distinct constituents adds up to a broad
community reinvestment movement aiming, in general, to increase access to private capital for disadvantaged places and people within a city. The CRA policy
design thus catalyzes the formation of community reinvestment coalitions—
groups join together to challenge local lenders and to engage in negotiations to
bolster lenders' community reinvestment performance.

But once coalitions succeed at convincing local lenders to change lending
practices and to fund the work of community groups, this success may threaten
the political coalition itself. Using the law threatens community reinvestment
coalitions by dividing the collective and self-interests of member groups. For example, in the case cities, as member groups secured program dollars or lending
commitments from specific banks, their incentive waned to maintain the vigilant
CRA monitoring that could work to hold all local banks accountable to the community on an ongoing basis. Tensions emerged in particular between consumer
and poor people's advocates and community development corporations, which
applied different criteria when they assessed the performance of particular banks.
This fault line was obvious, for example, during 1998 public hearings in Minneapolis on the proposed merger of Norwest and Wells Fargo banks. Consumer
advocates including ACORN and the Public Interest Research Group, joined by
elected officials from poor neighborhoods, criticized Norwest's banking services
for shutting out the poor.[24] They urged the regulators to deny permission for the
merger. A host of CDCs, on the other hand, praised the bank for its participation
in their affordable housing projects. They urged regulators to grant approval.

The collective good might be better served by a single-issue group focusing
on community reinvestment, but the CRA policy design offers no material help
to support such a group. It does not incorporate advocacy groups as legitimate
enforcement agents through provision of operational support, as the fair housing
policy design does, so community reinvestment coalitions face the challenge of
holding together nonspecialist groups with different constituencies. In some
cities, coalitions have succeeded in doing this (e.g., Chicago), but in Denver and
Minneapolis, they did not. Consequently, in both cities, CRA agreements were
outdated and had not been renewed. One leader of a defunct community reinvestment coalition in Denver said, "If we heard that a bank was doing poorly,
would I be able to gather up the individuals like we did before? Honest to God,
my guess is no." As community reinvestment advocacy coalitions have partial
successes in securing bank responsiveness to CRA, this splintering of the coalitions lurks as a possibility. Coalition partners whose demands are met abandon
the others, eroding the coalition's ability to mobilize in the future when the banking landscape shifts. Rather than building cooperation among local advocacy

groups, success in using community reinvestment policy resources creates tensions among them.

Fair Housing. A key challenge that fair housing groups face when trying to generate alliances is the general public presumption that racial discrimination in housing transactions no longer occurs, a perception challenged by social scientific research and the daily experiences of fair housing organizations.[25] Yet several aspects of fair housing policy's resource structure create disincentives for fair housing groups to publicize the prevalence of the problem in their communities. The method that advocacy groups use to identify discriminatory practices—fair housing testing—provides several examples of this problem. Testing is recognized by the courts and HUD as proof of discrimination, and HUD funds groups to engage in testing; part of my field research included working as a fair housing tester for about one year.

A fair housing test is a paired-comparison experiment in which individuals similar in all ways but race or ethnicity seek to buy or rent a home. These "testers" complete reports about their experiences, how they were treated and the information they were given. Comparing these reports can identify differential and discriminatory treatment. Usually a fair housing group will conduct several tests at a particular location when building a legal case or administrative claim. The anonymity of fair housing testers is critical to the success of this method of identifying discrimination; if a leasing agent or broker suspects someone to be a tester, he or she may behave differently during a housing transaction. Thus, fair housing groups must keep their testing initiatives and personnel confidential. Confidentiality also arises as an imperative in many fair housing cases settled out of court. The public may never learn the details about the practices that a defendant engaged in or the damages won by the plaintiff and nonprofit group. Advocates' work thus can remain invisible to most city residents.

Another reason fair housing groups keep the details of their testing programs private is that local real estate agents tend to fear the practice and worry that they may be "entrapped" unfairly. As part of my field research, I attended several fair housing training sessions for industry members and interviewed some fair housing trainers. When real estate agents talk at industry gatherings, it is clear that their sense of the size of a fair housing group's testing program is exaggerated. Nonprofit groups actually struggle to maintain a qualified pool of volunteer testers and conduct a rather limited number of tests each year, relative to the number of housing transactions that occur. Yet advocates think that if housing professionals fear being tested at any time, they may be more likely to comply with fair housing laws. Advocacy groups are thus less likely to publicize the weaknesses of their testing programs as a way of attracting more support for them and are more likely to work behind the scenes to garner resources.

Finally, the incentive to keep testing results confidential diminishes a fair housing group's ability to convert volunteer testers into political advocates. Because the results of any test may become evidence in litigation and a tester may be called as a witness to describe his or her experience seeking housing, fair housing groups do not inform testers about the outcome of a test because they fear contaminating the evidence. Volunteer testers rarely know whether they have helped to uncover and punish discrimination, or if the tests found no illegal practices at all. These volunteers may gain little sense of the extent of discrimination in their own communities, yet unlike the group's staff members, whose lobbying activities are restricted by federal funding, volunteers could freely lobby or attempt to mobilize support.

Mechanisms of allocating funding create disincentives for cooperation among fair housing groups in a community. Federal funding is awarded on a competitive basis, thus pitting local groups against one another. In addition, when several groups work together on a successful lawsuit, the legal damages and attorneys' fees must be shared among them. To some extent, groups have an incentive to work alone and many end up working out of the public eye. This isolation may help them develop strong fair housing cases and claims and may act to deter the private real estate industry from some discrimination, but it also keeps the problem off the public agenda, thus undermining the development of public support and the extent to which these groups effectively represent their constituency.

IMPLICATIONS

In this chapter I have compared the case studies and the elements of the two national policies to explain similarities and differences in four local struggles for housing equality: fair housing and community reinvestment movements in Minneapolis and Denver. My aim has been to understand how, and whether, national policy interacts with local context to shape local housing advocacy. I showed that, broadly speaking, different policy designs gave rise to different movements. The types of groups involved, their definitions of discrimination, their actions and relationships, varied in ways consistent with differences in the two national policy designs. Studying fair housing and community reinvestment movements across cities largely means studying two worlds in which two spheres of activity rarely overlap. Both fair housing and community reinvestment groups worry about the prevalence of housing discrimination in their communities, but they seldom interact with one another. Fair housing tends to be a world of lawyers, community reinvestment, neighborhood organizers, and community developers. But even when fair housing advocates adopt organizing strategies, as in Minneapolis, groups still do not cross these lines to work together. The second section of this chapter showed that national policy designs varied in the extent to which they interacted with local contexts. Community reinvestment advocacy groups responded similarly to national policy designs, whereas Minneapolis and

Table 6.5. Impact of Policy Design on Nonprofits

	Fair Housing Groups	Community Reinvestment Groups
Challenge of legitimacy	Positive	Negative
Challenge of alliance	Negative	Positive, then negative
Challenge of adaptability	Mixed	Negative

Denver fair housing movements differed significantly from one another. Elements of the local contexts of Denver and Minneapolis help explain why fair housing movements took different forms in these cities. Theoretically, this difference suggests that some policy designs have a stronger effect on local advocacy than others; some designs seem less permeable to local variations in constituencies and conditions.

A third way of comparing the case studies and policy designs focused on the link between national policy resources, movement uniformity or variability, and movement trajectories. A wider mix of fair housing resources that includes funding opportunities seems to enable fair housing groups to maintain activity, to compensate for local deficiencies, and to adapt national resources to local needs. The result is partial use of policy design resources—advocates in one city do not always use fair housing resources as comprehensively as they might. By contrast, community reinvestment policy throws up barriers for advocacy groups. These movements have trouble adapting both to changing conditions and local constituencies.

More generally, my analysis identifies specific public policy mechanisms that vary in the extent to which they support local groups, differentially affecting their capacity to build political strength and to sustain themselves. Table 6.5 summarizes the impact that fair housing and community reinvestment policy resources have on advocacy groups' ability to generate political strength. Although the fair housing policy design can help to sustain a movement by offering funding and legitimacy, the design poses challenges for groups in the important effort of forging local alliances. This deficiency is especially damaging when local groups rely heavily on national policy resources rather than alternative local resources. The community reinvestment design poses serious challenges to advocacy groups because using the policy resources threatens the survival of advocacy activity. It throws up obstacles to a movement's legitimacy, adaptability, and the creation of lasting coalitions.

7

Advancing the Struggle for Housing Equality: Opportunities and Constraints

Are we closer to racial equality in the post–civil rights era? Formal structures of segregation no longer exist, white people and diverse peoples of color encounter one another daily in myriad social interactions, racial and ethnic intermarriage rates are rising, and conceptions of racial identity are increasingly fluid.[1] In many respects the position of racial and ethnic minorities in American society has improved since 1960. Many indicators of occupational status, income, and educational outcomes show progress. Evidence of political participation demonstrates increased rates of voting and greater numbers of black, Latino, and Asian elected officials. Signs of progress are easy to find, but so are patterns of persistent, and in some cases growing, disparities between white people and people of color, including inequalities in health, wealth, educational achievement, and unemployment rates. Although it is natural to wonder whether race relations are getting better or worse, a linear model describing race relations as a steady march toward equality is misleading. It obscures the complexity of racial and ethnic inequality in the United States. As older forms of inequality disappear, new forms emerge to take their place.[2] Thus, we can think of improvements in the position of racial minorities relative to whites coexisting with some persistent and some growing inequalities.

For example, surveys indicate that levels of racial prejudice have declined over time. But research also shows that deeply rooted negative stereotypes underpin the white public's opposition to policies that they perceive help black people, such as welfare.[3] The rise in numbers of middle-class blacks coexists with a rise in numbers of poor black households.[4] The states where racial minorities are, by absolute indicators, doing the best are also the states with the highest gaps between whites and minorities. Thus, minorities may have high rates of high school graduation in states such as Minnesota and Wisconsin, but the gaps between graduation rates of white and minority students are greater in these places than elsewhere.[5] Explicit racist behavior occurs less often, but studies repeatedly show that minorities experience subtle forms of discrimination on a daily basis.[6] Greater numbers of black and Latino elected officials accompany a consistent erosion of civil rights programs such as affirmative action and school desegregation.[7] More minorities have been elected mayors of U.S. cities, but cities generally are declining relative to suburbs in metro areas, leading some to ask whether holding power is a hollow prize.[8]

Respondents, especially those of color, understood this mixed landscape of equality and inequality. During my interviews, I asked for descriptions of a city with perfectly fair housing. One black real estate agent who volunteers as a fair housing trainer answered this way: "It's like creating a utopia, and they don't exist. I understand the question, but it's not possible. I could dream of a utopia where nobody would care what color my skin was. I could live where I wanted to, play where I wanted to, and never feel that kind of inner sense, deep-rooted, that you don't want me here. And you don't want me here just because I'm black. I would say we do have fair housing in Denver. I live where I want to live, where I choose to live. But I meet people all the time, and it's still there. People aren't screaming at me and calling names, but it's there."

In the arena of housing, just as in other arenas, we see greater equality in some respects and new or persistent disparities in others. In the years since landmark laws on fair housing and community reinvestment were passed, there are signs that these policies have contributed to positive changes. There are also indications that much work remains to be done and that new threats to progress have emerged.

The majority of the public agrees with the objectives of fair housing law; they do not think a property owner should be able to discriminate on the basis of race when selling or renting a home.[9] In addition, most people know that such practices are illegal.[10] Some of the people who believe they have been victims of discrimination are using the law. From 1989 to 1997, HUD received more than 81,000 complaints of housing discrimination and continues to receive about 10,000 new claims each year; 43 percent are claims of racial discrimination.[11] The Department of Justice's litigation in fair lending cases has brought $33.4 million in relief; its fair housing cases have brought $1.2 million in civil penalties and $6.3 million in relief to individuals; from 1990 to 1998, nonprofit fair housing organizations have worked on nearly 1,400 private lawsuits, resulting in a total of $116 million in recovery.[12] But recent research documents a lack of confidence in fair housing law, so the number of claims that HUD and other groups receive is likely to understate the extent of the problem. In a national survey, about a quarter of black and Latino respondents reported that they thought they had been a victim of discrimination; 83 percent did nothing about it. Most said they did not think action would be worth the effort. Only 3 percent sought help from a fair housing organization, only 1 percent filed a complaint with government, and only 1 percent talked to a lawyer.[13]

The most recent national audit study found a lower incidence of consistently discriminatory treatment against black and Hispanic home seekers than had been found ten years earlier. Although consistent adverse treatment throughout the interaction between minority buyers and a housing agent occurred about 22 percent of the time, results also showed that some adverse treatment occurred during more than half of minorities' visits to sales and leasing agents. The study found that Hispanic renters faced the highest prospect of discrimination, and that geographic steering of prospective buyers based on their race occurred more often than in previous studies.[14] This study, too, has limitations that may understate the prevalence of discriminatory treatment. The authors point out that it focused on a limited number of metro areas, drew samples of real estate and rental agents from newspaper ads, and assigned economic characteristics of testers to the characteristics of housing units advertised. It examined only the initial interaction between home seeker and agent.[15]

The volume of home loans to minority and low-income borrowers is rising, as are homeownership rates. Yet disparities for both loans and homeownership between whites and people of color remain. Banks required to comply with the Community Reinvestment Act do have higher rates of lending to low- and moderate-income people and neighborhoods, and studies show that these neighborhoods do have higher property values than comparable ones, indicating reinvestment has occurred.[16] Research has found that where nonprofit advocacy groups have taken action on community reinvestment and when regulators require high standards of compliance, banks have better performance records. But a growing share of mortgage loans are made by lenders not subject to the law. Loans made by CRA-covered lenders constituted only about a quarter of all mortgage loans to blacks and Latinos. Lawmakers so far have not been willing to expand CRA requirements to cover a broader set of lenders. In addition, some banks have rolled back their community reinvestment commitments, and some agreements with advocacy groups are outdated and have not been renewed.

Evidence about racial and ethnic segregation is also mixed. Today, a black person is likely to live in a neighborhood where 51 percent of the households are black, 33 percent are white, 11 percent are Latino, and 3 percent are Asian. This breakdown contrasts with the typical white person's neighborhood, where 80 percent of households are white, 7 percent are black, 8 percent are Hispanic, and 4 percent are Asian.[17] The black-white segregation index for metropolitan areas in 2000 was 65, meaning that on average, 65 percent of black people would have to move to achieve more even housing patterns.[18] This level has dropped somewhat over the past twenty years, but at a slow rate, averaging 5.5 percent. Asians and Hispanics are less residentially segregated from whites, although their segregation increased between 1980 and 2000.[19] Whether they live in cities or suburbs, these groups are more isolated from whites today than they were twenty years ago. School segregation rates increased during the 1990s.[20]

Yet segregation varies substantially by region and city.[21] Some cities have seen significant declines in segregation during the 1990s, others more modest declines, and some have experienced increases. The West and South are more integrated, and cities there have seen the largest declines in recent decades; in the Midwest and Northeast, large cities have remained persistently segregated for decades. Racial and ethnic minorities constitute a larger portion of suburban populations than they did in 1990, moving to 27 percent from 19 percent.[22] Yet neighborhood conditions of the suburbs where most minorities live tend to be worse than those where most whites live.[23] Still, the number of racially integrated neighborhoods is growing, as is the stability of the population mix.[24] In fact, the concept of segregation has become more complex as the United States grows more diverse. As Dreier, Mollenkopf, and Swanstrom put it, suburbs and cities are becoming less white *and* less black, largely a product of the immigration that has brought at least 23 million people to the country since 1965.[25]

Although they are not the only factors driving positive changes in housing markets, public policies and the work of advocacy groups certainly contribute. Studies have shown that where groups have negotiated CRA agreements, regulated banks' practices improve.[26] While no research exists on the impact of fair housing groups, the lower incidence of consistent discriminatory treatment may be linked to their education and outreach efforts, as well as to the deterrence effect of litigation that brings costly damages. In cities with community reinvestment and fair housing advocacy groups, we can point to programs or local policy developments that they have influenced, such as the *Hollman* case in Minneapolis that is dispersing subsidized units or the insurance task force in Denver that is creating opportunities for homeowners in neighborhoods once ignored by insurers. Thus, it is likely that with stronger and continuous advocacy, we would see more positive changes and creative responses to old problems and new challenges.

OVERVIEW OF RESEARCH

As the above discussion indicates, complacency about race relations is far from warranted. Inequality does not so much decline as transform; the need for advocacy remains pressing. In this book I have examined how two landmark policies interact with advocacy for housing equality. On the one hand, I could argue that the persistence of housing inequality stems from the limitations of fair housing and community reinvestment laws. Why expect two policies that focus only on some aspects of the problem, and that allocate relatively few resources to it, to make a difference? Thinking about policies from a technical perspective such as this, it is hardly surprising that their successes are limited. But this research offers a different explanation, suggesting that the two public policies fall short not only technically but politically, and that these political consequences also serve to limit change.

Evaluating policies purely from a technical perspective is only a starting point to fully understand their impact. Considering the degree to which the policies offer adequate sanctions or target the appropriate causal factors builds important explanations for persisting problematic conditions. But these explanations insufficiently account for the laws' limited impacts because policies are not self-implementing. The fair housing and community reinvestment policy designs rely on the work of nonprofit advocacy groups for implementation and enforcement, so examining their influence on these groups is critical. In this book I argue that by shaping the fair housing and community reinvestment movements, these policies limit prospects for change to a deeper extent than previously understood. In this chapter, I take stock of the project, reviewing the major findings and considering their theoretical and substantive implications.

My research breaks new ground in several ways. I link policy to advocacy and identify political obstacles to fair housing and community reinvestment movements rooted in public policies. I also compare two public policies that many scholars, activists, and policy makers consider unrelated, too different to be legitimately compared, and argue that the fair housing and community reinvestment policy designs themselves have contributed to this impression. They address similar problems, but in very different ways, and have spawned separate advocacy efforts. In addition, the case cities of Denver and Minneapolis are nontraditional choices for an examination of race and housing politics. But all cities experience problems related to housing discrimination and segregation, so research that expands case studies beyond the often-studied larger, more polarized cities is important. The theoretical perspective I use, focusing on policy designs, has not been empirically applied in its entirety. I extend it by using it to study changes across government levels and focusing on the behavior of nonprofit groups rather than on social or target groups or on public agencies. I show that this theoretical approach offers a useful lens on urban politics and on the nature of inequality in the U.S. political system.

In this book I have examined two sets of relationships that unfold over time: the link between legislative process and policy design and the link between policy design and local advocacy groups. Broadly, the goal was to understand how political struggles among elected officials in Washington, D.C., created distinctive national policy designs, which in turn shaped the landscape for advocacy groups seeking to address pressing problems in their cities. Although my focus was on struggles for housing equality, these sets of relationships play out across policy issues. By analyzing fair housing and community reinvestment laws as policy designs, I illuminated key political consequences of these laws that other studies have overlooked, suggesting that applying this approach to additional issue areas would also be fruitful.

Policy designs are the powerful structures at the heart of this theoretical model. They capture ideas about problems and groups of people and bring them to life by establishing an enforcement structure that allocates resources consistent with them. These are not necessarily "good" ideas that represent "the best thinking of the time" about how to address a particular policy issue. Rather, they are highly contingent, reflecting the discursive strategies that legislators created to build support in a particular political context. The policy design perspective draws attention to the irony that these contingent, time-bound ideas can structure advocacy and problem solving for years until a new convergence of interests and ideas sets the stage for another round of political action that could change the policy design. By applying the policy design perspective to the cases of fair housing and community reinvestment, I showed two distinct paths to limited policy designs, with important consequences for advocacy at the local level.

Fair Housing

In the case of fair housing, I found that legislators supportive of a law prohibiting discrimination in housing faced a particularly hostile political context, marked by urban riots and black militancy, by declining political power for blacks, and by a powerful conservative coalition in Congress. Yet they were able to use this context to their advantage by crafting a persuasive strategy emphasizing that fair housing law would be a partial and incremental measure. Here Schneider and Ingram's notions about the social construction of target groups come vividly to life, as supporters and opponents evoked starkly different images of black Americans. Liberal Democrats and Republicans supporting the measure used the urban riots to justify the need for a fair housing law, but they created a new target group of beneficiaries as they depicted a small cadre of deserving black professionals whom fair housing would enable to escape the ghettos. They emphasized that, once race was removed as a determinant of housing choice, free-market processes would dictate who would leave the ghettos and where they would go. They thus predicted that a slow, small, and orderly stream of middle-class blacks would move into white city and suburban neighborhoods.

The fair housing policy design shows the price supporters paid for this rhetorical strategy. Certainly the Fair Housing Act was a long-overdue and much-needed measure that finally prohibited racial discrimination in housing. The law delineates and bans a range of practices that had been common ways of maintaining racial segregation in housing, assigns victims a right of action in civil court, and mandates that a national administrative process be established to handle claims. In contrast, the provision of the law affecting low-income housing is short and vague. The policy design offers vastly more resources to advocacy groups working to protect civil rights in private-sector housing by eliminating discrimination from housing transactions than for ensuring that affordable housing is available to minorities on a nondiscriminatory basis. The fair housing groups thriving at the local level are those working on enforcement of individual fair housing rights. Groups interested in promoting integrated housing patterns struggle or even disappear unless they can cultivate local resources to support them.

Community Reinvestment

In the case of community reinvestment, legislators navigated their political context quite differently than those active on fair housing nearly ten years earlier. Indeed, their context was not nearly so hostile, nor was it infused with the emotion attendant to the civil rights movement and to the rioting occurring during fair housing debate. Winners and losers here were places, not people—struggling, old, industrialized cities contrasted with the Sunbelt centers of a new economy as members of a Democratic-led Congress worked with a new president to forge an urban policy. Supporters of community reinvestment actually held the positions of power that fair housing's southern conservatives had controlled. Indeed, rather than having to develop a careful rhetorical strategy to attract swing voters, sponsors of community reinvestment did what they could to avoid extended debate. They used their positions of power to limit the visibility and controversy surrounding the measure. Reported out of the banking committee on a tied vote, this measure might have attracted opposition if it had been a more visible one.

When supporters did speak about the bill, they emphasized it as a remedy for urban decline. By discouraging banks from redlining poor neighborhoods, the law would ensure that they received financial services from the institutions that enjoyed the benefits of federal deposit insurance and other privileges. Senators avoided describing the people who would benefit from the Community Reinvestment Act, therefore avoiding the struggles to construct images of deserving groups of people that had marked the fair housing debate. Instead they sought to defuse opposition from bankers and from bank regulators by arguing that the measure would alter only slightly the existing framework of banking regulation. Banks would not have to submit "mountains of paperwork" to comply with CRA. Rather, community reinvestment was a low-cost solution to inner-city problems that reflected a new vision of urban policy emphasizing the importance of the private sector to the health of urban economies.

This package of arguments led to a policy design granting high discretion to regulators and to the private sector, one that did not "demand" anything of financial institutions but sought to "encourage" them to meet community credit needs. It mobilized existing processes of bank examinations and application reviews to monitor banks' interaction with the low- and moderate-income neighborhoods in their service areas. Low-income neighborhoods received a dubious benefit here, as the policy design included no incentives for regulators to enforce the law aggressively. For advocacy groups, resources included a procedural channel they could employ to express their dissatisfaction with the practices of local banks, a place where they could use the data that banks were required to disclose about their lending decisions. By and large, groups in the cities I studied utilized the resources available through the policy design, including the opportunity to define "community credit needs" and "community reinvestment" in their own terms. But ironically, the place-based policy design that theoretically might have inspired a common interest among constituencies within cities did not do so in a lasting way. Community reinvestment coalitions disintegrated fairly quickly in both places.

WHAT CAN WE LEARN FROM POLICY DESIGNS?

Policy design analysis brings together insights from postmodernism, institutional theories, and pluralist approaches. It guides the researcher to locate the actors involved and the ideas at stake in a legislative process, to trace how "winning" ideas and interests become embedded in policy, and to examine how policy allocates resources and thereby shapes subsequent action. In doing so, this approach pushes beyond the confines of traditional pluralist analysis to consider the consequences of compromises struck between competing interests. It answers a call to specify the relationship between ideas and political life by analyzing the mechanism of public policy. [27] It corrects for overdetermination in institutional analysis by examining how actors respond to and resist institutional forces such as public policy. This approach, applied to the politics of housing discrimination, generates insights about urban politics and the relationship between advocacy and policy.

Informing Urban Analysis

Urban scholarship theorizes local contextual factors and local government as critical forces shaping urban policy outcomes, driving variation in these outcomes across cities. It focuses particularly on economic factors. In several ways, my findings broaden this work. First, the contextual factors that influenced fair housing advocacy in Denver and Minneapolis are not rooted in local economies. By choosing cities similar in economic, demographic, and political characteristics, I was able to identify other important variables that influence local action. For example, the change in racial and economic diversity seemed more important than the fact of diversity in shaping fair housing advocacy. This is an important finding because more cities are becoming more diverse in the twenty-first century. We may see more affordable housing advocates using fair housing policy as their constituencies become more racially diverse. Also, past advocacy influenced present advocacy. The history and orientation of local policy networks affected how fair housing advocacy unfolded. Surprisingly, the absence of a fair housing network in Minneapolis did not dampen activity in the 1990s but allowed advocates more adaptability and freedom to address new aspects of housing problems.

Second, my research confirms the importance of analyzing both local and national politics and the influences each has on the other. On the one hand, the U.S. system of federalism and literature on urban politics lead us to expect variation in local responses to federal policy. I found more varied response to fair housing than to community reinvestment policy, which suggests that variation in local policy outcomes may depend on features of national policy designs. Some national policy designs are likely to have more direct effects on local groups than others; some sets of incentives and resources may leave more "room" for local adaptation. To some extent, therefore, in order to understand local action, we look back and up to the relevant national policy designs. Thus, changing local outcomes may require changes in national policy designs. It makes sense to consider how national policy changes would change the incentive structure locally and relative to advocacy groups. But the findings also offer the caveat that national design changes may not be enough to generate local change. The policy design approach, applied across scales, highlights the insufficiency of a "technical" fix—a stronger statute, less ambiguous language, a different set of policy tools; these will not be enough to bring about changes in local outcomes. We cannot predict in a straightforward way what the impact of national policy change will be because local conditions are also likely to shape local response.

Finally, city government did not emerge as an independent force directing local responses to fair housing and community reinvestment policy. Although studies of housing and economic development have identified differences in local government responses to federal policies, my research did not find local government to be a catalyst for action or a leader on housing equality. Neither fair housing nor community reinvestment were highly visible issues in city hall. Rather, local officials reacted to advocacy and to federal requirements in limited ways, but did not act independently of this pressure. A look at the national policy designs helps explain why: neither provides incentives for local officials to become more active and entrepreneurial.

City agencies in both Denver and Minneapolis began to review local banks' community reinvestment performance when choosing depositories for city funds, but when advocacy declined, so did their level of scrutiny. Both cities responded to national Community Development Block Grant requirements that they "affirmatively further fair housing" by offering limited funding to fair housing groups and preparing "Analyses of Impediments to Fair Housing." In Minneapolis, local officials are defendants in the *Hollman* settlement, so they have participated in its implementation. But in the absence of stringent federal requirements to aggressively address housing discrimination and segregation, local elected officials generally took little initiative.

Minneapolis and Denver were theoretically appropriate because aspects of their local context are similar such that my research could more easily focus on the impact of policy designs on local advocacy. And I argued that as two majority white cities, they diverged from the typical cities chosen for the many excellent studies of race and housing issues. On the one hand, it would be useful to examine the dynamics between advocacy and policy in such cities in order to discover the ways they converge and diverge from those studied here. This comparison would reveal more about the impact of demographics and the history of race relations on local housing advocacy. But I would expect groups in any city to confront the constraints posed by national policies that I was able to identify in this book. Variation may emerge in how and whether groups are able to overcome these constraints by drawing on local resources.

Informing Research on Advocacy

This research contributes to our understanding of how policies create politics, a core question in political science. Analyzing particular policies using a design framework identifies distinctive sets of structural challenges that advocacy groups face when they become active on certain issues and use specific policy resources. The research also shows policy feedback in action. National fair housing and community reinvestment movements have emerged since passage of these laws and work to preserve and expand related programs.

Although literature on nonprofits documents the differential levels of government funding available across broad policy areas,[28] it generally does not look beyond funding to identify the other ways in which government differentially affects nonprofit organizations. (It does consider the tax code, but this factor affects all nonprofit groups regardless of the sector in which they operate.) Scholarship on social movements has taken a broader approach to linking policy and advocacy, considering patterns in state repression and facilitation, the creation of spaces within the state apparatus where a social movement's issues are addressed, and the state's generation of "the stuff" of protest such as draft cards or draft boards.[29] My work fits into an emerging interest among social movement scholars to build theory that would guide research on "the web of interactions between challengers and the policies they challenge."[30] My analytic framework encourages attention to a range of policy resources that influence advocacy groups, expanding beyond funding mechanisms to problem definitions, tools, and arenas for action. It directs attention to how advocacy groups meet three types of political challenges: the challenge of gaining legitimacy, the challenge of building coalitions, and the challenge of adapting to changing contexts. Each policy design established a distinctive set of structural challenges for nonprofit groups.

Fair housing policy resources seem to promote legitimacy and enable adaptability, but create difficulties for building alliances. Community reinvestment policy resources create obstacles for legitimacy and adaptability and promote short-term coalitions at the expense of long-term ones. Especially as amended through the Fair Housing Initiatives Program, the fair housing design incorporates nonprofits as government partners in enforcement. But even before FHIP officially created a stream of funding for fair housing groups, the nature of the design's enforcement structure created an environment for partnership. In the claim-driven process, HUD's fair housing division needs claims in order to do its work, and nonprofits help to generate them. Especially under Secretary Cuomo,

who reorganized the fair housing division with the intention of boosting enforcement actions, HUD officials relied on the network of nonprofit groups to
help them fulfill their mission. Additionally, the original design, by establishing
a complainant's right to file suit in civil court, offered nonprofits this avenue as
well. Even when industry objects to claims of discrimination or attempts to shape
the nature of FHIP by working through its allies in Congress, nonprofits' basic
"right" to participate in the fair housing arena is not questioned. To be sure, this
legitimacy is tempered by other aspects of the policy design that serve to weaken
fair housing groups. HUD's political permeability means the agency is a rather
fragile partner to fair housing organizations. And certainly, nonprofits risk becoming dependent on FHIP funding, leaving themselves vulnerable to fluctua-
tions in funding levels.

Yet the situation contrasts with the community reinvestment design, in
which community groups have no explicit role in enforcement. Groups have utilized the design's tools and informational resources to create a role for themselves, using the threat of protesting bank mergers to get banks to the negotiating
table. But without explicit acknowledgment in the policy design, community
groups who intervene may be viewed as troublemakers, trying to scuttle a business deal. Yet this is their only avenue for participation—they have no alternative if they are to participate at all. The design not only falls short of granting
them an explicit enforcement role but also casts them in this position of inter-
vener, disrupting a process that is under way.

The policy design leaves groups' community reinvestment activities open to
challenge. Such a challenge occurred during the legislative process leading to the
1999 Financial Modernization Act, which imposed "sunshine" regulations on
community groups and scaled back some aspects of the Community Reinvestment Act. The chairman of the Senate Banking Committee, Senator Phil Gramm,
referred to the advocacy groups active in community reinvestment as extortionists engaging in "legalized bribery." The gains of advocacy groups are questioned in a way that legal damages paid to fair housing groups are not.

Additionally, community reinvestment policy may actually disadvantage
groups who use it by undermining the long-term potential of coalitions. More
broadly, a policy design's short-term and long-term impacts on advocacy may diverge. In the case of community reinvestment advocacy, initial bursts of activity
in my case cities gave way to group demobilization and limited capacity to monitor local banks' community reinvestment performance. As groups interact with
policy designs, the groups change in ways that influence how they will use policy resources in the future, even when no changes occur within the design itself.
Some policy designs help groups maintain action, others set off a trajectory of
demobilization. Thus, the interaction between groups and designs itself becomes
an engine of change.

The concept of policy feedback suggests that public policies stimulate the
formation of client groups that advocate for improvements to, or expansion of,

the original policy. This has happened in the arenas of community reinvestment and fair housing via the work of national fair housing and community reinvestment nonprofit organizations, to which many local advocacy groups belong. The National Fair Housing Alliance (NFHA) monitors fair housing implementation by HUD and the Department of Justice, staff members testify before Congress, and they advocate their position to members of Congress and the White House. They keep track of major fair housing litigation, conduct tests and file complaints and lawsuits, train industry and advocates on fair housing law and enforcement, and hold conferences yearly. The group, founded in 1988, has a membership of seventy-five local fair housing advocacy groups. To qualify for voting membership, groups must engage in fair housing enforcement; many NFHA members are FHIP grantees.[31] Other advocacy groups in Washington consider fair housing to be part of their mission and support NFHA when threats to fair housing programs arise; these include the Leadership Conference on Civil Rights and the Washington Lawyers' Committee for Civil Rights and Urban Affairs, among others.

The community reinvestment advocacy community is represented at the national level by the National Community Reinvestment Coalition (NCRC), ACORN, and the Center for Community Change, all with offices in Washington. With the exception of NCRC, these are multi-issue groups that include access to credit and fair lending as part of their agenda. National People's Action, a national coalition of neighborhood organizations and one of the original advocates of the law, is based in Chicago but holds annual conferences in Washington that include demonstrations at government offices. The Woodstock Institute, also based in Chicago, specializes in community reinvestment issues. Like their fair housing counterparts, these groups monitor implementation of the Community Reinvestment Act and pending legislation, testify before Congress, and advocate for stronger policy to elected officials. They mobilize member groups at the local level to contact Congress and the White House when threatening legislation is pending or when regulatory changes are in the works. They hold conferences where local groups exchange information and learn about national initiatives or developing problems. They offer technical assistance to local groups working on community reinvestment issues in their cities, such as analysis of HMDA data, help in submitting public comments to regulators, or negotiating CRA agreements.

These organizations have become part of the policy networks on fair housing and community reinvestment; government decision makers certainly know their views when considering statutory, programmatic, or regulatory changes. These national advocates push for changes that would enable both national and local groups to use the laws and programs more easily and effectively. Some of these efforts were noted in the discussion in Chapter 3 of the key changes to each policy design. National fair housing groups advocated for establishment of the Fair Housing Initiatives Program to fund nonprofit fair housing enforcement, and they discuss program implementation regularly with HUD staff. The civil rights groups involved in the legislative process resulting in the Fair Housing Amendments Act of 1988 pressed for changes that would boost relief for victims, punishments for offenders, and improve the capacity of attorneys to represent victims. The act removed limits on punitive damages so that steeper penalties are now possible, including in federal court both compensatory and punitive damages.[32] It allowed attorneys' fees to be granted and lengthened the statute of limitations. By establishing an administrative law system along with the court option, advocates hoped to offer speedier resolution of cases to clients. Community reinvestment advocates took part in the legislative process resulting in changes to the Community Reinvestment Act that required disclosure of examiners' ratings and a grading system focusing more on performance in categories of lending, investment, and service. This revision gives advocates more information, and, in theory, concrete performance standards could make banks more willing to respond to advocates' concerns.

As they do their work, these groups show policy feedback and path-dependence in action. That is, they primarily work within the frameworks created by the original policies, advocating for refinements or improvements rather than radical changes in government's approach to solving the problem. They press government to use the laws more often and to devote more money and staff to their implementation. Policy designs have been refined but policies have not been reframed. My point is not to criticize the important work of national advocacy groups, but rather to illustrate how policies institutionalize particular approaches to solving a problem and establish implementation and advocacy infrastructures that persist. In some respects, this process is a positive outcome for those concerned about housing inequality, but it also has drawbacks. As Pierson puts it, alternative solutions that once seemed possible become increasingly less possible and more "costly" over time as institutionalization unfolds. Thus, the dimensions of the problem that the original designs failed to incorporate remain outside of the mainstream approaches to addressing fair housing and community reinvestment. When groups do propose changes that depart from the policy design's logic or approach, they face a difficult challenge.

From its inception, fair housing policy has said little about integration or segregation, and its tools for the most part do not focus on promoting housing patterns. Today few advocacy groups concentrate on achieving integration with pro-integrative strategies; this work is not supported by federal funding. In the case of the Community Reinvestment Act, advocates and researchers know that regulated banks make smaller shares of mortgage loans today as the financial services industry changes. But lawmakers have not yet agreed to extend CRA requirements to other lenders. A part of the original logic for the law was that regulated banks benefited from the federal government and thus had an obligation to the public. Expanding CRA to currently nonregulated lenders would require a new logic. Similarly, industry changes including bank consolidation, Internet banking, and the increasing complexity of banking products strain the law's place-based logic that banks should reinvest in the communities where their customers live.[33] Advocates often point out that defining community has become increasingly problematic when banks serve hundreds of cities. CRA's role seems to become smaller as the industry changes; advocates are struggling to reframe the reinvestment issue.

LESSONS FOR ADVOCACY

In this book I have identified the constraints and opportunities that fair housing and community reinvestment policies pose to advocacy groups. I have shown how some groups have suffered from these constraints and how others have overcome them. In doing so, my research offers several lessons to advocacy groups working to advance fair housing and community reinvestment.

National policies are constraints, not straitjackets.[34] Advocacy groups can look beyond their internal resources (leaders, organization, and so on) to consider how policies affect their ability to develop key organizational resources and to address housing problems. They can then cultivate local resources that compensate for problematic national ones and vice versa. The groups in this study whose behavior did not conform to the contours of national policy had usually developed alternative sets of resources to supplement those available from national policy or even to make them irrelevant. The clearest example is the fair housing movement in Minneapolis, where groups focused on housing patterns with the goal of integrating affordable housing across the metro area. They focused on the public sector and government's role in housing choices rather than on the role of the private-housing sector. As I outlined in Chapter 6, a set of local conditions and resources enabled Minneapolis groups to use fair housing policy in this way. These included the extensive network of affordable housing advocates who had their own base of operational support. The fair housing movement in Minneapolis has evaded the cycle of invisibility that challenges Denver's movement, a problem that stems in part from national policy's funding requirements and approach to enforcement.

Advocates can think about how and whether policies foster or undermine their coalitions. The case of community reinvestment coalitions in my two case cities shows their vulnerability as well as how policy implementation has served to split the consumer and community development sides of the movement. As banks and community development corporations establish mutually beneficial working relationships, CDCs are less likely to challenge banks for disparities in mortgage lending or for other practices that result in lack of service to low-income consumers. Research on other cities can show how community reinvestment movements can overcome the challenge, which is rooted in the broad definition of "community reinvestment" and the high level of discretion that the original policy granted to regulators. On the one hand, this finding questions the extant literature on the community reinvestment movement that portrays it as growing and vibrant by warning that strong movements may exist in only some places. My research anticipates that where advocacy is sustained over time, non-profits have overcome the challenges posed by national policy by building on local resources, distinctive features of the local context. Chicago, with an extensive network of neighborhood groups and CDCs who work in coalition on community reinvestment issues, and North Carolina, where a statewide coalition exists, are interesting examples.

It may take both federal requirements and local pressure to move fair housing and community reinvestment up on local government agendas. Thus, a combination of local and national advocacy is important. The cases show several examples of city governments becoming responsive to housing advocates when doing so coincided with federal requirements. Similarly, withdrawal of federal requirements coincided with local government officials withdrawing their focus on these issues. When HUD changed its Community Development Block Grant (CDBG) requirements to include a stronger fair housing component, local governments funded groups to engage in fair housing research. But when the agency pulled back and did not monitor or demand action on the Analyses of Impediments to Fair Housing that it had required cities to compile, the two case cities took little action. When HUD supported Community Housing Resource Boards, local officials participated in them; when the agency discontinued its support, officials withdrew. When HUD changed its approach to litigation against the agency, advocates in Minneapolis were able to settle the *Hollman* case and city officials were required, as parties to the suit, to participate in desegregating public housing.

The Community Reinvestment Act, implemented by banking regulators who have no relationship with local government officials, has no mechanism equivalent to HUD's CDBG program that could, independent of advocacy pressure, push local governments to focus on disparities in access to financial services and other reinvestment issues. In Denver and Minneapolis, local officials' support stemmed in part from an interest in banks participating in city development programs. But without pressure from local groups speaking for key constituencies, mayors were not willing to take action that could alienate banks. Advocates might consider how federal requirements could be tied into reinvestment issues in such a way as to push community reinvestment higher on the local government agenda.

Recognize the value of legitimacy that arises from government partnerships. The partnerlike relationship that fair housing law establishes between advocacy groups and government affords advocates the legitimacy that community reinvestment advocates lack. As I noted above, CRA's resources undermine the legitimacy of advocacy groups that appear as troublemakers rather than valuable partners in enforcement. Advocacy groups should consider what policy changes would formalize, or at least officially recognize, the valuable role they have played in CRA enforcement. The original legislative process was notable for the absence of discussion about advocacy groups that had been working on reinvestment in many cities and were looking for tools to improve their efforts. But more than twenty years later, during debate in Congress on financial modernization legislation, lawmakers offered competing images of groups as neighborhood heroes and self-interested villains. The negative image prevailed, in that the 1999 Gramm-Leach-Bliley Act imposed "sunshine" requirements on groups to disclose how they benefit organizationally from relationships with banks. Advocates lamented this development, fearing the "chilling effect" it could have on advocacy groups' willingness to engage in community reinvestment work because of the reporting burden.[35] Ironically, now advocacy groups complain about the paperwork burdens that regulators and financial institutions always have criticized. Yet "sunshine" is the first statutory recognition that community groups play a role in advancing the goals of CRA. Disclosure, broadly conceived, could officially document this role, serving as a wedge that groups could use to move toward formal recognition of their part in the law's implementation. Groups should think about how to use "sunshine" as a political opportunity to advance their legitimacy as partners in CRA enforcement.

Choose allies not only based on shared interests or goals but also based on complementary political skills and resources. That is, groups can compensate for their weaknesses by seeking allies with complementary strengths. Fair housing and community reinvestment advocacy groups might overcome the challenges implicit in national policy designs by looking to one another and working together on common goals. Recognizing that external factors, such as public policies, keep them apart may help to build bridges across these movements. By and large, this cooperation has not happened in Minneapolis and Denver, although it has emerged to some extent at the national level and has occurred in other cities. National advocacy organizations recognize their common interests enough to support each other's legislative lobbying efforts; they sign each other's letters urging Congress to endorse various fair housing and community reinvestment reforms and attend each other's national conferences. Sometimes reaching across policy areas amounts to competing for resources; thus, the National Community Reinvestment Coalition received an FHIP grant to work on mortgage lending discrimination issues, and in Denver, the director of the fair housing–oriented Community Housing Resource Board was planning to begin fund-raising from local banks, making the argument that they could fulfill CRA obligations by funding her group.

But bridging the divide created by the policy designs can also mean expanding the capacity of a single nonprofit organization by expanding the tools available to address common problems. Combining community reinvestment and fair housing activities increases skills and strategies. Fair housing professionals have expertise in judicial processes and in conducting audits for discrimination, among other things; community reinvestment activists may have constituency-building or community organizing skills. Affordable housing advocates may be viable partners on low-income fair housing issues, as illustrated in the Minneapolis case where advocates had political skills that the average fair housing professional may lack. In Nevada and in Toledo, Ohio, fair housing groups negotiate CRA agreements and thus are able to address patterns of discrimination in addition to working on discriminatory practices that occur during housing transactions, which is the work best supported by the national fair housing design. In the Bronx, New York, the leader of a community reinvestment advocacy group (an attorney) has urged advocates to consider filing fair lending lawsuits against local banks with poor lending records in addition to using the typical CRA channels.

Despite the attractiveness of bridges between the movements, real challenges exist to building them. The two policy designs truly have created two worlds of action in which players operate with different understandings of discrimination and different judgments about remedies. They use distinct kinds of data and strategies to achieve their goals. For example, community reinvestment activists look at patterns of lending activity, whereas fair housing activists look for instances of discriminatory behavior toward individuals. This difference has given rise to situations where fair housing groups pursue litigation against local banks that are, relatively speaking, good community lenders from the perspective of community reinvestment activists. In addition, fair housing activists tend to be skeptical about the quality of lending pattern data, because it differs from their ways of identifying discrimination and may not satisfy the evidentiary standards they must meet in the courtroom.

Community reinvestment advocates typically hope to persuade banks to come to the negotiating table and ultimately begin to increase the flow of capital to poor and minority neighborhoods in their communities. When they begin a protest action against a bank whose merger is pending, the bank has an incentive to settle the matter quickly, so groups are used to relatively fast resolution—that is, if the banks respond to them. Fair housing activists are accustomed to much longer procedures—processing a claim through a court or an administrative system can take at least nine months and often much longer. HUD develops periodic backlogs in case processing, and lawsuits drag on for years, even decades. To a community reinvestment advocate, this delay looks like wasted time when the parties fight one another without any change in local housing conditions. To fair housing advocates, such lawsuits, when successful, are the ultimate deterrent because they raise large settlements or win significant punitive and compensatory damages as well as injunctive relief, thus sending a message to other industry members.

Still, recognizing these differences, advocates could find initiatives on which to collaborate, especially in light of the political obstacles that each type of group confronts when working alone. This collaboration has begun to happen with the issue of predatory lending, a concern to both fair housing and community reinvestment groups.[36] Together, fair housing and community reinvestment groups are using strategies of litigation, pressing for legislative change and community mobilization to address this emerging barrier to housing equality for the poor and for minority households. The developing interest in "smart growth" also involves issues of housing equality to which fair housing and community reinvestment groups might coordinate a joint response.

PROSPECTS FOR CHANGE

The Fair Housing Act and the Community Reinvestment Act were victories for politically weak groups and subjected powerful industries to burdens. Banks and the housing industry are critical actors in the private economy and have strong ties to political officials and government agencies. As the policy design perspective predicts, the fair housing and the community reinvestment designs tempered burdens on these groups in several ways through means such as minimal sanctions, delayed effective dates, and others. These are some of the reasons that housing discrimination and segregation persist in U.S. cities.

But the policy design perspective directs attention to the impacts of policy designs on politics as well as on problems. Indeed, by shaping political participation, policy designs shape the nature of democracy in our society. To fully understand how fair housing and community reinvestment policies influence prospects for limiting racial discrimination in housing markets, I have suggested considering the intervening role of advocacy groups. Examining how the two policy designs, in distinctive ways, both limit the capacity and political power of advocacy groups provides a further set of explanations for the persistence of discriminatory housing conditions and practices. Many cities and some states have no fair housing or community reinvestment advocacy groups. Many of the existing groups struggle to continue their work.

As policy agents, advocacy groups represent a crucial mechanism through which public policy influences citizens and vice versa. In addition, these groups often represent the interests of marginalized populations and serve as vehicles through which government responds. As they connect people to government, advocacy groups therefore influence the nature of democracy. This multidimensional approach to analyzing political viability helps pinpoint the specific weaknesses of sets of nonprofits working on particular issues and demonstrates that external factors such as public policies may be their source rather than—or in addition to—internal factors. Although I would argue that the political strength of the nonprofit and voluntary sector is a necessary condition for vigorous local democracy, it is, of course, not sufficient. Research on nonprofit organizations points to other factors that condition the democratic nature of a nonprofit's contribution to society such as a group's organizational structure, its inclusiveness, its decision-making procedures, the relationships between staff and "clients," and more.[37] Yet, these dimensions may also be products of public policy and can be probed with a design framework.

Enacting policies to benefit weak groups is notoriously difficult in the U.S. political system. The story I tell in this book is pessimistic in some respects because it suggests that when legislatures act to advance equality, the dynamics of the political process have long-standing and possibly harmful consequences for disadvantaged groups. That is, the inevitable competition over target images or policy rationales—strategies that legislators and advocates adopt in the heat of the moment to achieve the immediate goal of policy adoption—builds features into policy designs that can threaten the political strength of advocates in the future. Policies designed to reduce inequality thus sustain it. Yet the national legislature is only one locus of policy making in the U.S. system. If advocates can be aware of the multiple ways in which policy designs might affect them, they perhaps could change their strategies during the policy-making process. That is, they could advocate for changes not just in the technical content of policies but also in the civic content—in particular, design features that might improve their prospects for keeping up the fight for social justice.

Achieving positive change, though difficult, is not impossible. What policy scholars find is that radical policy changes tend to occur when reformers take advantage of (or help to create) shifts in discourse that highlight dimensions of a problem that were previously hidden. Unexpected events or crises can bring attention to an issue and enable new or marginal actors to take on key policy-making roles.[38] Advocates can creatively forge new political opportunities from changing conditions. The increasing diversity of the U.S. population, arising from record immigration rates, and the rapidly changing financial services industry in the context of globalization are among the changes that may become the basis for reframing and reinvigorating the struggle for housing equality.

Notes

CHAPTER 1. HOUSING DISCRIMINATION: PROBLEMS, POLITICS, POLICIES

1. Alex Kotlowitz, *There Are No Children Here* (New York: Anchor Books, 1991).

2. Ibid., 27.

3. Mary Pattillo-McCoy, *Black Picket Fences: Privilege and Peril among the Black Middle Class* (Chicago: University of Chicago Press, 1999).

4. John R. Logan, "Separate and Unequal: The Neighborhood Gap for Blacks and Hispanics in Metropolitan America," October 13, 2002, Lewis Mumford Center for Comparative Urban and Regional Research, SUNY–Albany, *www.albany.edu/mumford.*

5. Judith I. De Neufville and Stephen E. Barton, "Myths and the Definition of Policy Problems," *Policy Sciences* 20 (1987): 181–206.

6. Jennifer L. Hochschild, *Facing Up to the American Dream: Race, Class, and the Soul of the Nation* (Princeton: Princeton University Press, 1995).

7. Ibid.

8. Gregory D. Squires, Samantha Friedman, and Catherine E. Saidat, "Experiencing Residential Segregation: A Contemporary Study of Washington, D.C.," *Urban Affairs Review* 38, no. 2 (November 2002): 155–183.

9. Minnesota Fair Housing Center, *Housing Discrimination: A Report on the Rental Practices in Two Minneapolis Communities* (Minneapolis: Author, 1996).

10. John Yinger, *Closed Doors, Opportunities Lost: The Continuing Costs of Housing Discrimination* (New York: Russell Sage, 1995).

11. Ibid., 49.

12. Margery Austin Turner, Raymond J. Struyk, and John Yinger, *Housing Discrimination Study* (Washington, D.C.: U.S. Department of Housing and Urban Development, 1991).

13. Margery Austin Turner, Stephen L. Ross, George Galster, and John Yinger, *Discrimination in Metropolitan Housing Markets: National Results from Phase I HDS 2000* (Washington, D.C.: U.S. Department of Housing and Urban Development, November 2002), *www.huduser.org/publications/hsgfin/phase1.html.*

14. John Goering and Ron Wienk, eds., *Mortgage Lending, Racial Discrimination, and Federal Policy* (Washington, D.C.: Urban Institute Press, 1996); Yinger, *Closed Doors, Opportunities Lost.*

15. Robert B. Avery, Patricia E. Beeson, and Mark S. Sniderman, "Accounting for Racial Differences in Housing Credit Markets," in Goering and Wienk, eds., *Mortgage Lending, Racial Discrimination, and Federal Policy,* 75–141.

16. ACORN, "An Analysis of Racial and Economic Disparities in Home Purchase Mortgage Lending Nationally and in Sixty-Eight Metropolitan Areas," October 1, 2002; online at *www.acorn.org/acorn10/communityreinvestment/reports/HMDA2002/index.php.*

17. Yinger describes Munnell et al.'s study in John Yinger, "Discrimination in Mortgage Lending: A Literature Review," in Goering and Wienk, eds., *Mortgage Lending, Racial Discrimination, and Federal Policy,* 29–73.

18. Kathleen Day, "HUD Says Mortgage Policies Hurt Blacks; Home Loan Giants Cited," *Washington Post,* March 2, 2002, A1; and "Fannie Mae Vows More Minority Leasing," *Washington Post,* March 16, 2000, E1.

19. Robert Van Order, "Discrimination and the Secondary Market," in Goering and Wienk, eds., *Mortgage Lending, Racial Discrimination, and Federal Policy,* 335–363.

20. Amy S. Bogdon and Carol A. Bell, *Making Fair Lending a Reality in the New Millenium: Proceedings* (Washington, D.C.: Fannie Mae Foundation, 2000).

21. Ibid.

22. Ibid.

23. Goering and Wienk, eds., *Mortgage Lending, Racial Discrimination, and Federal Policy.*

24. Gregory Squires, ed., *Insurance Redlining: Disinvestment, Reinvestment, and the Evolving Role of Financial Institutions* (Washington, D.C.: Urban Institute Press, 1997).

25. Shanna L. Smith and Cathy Cloud, "Documenting Discrimination by Homeowners Insurance Companies through Testing," in Squires, ed., *Insurance Redlining,* 97–117.

26. Robert G. Schwemm, "Housing Discrimination and the Appraisal Industry," in Goering and Wienk, eds., *Mortgage Lending, Racial Discrimination, and Federal Policy,* 365–397; Yinger, "Discrimination in Mortgage Lending: A Literature Review."

27. Melvin L. Oliver and Thomas M. Shapiro, *Black Wealth/White Wealth: A New Perspective on Racial Inequality* (New York: Routledge, 1997).

28. Joint Center for Housing Studies, "The State of the Nation's Housing, 2002," Harvard University, *www.jchs.harvard.edu.*

29. Oliver and Shapiro, *Black Wealth/White Wealth.*

30. Ibid.

31. Others include national and local policies and whites' preferences for limited integration. These factors are described in R. D. Bullard, J. E. Grigsby III, and C. Lee, eds., *Residential Apartheid: The American Legacy* (Los Angeles: Center for Afro-American Studies, UCLA, 1994); R. Farley and W. H. Frey, "Changes in the Segregation of Whites from Blacks during the 1980s: Small Steps toward a More Integrated Society," *American Sociological Review* 59 (1994): 23–45; George Galster, "Racial Steering in Urban Housing Markets: A Review of the Audit Evidence," *Review of Black Political Economy* 18 (1990): 105–129; John M. Goering, ed., *Housing Desegregation and Federal Policy*

(Chapel Hill: University of North Carolina Press, 1986); Douglas S. Massey and Nancy A. Denton, *American Apartheid: Segregation and the Making of the Underclass* (Cambridge: Harvard University Press, 1993); H. Schuman and L. Bobo, "Survey-based Experiments on White Racial Attitudes toward Residential Integration," *American Journal of Sociology* 94 (1988): 273–299; G. A. Tobin, ed., *Divided Neighborhoods: Changing Patterns of Racial Segregation* (Newbury Park, Calif.: Sage Publications, 1987); Yinger, *Closed Doors, Opportunities Lost*.

32. Paul A. Jargowsky, *Poverty and Place: Ghettos, Barrios, and the American City* (New York: Russell Sage Foundation, 1997).

33. Ibid., 62.

34. The Lewis Mumford Center, "Ethnic Diversity Grows, Neighborhood Integration Lags Behind," December 18, 2001, SUNY–Albany, *www.albany.edu/mumford/census*.

35. Ibid.

36. Ibid.; Nancy A. Denton, "Half Empty or Half Full: Segregation and Segregated Neighborhoods 30 Years after the Fair Housing Act," *Cityscape* 4 (1999): 107–122.

37. George C. Galster, "Housing Discrimination and Urban Poverty of African Americans," *Journal of Housing Research* 2 (1991): 87–113; Jargowsky, *Poverty and Place;* W. Dennis. Keating, *The Suburban Racial Dilemma: Housing and Neighborhoods* (Philadelphia: Temple University Press, 1994); Douglas S. Massey, Gretchen A. Condran, and Nancy A. Denton, "The Effect of Residential Segregation on Black Social and Economic Well-Being," *Social Forces* 66 (1987): 29–56; Massey and Denton, *American Apartheid;* Loic J. Wacquant and William J. Wilson, "The Cost of Racial and Class Exclusion in the Inner City," *Annals, AAPS* 501 (1989): 8–25; Yinger, *Closed Doors, Opportunities Lost*.

38. Logan, "Separate and Unequal."

39. Yinger, *Closed Doors, Opportunities Lost.*

40. Although my focus here is on the negative consequences of residential segregation, many scholars have noted that this pattern may sometimes offer advantages to racial and ethnic minorities, such as opportunities for political representation, economic advantages such as job opportunities secured through local networks, and cultural identity emerging from ethnic enclaves. Assumptions that segregation is purely negative arise primarily from analyses of African-Americans' experiences in U.S. cities. Patterns need to be evaluated on a place by place basis to determine the mix of advantages and disadvantages arising for particular groups. See, for example, David H. Kaplan and Steven R. Holloway, "Contingency and Segregation: Making Sense of a Global Phenomenon," presentation at the annual meeting of the Urban Affairs Association, Los Angeles, May 2000.

41. Rachel G. Bratt, Chester Hartman, and Ann Meyerson, eds., *Critical Perspectives on Housing* (Philadelphia: Temple University Press, 1986).

42. Center for Responsive Politics Web site, *opensecrets.org*. Although donations were split evenly from 1990 to 1995, the trend since 1996 has been for about 60 percent of the sector's contributions to go to Republicans.

43. Jean E. Dubofsky, "Fair Housing: A Legislative History and a Perspective," *Washburn Law Journal* 8 (1969): 149–166; Massey and Denton, *American Apartheid;* Yinger, *Closed Doors, Opportunities Lost.*

44. Calvin Bradford and Gale Cincotta, "The Legacy, the Promise, and the Unfin-

ished Agenda," in Gregory D. Squires, ed., *From Redlining to Reinvestment: Community Responses to Urban Disinvestment* (Philadelphia: Temple University Press, 1992), 228–286; Gregory D. Squires, "Community Reinvestment: The Privatization of Fair Lending Law Enforcement," in Bullard, Grigsby, and Lee, eds., *Residential Apartheid,* 257–286.

45. Martin D. Abravanel and Mary K. Cunningham, "How Much Do We Know? Public Awareness of the Nation's Fair Housing Laws," prepared for the U.S. Department of Housing and Urban Development, Office of Policy Development and Research, by the Urban Institute, Washington, D.C., April 2002, *www.huduser.org.*

46. Bill Lann Lee, "An Issue of Public Importance: The Justice Department's Enforcement of the Fair Housing Act," *Cityscape* 4, no. 3 (1999): 35–56; Fair Housing Center of Metropolitan Detroit, "$115,000 and Counting: A Summary of Housing Discrimination Lawsuits That Have Been Assisted by the Efforts of Private, Non-Profit Fair Housing Organizational Members of the National Fair Housing Alliance," June 26, 1999.

47. Robert C. Lieberman, Anne L. Schneider, and Helen Ingram, "Social Construction (Continued)," *American Political Science Review* 89 (1995): 437–446; Anne Larason Schneider and Helen Ingram, "Social Constructions and Target Populations: Implications for Politics and Policy," *American Political Science Review* 87 (1993): 334–347; Anne Larason Schneider and Helen Ingram, *Policy Design for Democracy* (Lawrence: University Press of Kansas, 1997).

48. Schneider and Ingram, *Policy Design for Democracy,* 53, chap. 3.

49. Helen Ingram and Anne Schneider, "Public Policy and the Social Construction of Deservedness," in Schneider and Ingram, eds., *Deserving and Entitled: Social Constructions and Public Policy* (Albany: State University of New York Press, forthcoming).

50. Harold D. Lasswell, *A Pre-View of Policy Sciences* (New York: Elsevier, 1971).

51. Susan E. Clarke, "Interests, Ideas, and Institutions in Urban Education Politics," in *The New Educational Populism: The Multi-ethnic Politics of School Reform,* ed. Susan E. Clarke, Rodney E. Hero, Mara S. Sidney, Bari Anhalt Erlichson, and Luis Fraga (Durham, N.C.: Duke University Press, forthcoming); Hugh Heclo, "Ideas, Interests, and Institutions," in *The Dynamics of American Politics,* ed. Lawrence C. Dodd and Calvin Jillson (Boulder, Colo.: Westview Press, 1994), 366–392; Mark I. Lichbach, "Social Theory and Comparative Politics," in *Comparative Politics: Rationality, Culture, and Structure,* ed. Mark I. Lichbach and Alan S. Zuckerman (Cambridge: Cambridge University Press, 1997), 239–276.

52. Heclo, "Ideas, Interests, and Institutions," in Dodd and Jillson, eds., *Dynamics of American Politics,* 383.

53. Schneider and Ingram, *Policy Design for Democracy.*

54. Ibid., 3.

55. Robert A. Dahl and Charles E. Lindblom, *Politics, Economics, and Welfare* (New York: Harper, 1953).

56. Ellen M. Immergut, "The Theoretical Core of the New Institutionalism," *Politics and Society* 26 (1998): 5–34.

57. Schneider and Ingram, *Policy Design for Democracy,* chap. 4.

58. Murray Edelman, *Constructing the Political Spectacle* (Chicago: University of Chicago Press, 1988); Peter A. Hall, "The Role of Interests, Institutions, and Ideas in the

Comparative Political Economy of the Industrialized Nations," in Lichbach and Zucker-man, eds., *Comparative Politics,* 174–207.

59. R. Cobb and C. D. Elder, *Participation in American Politics: The Dynamics of Agenda Building* (Baltimore: Johns Hopkins University Press, 1972); E. E. Schattschnei-der, *The Semi-Sovereign People* (New York: Rinehart and Wilson, 1960).

60. Frank Fischer and John Forester, eds., *The Argumentative Turn in Policy Analy-sis and Planning* (Durham, N.C.: Duke University Press, 1993); D. Rochefort and R. W. Cobb, "Problem Definition: An Emerging Perspective," in *The Politics of Problem Defin-ition,* ed. D. Rochefort and R.W. Cobb (Lawrence: University Press of Kansas, 1994); Schneider and Ingram, "Social Constructions and Target Populations"; Deborah Stone, "Causal Stories and the Formation of Policy Agendas," *Political Science Quarterly* 104 (1989): 281–300.

61. Herbert A. Simon, *The Sciences of the Artificial* (Cambridge, Mass.: MIT Press, 1996).

62. Bryan D. Jones, *Reconceiving Decision-Making in Democratic Politics: Atten-tion, Choice, and Public Policy* (Chicago: University of Chicago Press, 1994); Simon, *The Sciences of the Artificial.*

63. Joe Soss, "Lessons of Welfare: Policy Design, Political Learning, and Political Action," *American Political Science Review* 93 (1999): 363–380.

64. Paul Pierson, *Dismantling the Welfare State? Reagan, Thatcher, and the Politics of Retrenchment* (Cambridge: Harvard University Press, 1994), 39–46.

65. Ibid.

66. Schneider and Ingram, *Policy Design for Democracy,* chap. 5; Ingram and Schneider, "Public Policy and the Social Construction of Deservedness."

67. John H. Mollenkopf, *The Contested City* (Princeton: Princeton University Press, 1983); see also J. D. Greenstone and P. E. Peterson, *Race and Authority in Urban Politics: Community Participation and the War on Poverty* (New York: Russell Sage Foundation, 1973).

68. Steven Gregory, *Black Corona: Race and the Politics of Place in an Urban Community* (Princeton: Princeton University Press, 1998).

69. Martha Derthick, *New Towns In-Town: Why a Federal Program Failed* (Wash-ington, D.C.: Urban Institute, 1972); John R. Logan and Todd Swanstrom, eds., *Beyond the City Limits: Urban Policy and Economic Restructuring in Comparative Perspective* (Philadelphia: Temple University Press, 1990); Michael J. Rich, *Federal Policymaking and the Poor: National Goals, Local Choices, and Distributional Outcomes* (Princeton: Princeton University Press, 1993).

70. Derthick, *New Towns In-Town,* 97.

71. Helen Ingram, "Policy Implementation through Bargaining: The Case of Federal Grants-in-Aid," *Public Policy* 25 (1977): 499–526.

72. Elizabeth T. Boris and C. Eugene Steuerle, eds., *Nonprofits and Government: Collaboration and Conflict* (Washington, D.C.: Urban Institute Press, 1999); Lester M. Salamon, ed., *Beyond Privatization: The Tools of Government Action* (Washington, D.C.: Urban Institute Press, 1989).

73. Lester M. Salamon, "Partners in Public Service: The Scope and Theory of Gov-ernment-Nonprofit Relations," in *The Nonprofit Handbook,* ed. Walter W. Powell (New Haven: Yale University Press, 1987), 99–117; Dennis R. Young, "Complementary, Sup-

plementary, or Adversarial? A Theoretical and Historical Examination of Nonprofit-Government Relations in the United States," in Boris and Steuerle, eds., *Nonprofits and Government,* 31–67.

74. Steven Rathgeb Smith and Michael Lipsky, *Nonprofits for Hire: The Welfare State in the Age of Contracting* (Cambridge: Harvard University Press, 1993).

75. Elizabeth J. Reid, "Nonprofit Advocacy and Political Participation," in Boris and Steuerle, eds., *Nonprofits and Government,* 291–325; Steven Rathgeb Smith, "Government Financing of Nonprofit Activity," in Boris and Steuerle, eds., *Nonprofits and Government,* 177–210.

76. Ingram and Schneider, "Public Policy and the Social Construction of Deservedness."

77. David S. Meyer, "Social Movements and Public Policy: Eggs, Chickens, and Theory," prepared for the workshop "Social Movements, Public Policy, and Democracy," University of California–Irvine, January 11–13, 2002.

78. Ibid.

79. Ibid.

80. Ibid.

81. Richard Chin, "For Twin Cities Blacks, Home Loans Hard to Get," *St. Paul Pioneer Press,* April 25, 1993, 1A; Karl H. Flaming and Richard H. Anderson, *Mortgage Practices in Colorado* (Denver: Civil Rights Division, State of Colorado, 1993); Karl H. Flaming, Richard H. Anderson, and Margaret Lake, *Mortgage Practices in Colorado: A Second Look* (Denver: Civil Rights Division, State of Colorado, 1997); Franklin J. James, "Minority Suburbanization in Denver," in Bullard, Grigsby, and Lee, eds., *Residential Apartheid,* 95–121; Minnesota Fair Housing Center, *Housing Discrimination.*

82. James, "Minority Suburbanization in Denver"; Myron Orfield, *Metropolitics: A Regional Agenda for Community and Stability,* rev. ed. (Washington, D.C.: Brookings Institution Press, 1997).

CHAPTER 2. CRAFTING HOUSING POLICY IN SPOTLIGHT AND SHADOW

1. This description is drawn from Jude Wanniski, "How the Civil-Rights Victory Was Won," *National Observer,* March 11, 1968.

2. Rochelle L. Stanfield, "If Baroni's at HUD, the Neighborhoods Are Looking Up," *National Journal,* June 4, 1977, 860.

3. Schneider and Ingram, *Policy Design for Democracy.*

4. Ibid., chap. 5.

5. Mark C. Donovan, "Social Constructions of People with AIDS: Target Populations and United States Policy, 1981–1990," *Policy Studies Review* 12 (1993): 3–26.

6. Schneider and Ingram, *Policy Design for Democracy,* 341.

7. Data for context analysis come from contemporary media accounts including publications that cover Congress, from transcripts of congressional hearings, and from secondary sources. I also use transcripts from twenty-five interviews with government officials and national-level advocates conducted in Washington, D.C., from 1998 to 2000. Data for discourse analysis come from the *Congressional Record* transcripts of debates. I coded each statement for support or opposition and for mentions of target groups, agents,

rationales, and policy logic. Data for policy design analysis consist of texts of the bills first proposed, the versions reported out of committee, the versions amended or substituted on the floor or both (in the case of fair housing) or reported out of conference committee (in the case of community reinvestment), and the versions signed into law.

8. P.L. 90-284.

9. Ronald H. Bayor, *Race and the Shaping of Twentieth-Century Atlanta* (Chapel Hill: University of North Carolina Press, 1996); Congressional Quarterly, *Revolution in Civil Rights* (Washington, D.C.: Congressional Quarterly Service, 1968); Arnold R. Hirsch, *Making the Second Ghetto: Race and Housing in Chicago, 1940–1960* (Cambridge: Cambridge University Press, 1983); Duane Lockard, *Toward Equal Opportunity* (New York: Macmillan, 1968); Raymond A. Mohl, "Making the Second Ghetto in Metropolitan Miami, 1940–1960," in *The New African American Urban History,* ed. K. W. Goings and R. A. Mohl (Thousand Oaks, Calif.: Sage Publications, 1996), 266–298; Christopher Silver and John V. Moeser, *The Separate City: Black Communities in the Urban South, 1940–1968* (Lexington: University Press of Kentucky, 1995); Thomas J. Sugrue, *The Origins of the Urban Crisis: Race and Inequality in Postwar Detroit* (Princeton: Princeton University Press, 1996).

10. Citizens Commission on Civil Rights, "The Federal Government and Equal Housing Opportunity: A Continuing Failure," in *Critical Perspectives on Housing,* ed. R. G. Bratt, C. Hartman, and A. Meyerson (Philadelphia: Temple University Press, 1986), 296–324.

11. Jean E. Dubofsky, "Fair Housing: A Legislative History and a Perspective," *Washburn Law Journal* 8 (1969): 149–166.

12. Wanniski, "How the Civil-Rights Victory Was Won."

13. Doug McAdam, *Political Process and the Development of Black Insurgency, 1930–1970* (Chicago: University of Chicago Press, 1982).

14. Ibid., 182.

15. Keesing's Research Report, *Race Relations in the USA: 1954–68* (New York: Charles Scribner's Sons, 1970).

16. Robert Weisbrot, *Freedom Bound: A History of America's Civil Rights Movement* (New York: W. W. Norton, 1990).

17. James L. Sundquist, *Politics and Policy: The Eisenhower, Kennedy, and Johnson Years* (Washington, D.C.: Brookings Institution, 1968).

18. Ibid., 281.

19. Ibid.; James L. Sundquist, *Dynamics of the Party System: Alignment and Realignment of Political Parties in the United States* (Washington, D.C.: Brookings Institution, 1983).

20. McAdam, *Political Process and the Development of Black Insurgency.*

21. Hugh Davis Graham, *The Civil Rights Era: Origins and Development of National Policy, 1960–1972* (New York: Oxford University Press, 1990); Weisbrot, *Freedom Bound.*

22. Rachel G. Bratt, Chester Hartman, and Ann Meyerson, eds., *Critical Perspectives on Housing* (Philadelphia: Temple University Press, 1986); J. Paul Mitchell, *Federal Housing Policy and Programs: Past and Present* (New Brunswick, N.J.: Center for Urban Policy Research, 1985).

23. Graham, *The Civil Rights Era.*

24. Lockard, *Toward Equal Opportunity*.

25. Congressional Quarterly, *Revolution in Civil Rights;* Graham, *The Civil Rights Era.*

26. Ibid.

27. Ibid.

28. Schneider and Ingram, "Social Constructions and Target Populations."

29. Wanniski, "How the Civil-Rights Victory Was Won."

30. Ibid.

31. Graham, *The Civil Rights Era.*

32. Mara S. Sidney, "The Origin of U.S. Fair Housing Policy: Images of Race, Class, and Markets," *Journal of Policy History* 13, no. 2 (Spring 2001): 181–214.

33. Rep. Smith (D-Va.), in *Congressional Record,* 89th Cong., 2d sess., 1966, 112, pts. 13–14: 16834.

34. Ibid., 17229.

35. *Congressional Record,* 90th Cong., 2d sess., 1968, 114, pts. 2–5: 2274.

36. Ibid., 2279.

37. U.S. Congress, *Fair Housing Act of 1967: Hearings before the Subcommittee on Housing and Urban Affairs of the Committee on Banking and Currency, United States Senate, 90th Congress, First Session, on S. 1358, S. 2114, and S. 2280 Relating to Civil Rights and Housing, August 21, 22, and 23, 1967* (Washington, D.C.: Government Printing Office, 1967), 194.

38. Ibid., 99.

39. Ibid., 116.

40. Ibid., 377.

41. *Congressional Record,* 114, pts. 2–5: 2279.

42. Ibid., 3421.

43. Ibid., 3421.

44. Ibid., 3422.

45. U.S. Congress, *Hearings before Subcommittee No. 5 of the Committee on the Judiciary, House of Representatives, 89th Congress, Second Session, on Miscellaneous Proposals Regarding the Civil Rights of Persons within the Jurisdiction of the United States* (Washington, D.C.: Government Printing Office, 1966).

46. Jean Pogge, "Reinvestment in Chicago Neighborhoods: A Twenty-Year Struggle," in *From Redlining to Reinvestment: Community Responses to Urban Disinvestment,* ed. Gregory D. Squires (Philadelphia: Temple University Press, 1992), 134.

47. Squires, *From Redlining to Reinvestment,* especially Cincotta and Bradford, "The Legacy, The Promise, and the Unfinished Agenda."

48. Joseph P. Fried, "The Struggle over Redlining Is Intensifying," *New York Times,* May 1, 1977, 7.

49. P.L. 95-128.

50. John H. Mollenkopf, *The Contested City* (Princeton: Princeton University Press, 1983).

51. Ibid., 213.

52. Dennis R. Judd and Todd Swanstrom, *City Politics: Private Power and Public Policy* (New York: HarperCollins College Publishers, 1994).

53. Mollenkopf, *The Contested City.*

54. Judd and Swanstrom, *City Politics*.

55. Susan S. Fainstein, "Urban Redevelopment," in *The Encyclopedia of Housing*, ed. Willem van Vliet-- (Thousand Oaks, Calif.: Sage Publications, 1998), 614–617.

56. John Emmeus Davis, *Contested Ground: Collective Action and the Urban Neighborhood* (Ithaca: Cornell University Press, 1991); Neil Smith, "Gentrification," in van Vliet--, ed., *The Encyclopedia of Housing*, 198–199.

57. Congressional Quarterly, *Congress and the Nation, 1977–1980* (Washington, D.C.: Congressional Quarterly Service, 1981).

58. Congressional Quarterly, *CQ Almanac* (Washington, D.C.: Congressional Quarterly, 1975).

59. Marilyn R. Christiano, "The Community Reinvestment Act: The Role of Community Groups in the Formulation and Implementation of a Public Policy" (Ph.D. diss., University of Maryland, 1995).

60. Ibid.

61. Eric Moskowitz, "The National Politics of Neighborhood Reinvestment," presentation at the Midwest Political Science Association annual meeting, Chicago, April 19–21, 1979.

62. George S. Eccles, *The Politics of Banking* (Salt Lake City: Graduate School of Business, University of Utah, 1982); Kenneth Spong, *Banking Regulation: Its Purposes, Implementation, and Effects* (Kansas City, Mo.: Federal Reserve Bank of Kansas City, 1994).

63. Anne M. Khademian, *Checking on Banks: Autonomy and Accountability in Three Federal Agencies* (Washington, D.C.: Brookings Institution Press, 1996).

64. Ibid.

65. U.S. Senate, *Community Credit Needs: Hearings before the Committee on Banking, Housing, and Urban Affairs, United States Senate, 95th Congress, First Session, on S. 406, March 23–25* (Washington, D.C.: Government Printing Office, 1977).

66. *Congressional Record*, 95th Cong., 1st sess., 1977, 123: 17635.

67. Norman J. Ornstein, Thomas E. Mann, and Michael J. Malbin, *Vital Statistics on Congress: 1995–1996* (Washington, D.C.: Congressional Quarterly, 1996).

68. Steven S. Smith and Christopher J. Deering, *Committees in Congress* (Washington, D.C.: CQ Press, 1990).

69. John E. Owens, "Good Public Policy Voting in the U.S. Congress: An Explanation of Financial Institutions Politics," *Political Studies* 43 (1995): 66–91.

70. Christiano, "The Community Reinvestment Act."

71. Ibid.; Congressional Quarterly, *CQ Almanac* (Washington, D.C.: Congressional Quarterly, 1977).

72. Committee on Banking, Finance, and Urban Affairs, House of Representatives, *Compilation of the Housing and Community Development Act of 1977* (Washington, D.C.: Government Printing Office, 1977).

73. Christiano, "The Community Reinvestment Act."

74. *Congressional Record*, 123: 17630; emphasis added.

75. Ibid., 17628–17629.

76. Ibid., 17630; emphasis added.

77. Ibid..

78. Ibid., 17603.

79. Christiano, "The Community Reinvestment Act"; Congressional Quarterly, *CQ Almanac* (Washington, D.C.: Congressional Quarterly, 1975).

80. *Congressional Record,* 123: 17633.

81. Christiano, "The Community Reinvestment Act"; Squires, *From Redlining to Reinvestment.*

82. Squires, *From Redlining to Reinvestment.*

83. Senate, *Community Credit Needs;* see statements by Ralph Nader, Gale Cincotta, Conrad Weiler, and Ronald Grzywinski.

84. *Congressional Record,* 123: 17630.

85. Khademian, *Checking on Banks.*

86. Ibid.

87. Ibid.

CHAPTER 3. LINKING HOUSING POLICY TO ADVOCACY

1. "Los Angeles Federal Jury Awards $500,000 to Mixed Race Family Denied Rental House," *National Fair Housing Advocate* 10, no. 2 (August 2002): 1, 3; *www. fairhousing.com.*

2. "Toledo Fair Housing Center, along with Other Fair Housing Groups, Sues Citigroup/Travelers/Aetna Alleging Discrimination against African American and Latino Homeowners," in New Developments, the Toledo Fair Housing Center Web site, *www. toledofhc.org.*

3. "New Member Helps on Fair Housing Rules," *Reinvestment Works* (Summer 2002): 10; *www.ncrc.org.*

4. "National Fair Housing Alliance Documents Continued Discrimination in Housing: Only 1 Percent of Illegal Housing Discrimination Reported," press release dated April 3, 2002, *www.nationalfairhousing.org.*

5. "Fair Banking and Community Reinvestment," New Jersey Citizen Action Web site, *www.njcitizenaction.org.*

6. "Community Reinvestment and Fair Lending," Center for Community Change Web site, *www.communitychange.org.*

7. "Community Reinvestment: What's Happening Now—Study Shows Increased Racial Disparity in Mortgage Lending," news item dated October 17, 2002, Association of Community Organizations for Reform Now (ACORN) Web site, *www.acorn.org.*

8. Inner City Press Web site, *www.innercitypress.org.*

9. Calvin Bradford and Gale Cincotta, "The Legacy, the Promise, and the Unfinished Agenda," in Squires, ed., *From Redlining to Reinvestment,* 228–286; Christiano, "The Community Reinvestment Act"; Allen J. Fishbein, "The Ongoing Experiment with 'Regulation from Below': Expanded Reporting Requirements for HMDA and CRA," *Housing Policy Debate* 3 (1992): 601–638; Massey and Denton, *American Apartheid;* Shanna L. Smith, "The National Fair Housing Alliance at Work," in Bullard, Grigsby, and Lee, eds., *Residential Apartheid,* 237–256; Gregory D. Squires, "Friend or Foe? The Federal Government and Community Reinvestment," in *Revitalizing Urban Neighborhoods,* ed. W. D. Keating, N. Krumholz, and P. Star (Lawrence: University Press of Kansas, 1996), 224–234; Gregory D. Squires, "Community Reinvestment: The Privatization of

Fair Lending Law Enforcement," in Bullard, Grigsby, and Lee, eds., *Residential Apartheid*, 257–286.

10. Robert C. Art, "Social Responsibility in Bank Credit Decisions: The Community Reinvestment Act One Decade Later," *Pacific Law Journal* 18 (1987): 1071; Squires, "Community Reinvestment," in Bullard, Grigsby, and Lee, eds., *Residential Apartheid*, 257–286.

11. Smith, "The National Fair Housing Alliance at Work."

12. Robert G. Schwemm, "Fair Housing Amendments Act of 1988," in van Vliet--, ed., *The Encyclopedia of Housing*.

13. For example, Committee on Banking, Finance, and Urban Affairs, *Discrimination in Federally Assisted Housing Programs: Hearings before the Subcommittee on Housing and Community Development of the Committee on Banking, Finance, and Urban Affairs, House of Representatives, 99th Congress, Second Session, Part 1, November 21, 1985, January 30, 1986* (Washington, D.C.: Government Printing Office, 1986); Committee on Banking, Finance, and Urban Affairs, *Discrimination in Federally Assisted Housing Programs: Hearings before the Subcommittee on Housing and Community Development of the Committee on Banking, Finance, and Urban Affairs, House of Representatives, 99th Congress, Second Session, Part 2, February 27, May 6 and 13* (Washington, D.C.: Government Printing Office, 1986); Committee on Banking, Finance, and Urban Affairs, *Issues Relating to Fair Housing: Hearings before the Subcommittee on Housing and Community Development of the Committee on Banking, Finance, and Urban Affairs, House of Representatives, 100th Congress, Second Session, January 27 and February 4* (Washington, D.C.: Government Printing Office, 1988); Committee on the Judiciary, *Fair Housing Act: Hearings before the Subcommittee on Civil and Constitutional Rights of the Committee of the Judiciary, House of Representatives, 95th Congress, Second Session, on H.R. 3504 and H.R. 7787, February 2, 9, May 10, 11, 15, June 7, and July 27* (Washington, D.C.: Government Printing Office, 1978); Committee on the Judiciary, *Fair Housing Amendments Act of 1979: Hearings before the Subcommittee on Civil and Constitutional Rights of the Committee on the Judiciary, House of Representatives, 96th Congress, First Session, on H.R. 2540, April 6, 25, 26, May 3, 16, 23, 31, and June 14* (Washington, D.C.: Government Printing Office, 1979); Committee on the Judiciary, *Fair Housing Amendments Act of 1979: Hearings before the Subcommittee on the Constitution of the Committee on the Judiciary, United States Senate, 96th Congress, First Session, on S. 506, March 21, 22, May 2, June 5, 11, and September 17* (Washington, D.C.: Government Printing Office, 1979); Committee on the Judiciary, *Fair Housing Amendments Act: Hearing before the Subcommittee on Civil and Constitutional Rights of the Committee on the Judiciary, Housing of Representatives, 99th Congress, Second Session, on H.R. 4119, Fair Housing Amendments Act, July 17 and 18* (Washington, D.C.: Government Printing Office, 1986); Committee on the Judiciary, *Fair Housing Amendments Act of 1987: Hearings before the Subcommittee on Civil and Constitutional Rights of the Committee on the Judiciary, House of Representatives, 100th Congress, First Session, on H.R. 1158, April 22, 29, May 6, 7, 12, and 14* (Washington, D.C.: Government Printing Office, 1987); Committee on the Judiciary, *Fair Housing Amendments Act of 1987: Hearings before the Subcommittee on the Constitution of the Committee on the Judiciary, United States Senate, 100th Congress, First Session, on S. 558, March 31, April 2, 7, 9, June 9, and July 1* (Washington, D.C.: Government Printing Office, 1987); U.S. Commission on Civil Rights, *Federal Civil Rights Enforcement Effort* (Washington, D.C.: Government Printing

Office, 1971); U.S. Commission on Civil Rights, *The Federal Civil Rights Enforcement Effort—1974; Volume II: To Provide for Fair Housing* (Washington, D.C.: Government Printing Office, 1974); U.S. Commission on Civil Rights, *The Federal Fair Housing Enforcement Effort* (Washington, D.C.: Government Printing Office, 1979); U.S. Commission on Civil Rights, *A Sheltered Crisis: The State of Fair Housing in the Eighties; Presentations at a Consultation Sponsored by the United States Commission on Civil Rights, Washington, D.C., September 26–27, 1983* (Washington, D.C.: Government Printing Office, 1983).

14. For example, see essays by advocates including Wade J. Henderson of the ACLU, Patricia Horton, former director of the Fair Housing Council of Greater Washington, Avery S. Friedman, former chief counsel, the Housing Advocates Inc., Althea T. L. Simmons, director of the NAACP Washington bureau, in "Should Congress Approve the Fair Housing Amendments Act of 1987?" *Congressional Digest*, June–July 1998, 170–191.

15. Ron Wienk, John Simonson, Robin Ross Smith, Martha Kuhlman, and Jennifer Pack, *An Evaluation of the FHIP Private Enforcement Initiative Testing Demonstration* (Washington, D.C.: U.S. Department of Housing and Urban Development, 1994).

16. "Compromise Fair-Housing Bill Is Cleared," *CQ Almanac* 44 (1988): 68–74, and my interviews.

17. Fishbein, "The Ongoing Experiment with 'Regulation from Below,'" 613.

18. Stephen Labaton, "Midnight Talks Helped to Close Deal on Banks," *New York Times*, October 24, 1999, 1, 22; National Community Reinvestment Coalition, "President Signs Bill Giving Financial Freedom to Wall Street, NCRC Urges the Same for Main Street," press release, Washington, D.C., November 12, 1999.

19. Elizabeth T. Boris and C. Eugene Steuerle, eds., *Nonprofits and Government: Collaboration and Conflict* (Washington, D.C.: Urban Institute Press, 1999); Lester M. Salamon, ed., *Beyond Privatization: The Tools of Government Action* (Washington, D.C.: Urban Institute Press, 1989); Steven Rathgeb Smith and Michael Lipsky, *Nonprofits for Hire: The Welfare State in the Age of Contracting* (Cambridge: Harvard University Press, 1993).

20. Schneider and Ingram, *Policy Design for Democracy*.

21. Smith and Lipsky, *Nonprofits for Hire*.

22. Ellen M. Immergut, "The Theoretical Core of the New Institutionalism," *Politics and Society* 26 (1998): 5–34; Salamon, *Beyond Privatization;* Schneider and Ingram, *Policy Design for Democracy*.

23. Salamon, *Beyond Privatization;* Smith and Lipsky, *Nonprofits for Hire*.

24. Schwemm, "Fair Housing Amendments Act of 1988."

25. A concept from Robert C. Lieberman, *Shifting the Color Line: Race and the American Welfare State* (Cambridge: Harvard University Press, 1998).

26. Judd and Swanstrom, *City Politics,* 246.

27. Schwemm, "Fair Housing Amendments Act of 1988."

28. Wienk et al., *An Evaluation of the FHIP Private Enforcement Initiative Testing Demonstration.*

29. U.S. General Accounting Office, *Fair Housing: Funding and Activities under the Fair Housing Initiatives Program* (Washington, D.C.: Author, 1997).

30. John E. Owens, "Good Public Policy Voting in the U.S. Congress: An Explanation of Financial Institutions Politics," *Political Studies* 43 (1995): 66–91.

31. Allen J. Fishbein, "The Community Reinvestment Act after Fifteen Years: It Works, But Strengthened Federal Enforcement Is Needed," *Fordham Urban Law Journal* 20 (1993): 293–310.

32. Ibid.; National Community Reinvestment Coalition, *Advanced CRA Manual* (Washington, D.C.: Author, 2000).

33. National Community Reinvestment Coalition, *Advanced CRA Manual.*

34. U.S. General Accounting Office, *Fair Housing.*

35. Ibid.

36. George R. Metcalf, *Fair Housing Comes of Age* (New York: Greenwood Press, 1988); U.S. Commission on Civil Rights, *The Fair Housing Amendments Act of 1988: The Enforcement Report* (Washington, D.C.: Government Printing Office, 1994).

37. Schwemm, "Fair Housing Amendments Act of 1988."

38. Sarah Rigdon Bensinger, "Maximizing Damages for Fair Housing Organizations under the Fair Housing Act," *Journal of Affordable Housing* 5 (1996): 227–235.

39. Michael H. Schill and Samantha Friedman, "Fair Housing Strategies for the Future: A Balanced Approach," *Cityscape* 4 (1999): 57–78.

40. Beth J. Lief and Susan Goering, "The Implementation of the Federal Mandate for Fair Housing," in Tobin, ed., *Divided Neighborhoods,* 227–267; Florence Wagman Roisman, "Long Overdue: Desegregation Litigation and Next Steps to End Discrimination and Segregation in the Public Housing and Section 8 Existing Housing Programs," *Cityscape* 4 (1999): 171–196.

41. Ibid.

42. Roisman, "Long Overdue"; Timothy L. Thompson, "Promoting Mobility and Equal Opportunity: *Hollman v. Cisneros," Journal of Affordable Housing* 5 (1996): 237–260.

43. Fishbein, "The Ongoing Experiment with 'Regulation from Below.'"

44. National Community Reinvestment Coalition, *Advanced CRA Manual.*

45. Goering and Wienk, *Mortgage Lending, Racial Discrimination, and Federal Policy.*

46. Christiano, "The Community Reinvestment Act"; Fishbein, "The Ongoing Experiment with 'Regulation from Below.'"

47. National Community Reinvestment Coalition, *Advanced CRA Manual;* John Yinger, *Closed Doors, Opportunities Lost: The Continuing Costs of Housing Discrimination* (New York: Russell Sage, 1995).

48. Fishbein, "The Community Reinvestment Act after Fifteen Years."

49. Squires, *From Redlining to Reinvestment.*

50. Fishbein, "The Community Reinvestment Act after Fifteen Years."

51. National Community Reinvestment Coalition, *Advanced CRA Manual.*

52. Fishbein, "The Community Reinvestment Act after Fifteen Years."

53. This distinction between process and outcome draws on Yinger, *Closed Doors, Opportunities Lost.*

54. Ibid.

55. Lief and Goering, "The Implementation of the Federal Mandate for Fair Housing."

56. Fishbein, "The Community Reinvestment Act after Fifteen Years."

57. Ibid.; Committee on Banking, Finance, and Urban Affairs, *Current Status of the*

Community Reinvestment Act: Hearings before the Subcommittee on Housing and Urban Affairs of the Committee on Banking, Housing, and Urban Affairs, United States Senate, 102d Congress, Second Session, September 15, 1992 (Washington, D.C.: Government Printing Office, 1992).

58. Fishbein, "The Community Reinvestment Act after Fifteen Years."

59. Khademian, *Checking on Banks.*

60. Art, "Social Responsibility in Bank Credit Decisions."

61. Khademian, *Checking on Banks,* 154.

62. Ibid., 149.

63. Art, "Social Responsibility in Bank Credit Decisions"; Fishbein, "The Community Reinvestment Act after Fifteen Years"; Khademian, *Checking on Banks.*

64. Khademian, *Checking on Banks.*

65. American Bankers Association, *www.aba.com;* Fishbein, "The Community Reinvestment Act after Fifteen Years."

66. Fishbein, "The Community Reinvestment Act after Fifteen Years."

67. Committee on Banking, Finance, and Urban Affairs, *Current Status of the Community Reinvestment Act.*

CHAPTER 4. ADVOCACY FOR HOUSING EQUALITY IN MINNEAPOLIS

1. Data for analysis of local action were collected during field research in Minneapolis from September 1998 through January 2000, consisting of interviews, archival research, and participant observation. I conducted forty-six in-person semistructured interviews with past and present civil rights, fair housing, community reinvestment, and housing activists and with government officials at the local, state, and federal levels, both elected and civil servants. I attended related events and workshops and consulted archival materials, including government documents, local newspapers, and advocacy group archives.

2. Daniel J. Elazar, Virginia Gray, and Wyman Spano, *Minnesota Politics and Government* (Lincoln: University of Nebraska Press, 1999); Joseph Galaskiewicz, *Social Organization of an Urban Grants Economy* (Orlando, Fla.: Academic Press, 1985).

3. Elazar, Gray, and Spano, *Minnesota Politics and Government.*

4. Timothy N. Thurber, *The Politics of Equality: Hubert H. Humphrey and the African American Freedom Struggle* (New York: Columbia University Press, 1999).

5. Jon Jeter, "In Minnesota, Political Views Change with Minority Influx," *Washington Post,* March 3, 1998, A1; "The Minneapolis Spirit," editorial, *Star Tribune,* September 14, 1997, 26A.

6. Rodney E. Hero, *Faces of Inequality: Social Diversity in American Politics* (New York: Oxford University Press, 1998).

7. Thurber, *The Politics of Equality,* 27.

8. Dick Cunningham, "Problem of Twin Cities Negro Few Ignored, Rights Aides Say," *Minneapolis Morning Tribune,* August 23, 1967, 1, 3.

9. Marilyn Cathcart, *The Unseen City: A Status Report on Minorities in Minneapolis* (Minneapolis: Urban Coalition, 1984).

10. David Peterson, "Racial Friction in the Land of Liberals," *Star Tribune,* June 16, 1990.

11. Denise R. Nickel, "The Progressive City? Urban Redevelopment in Minneapolis," *Urban Affairs Review* 30 (1995): 355–377.

12. Ibid.

13. Ibid.

14. Monika Bauerlein, "Civil Disservice," *City Pages,* August 14, 1991, 10–15; Mark Engebretson, "Budget Cutters Target Civil Rights Department, Others," *Surveyor,* October 1993, 1, 11; Rose Farley, "A Department without Rights," *Twin Cities Reader,* December 15, 1993.

15. U.S. Bureau of the Census, Census of Population, 1970, 1980, 1990, 2000.

16. League of Women Voters, *Housing Problems in Minneapolis and Its Hennepin County Suburbs* (Minneapolis: Author, 1969).

17. Ibid.

18. Ibid., 18.

19. Ibid., 1.

20. Institute on Race and Poverty, *Examining the Relationship between Housing, Education, and Persistent Segregation* (Minneapolis: Author, 1998).

21. Minnesota Fair Housing Center, *Housing Discrimination: A Report on the Rental Practices in Two Minneapolis Communities* (Minneapolis: Author, 1996); Trellis A. Powell and Yu Zhou, *People of Phillips Fair Housing Report* (Minneapolis: People of Phillips, 1991).

22. Richard Chin, "For Twin Cities Blacks, Home Loans Hard to Get," *St. Paul Pioneer Press,* April 25, 1993, 1A.

23. Myron Orfield, *Metropolitics: A Regional Agenda for Community and Stability,* rev. ed. (Washington, D.C.: Brookings Institution Press, 1997), 18.

24. Sanders Korenman, Leslie Dwight, and John E. Sjaastad, "The Rise of African American Poverty in the Twin Cities, 1980 to 1990," *CURA Reporter* 27 (1997): 1–12. These authors define "ghetto" as a place where the black poverty rate exceeds 40 percent.

25. Minneapolis Planning Department, *2000 Census Report: Population, Race, and Ethnicity, Publication 1* (Minneapolis: Author, October 2001).

26. David Peterson, "Census 2000: Segregation Eases, but a Divide Remains," *Star Tribune,* March 30, 2001.

27. Minneapolis Planning Department, *2000 Census Report.*

28. Affordable Housing Task Force, *Minneapolis Affordable Housing Task Force Report* (Minneapolis: City of Minneapolis, 1999).

29. Family Housing Fund, *The Need for Affordable Housing in the Twin Cities* (Minneapolis: Author, 1997).

30. Affordable Housing Task Force, *Minneapolis Affordable Housing Task Force Report;* Family Housing Fund, *The Need for Affordable Housing in the Twin Cities.*

31. Minneapolis Affordable Housing Task Force, 1999.

32. Bradley L. Morison, "City Negroes Caught in Housing 'Pockets,'" *Minneapolis Tribune,* July 20, 1959, 6.

33. Affidavit of W. Harry A. Davis, *Hollman v. Cisneros,* 1992.

34. D. J. Hafrey, "Legislators Hear Church Plea for Fair Housing Law," *Minneapolis Morning Tribune,* January 19, 1961, 7.

35. D. J. Hafrey, "Senate, House Get Bill on Fair Housing," *Minneapolis Morning Tribune,* March 25, 1961, 1.

36. Bernie Shellum, "City Extends Open Housing to Duplexes," *Minneapolis Morning Tribune,* August 26, 1967, 1.

37. Greater Minneapolis Council of Churches, n.d.

38. Powell and Zhou, *People of Phillips Fair Housing Report.*

39. Timothy L. Thompson, "Promoting Mobility and Equal Opportunity: *Hollman v. Cisneros,*" *Journal of Affordable Housing* 5 (1996): 237–260.

40. Education and Housing Equity Project, *Submission to the President's Initiative on Race: Summary of "Promising Practice" Twin Cities Community Circles on Schools, Housing and Race,* n.d.

41. Maya Beckstrom, "Houses of Worship to Teach about Housing," *St. Paul Pioneer Press,* 1999, 2G.

42. Orfield, *Metropolitics.*

43. Iric Nathanson, "Negotiating for Neighborhood Development Capital in the Twin Cities, Minnesota," n.p., n.d.

44. Ibid.

45. Ibid.

46. Edward G. Goetz and Mara Sidney, "Community Development Corporations as Neighborhood Advocates: A Study of the Political Activism of Nonprofit Developers," *Applied Behavioral Science Review* 3 (1995): 1–20.

47. Paul Klauda and Neal St. Anthony, "Minneapolis Minority Neighborhoods Get Fewer Home Loans from Banks," *Star Tribune,* 1990, 1A.

48. National Community Reinvestment Coalition, *Advanced CRA Manual.*

49. Neal St. Anthony, "Minorities, Mortgages: Metro-Area Bankers, Housing Activists Say Loan Outreach Effort Starting to Take Hold," *Star Tribune,* November 4, 1992, 1D.

50. Neal St. Anthony and Paul Klauda, "Helping Minorities Buy Home Is a Job for Many," *Star Tribune,* June 18, 1990, 10A.

51. Chin, "For Twin Cities Blacks, Home Loans Hard to Get."

52. Ibid.

53. Dee DePass, "Federal Reserve Will Conduct Hearing on Merger of Norwest and Wells Fargo," *Star Tribune,* September 1, 1998, 3D.

54. Dee DePass, "Group Protests Norwest's New Bounced Check Fee," *Star Tribune,* June 13, 1998, 2D.

55. Federal Reserve Board, public meeting regarding Norwest Corporation and Wells Fargo and Company, 1998, *www.bog.frb.fed.us/events/publicmeeting/19980917/.*

56. Ibid.

57. Ibid.

CHAPTER 5. ADVOCACY FOR HOUSING EQUALITY IN DENVER

1. Data were collected through interviews, archival research, and participant observation during field research in Denver from March 1999 to January 2000. I conducted twenty-four in-person semistructured interviews with past and present civil rights, fair housing, community reinvestment, and housing activists and with government officials at

the local, state, and federal levels, both elected and civil servants. I attended related events and workshops and consulted archival materials, including government documents, local newspapers, and advocacy group archives.

2. Susan E. Clarke and Martin Saiz, "From Waterhole to World City: Place-Luck and Public Investment Agendas in Denver," presentation at the North American Institute for Comparative Urban Research conference, Barcelona, Spain, January 2000; Dennis R. Judd and Randy L. Ready, "Entrepreneurial Cities and the New Policies of Economic Development," in *Reagan and the Cities,* ed. George E. Peterson and Carol W. Lewis (Washington, D.C.: Urban Institute Press, 1986), 209–247; Stephen J. Leonard and Thomas J. Noel, *Denver: Mining Camp to Metropolis* (Niwot: University Press of Colorado, 1990); Tony Robinson, "Denver's LoDo, Denver's NoDo, and San Francisco's Tenderloin: The Possibilities and Limitations of Inner-City Rejuvenation," presentation at the American Political Science Association annual meeting, San Francisco, August 1996.

3. This discussion draws on Rodney E. Hero and Susan E. Clarke, "Latinos, Blacks, and Multiethnic Politics in Denver: Realigning Power and Influence in the Struggle for Equality," in *Racial Politics in American Cities,* ed. Rufus P. Browning, Dale Rogers Marshall, and David H. Tabb (New York: Longman, 2003), 309–330, and Judd and Ready, "Entrepreneurial Cities and the New Policies of Economic Development."

4. Leonard and Noel, *Denver: Mining Camp to Metropolis.*

5. Ibid., 190.

6. Ibid.

7. Alexander L. Crosby, *In These 10 Cities: Discrimination in Housing* (New York: National Committee against Discrimination in Housing, 1951).

8. City of Denver Commission on Human Relations, *Fourth Report,* 1957.

9. Susan Greene, "'73 Showdown Still Wounds: Book Examines Young Chicano's Death, Legacy," *Denver Post,* March 14, 1999, 1, 27A.

10. Rodney E. Hero, *Latinos and the U.S. Political System: Two-Tiered Pluralism* (Philadelphia: Temple University Press, 1992).

11. Ibid.

12. Ibid.

13. Hero and Clarke, "Latinos, Blacks, and Multiethnic Politics in Denver," in Browning, Marshall, and Tabb, eds., *Racial Politics in American Cities.*

14. Ibid.

15. J. Sebastian Sinisi, "City Housing Squeeze Tightens," *Denver Post,* March 20, 2000, 1, 6B.

16. Hero and Clarke, "Latinos, Blacks, and Multiethnic Politics in Denver," in Browning, Marshall, and Tabb, eds., *Racial Politics in American Cities,* 318.

17. Ibid.

18. Mayor's Interim Survey Committee on Human Relations, *A Report of Minorities in Denver with Recommendations* (Denver: Author, 1947), 44.

19. Ibid.

20. Denver Commission on Human Relations, *Inventory of Human Relations,* September–October 1954.

21. Franklin J. James, Betty L. McCummings, and Eileen A. Tynan, *Discrimination, Segregation, and Minority Housing in Sunbelt Cities: A Study of Denver, Houston, and*

Phoenix, Center for Public-Private Sector Cooperation, Graduate School of Public Affairs, University of Colorado at Denver, March 1983.

22. City of Denver Commission on Human Relations, *Fourth Report,* 4.

23. Edward L. Glaeser and Jacob L. Vigdor, "Racial Segregation in the 2000 Census: Promising News," Brookings Institution, Survey Series, April 2001, *www.brookings. edu/urban;* the Lewis Mumford Center, "Ethnic Diversity Grows, Neighborhood Integration Lags Behind."

24. The Piton Foundation, "Neighborhood Facts," *www.piton.org.*

25. James, McCummings, and Tynan, *Discrimination, Segregation, and Minority Housing in Sunbelt Cities,* 7.

26. Franklin J. James, "Minority Suburbanization in Denver," in Bullard, Grigsby, and Lee, eds., *Residential Apartheid,* 95–121.

27. John Accola, "Denver Banks Deny Claims of Redlining," *Rocky Mountain News,* April 16, 1995.

28. Flaming and Anderson, *Mortgage Practices in Colorado;* Flaming, Anderson, and Lake, *Mortgage Practices in Colorado.*

29. Eleanor Crow, Donna Hilton, Clyda Stafford, Franklin James, and Patrick Goff, *Discrimination in Homeowners/Property Insurance in Denver* (Denver: Housing for All, Graduate School of Public Affairs, University of Colorado at Denver, 1997), 1.

30. Colorado Affordable Housing Partnership, "Affordable Housing Needs in Metro Denver," November 6, 2002, *www.coloradoaffordablehousing.org/facts.htm#metro;* Sinisi, "City Housing Squeeze Tightens."

31. Colorado Affordable Housing Partnership, "Affordable Housing Needs in Metro Denver."

32. Art Branscombe and Bea Sutton Branscombe, "Park Hill History—A Treasury of Memories," *Greater Park Hill News* 31, nos. 6–13; 32, nos. 1–8, 10–12; 33, nos. 1–3 (1993–1995).

33. Katherine Woods, "Park Hill, Denver," *Cityscape* 4 (1998): 89–103.

34. City of Denver Commission on Human Relations, *Fourth Report.*

35. Woods, "Park Hill, Denver."

36. Andrew Wiese, "Neighborhood Diversity: Social Change, Ambiguity, and Fair Housing since 1968," *Journal of Urban Affairs* 17 (1995): 107–129; Donald L. DeMarco and George C. Galster, "Prointegrative Policy: Theory and Practice," *Journal of Urban Affairs* 15 (1993): 141–160; Thomas W. Simon, "Double Reverse Discrimination in Housing: Contextualizing the Starrett City Case," *Buffalo Law Review* 39 (1991): 803–853; Richard A. Smith, "Creating Stable Racially Integrated Communities: A Review," *Journal of Urban Affairs* 15 (1993): 115–140.

37. Juliet Z. Saltman, *Open Housing: Dynamics of a Social Movement* (New York: Praeger Publishers, 1978).

38. Juliet Z. Saltman, *Open Housing as a Social Movement: Challenge, Conflict, and Change* (Lexington, Mass.: Heath Lexington Books, 1971), 253.

39. Ibid.

40. Alex Berenson, "Bank Given Good Grades after Inquiry," *Denver Post,* February 23, 1995: C-1.

41. Stephen Keating, "Norwest OKs Deal on Minority Loans," *Denver Post,* February 3, 1995, C-2.

42. Alex Berenson, "Banks' Minority Lending Praised," *Denver Post,* January 25, 1996, B8.

43. Denver Community Reinvestment Partnership, "Executive Summary," unpublished document, 1993.

44. Center for Community Development, 1994.

45. Alex Berenson, "Bank Baffles Denver by Dropping Out of Partnership," *Denver Post,* May 30, 1996, D2.

CHAPTER 6. A COMPARATIVE ANALYSIS

1. Schneider and Ingram, *Policy Design for Democracy.*

2. Derthick, *New Towns In-Town;* Jeffrey L. Pressman and Aaron Wildavsky, *Implementation: How Great Expectations in Washington Are Dashed in Oakland* (Berkeley: University of California Press, 1984).

3. Susan E. Clarke, "More Autonomous Policy Orientations: An Analytic Framework," in *The Politics of Urban Development,* ed. Clarence N. Stone and Heywood T. Sanders (Lawrence: University Press of Kansas, 1987), 105–124; Susan E. Clarke and Gary L. Gaile, *The Work of Cities* (Minneapolis: University of Minnesota Press, 1998); Edward G. Goetz, "Expanding Possibilities in Local Development Policy: An Examination of U.S. Cities," *Political Research Quarterly* 47 (1994): 85–109.

4. Edward G. Goetz, "The Politics of Poverty Deconcentration," *Journal of Urban Affairs* 22 (2000): 157–173.

5. Hero and Clarke, "Latinos, Blacks, and Multiethnic Politics in Denver," in Browning, Marshall, and Tabb, eds., *Racial Politics in American Cities;* Minneapolis Planning Department, *2000 Census Report: Population, Race, and Ethnicity, Publication 1.*

6. Edward G. Goetz, "Race, Class, and Metropolitan Housing Strategies: A Look at the Minneapolis–St. Paul Region," presentation at the Urban Affairs Association annual meeting, Fort Worth, Texas, April 22–25, 1998.

7. Minneapolis Planning Department, *2000 Census Report: Population, Race, and Ethnicity.*

8. William J. Craig, "New Languages in Minnesota," *CURA Reporter* 27 (1997): 6–10.

9. Dennis A. Ahlburg, "Characteristics of Poverty in Minnesota," *CURA Reporter* 28 (1998): 7–11.

10. Ibid.

11. Korenman, Dwight, and Sjaastad, "The Rise of African American Poverty in the Twin Cities," 1–12.

12. Ibid. These authors define "ghetto" as a place where the black poverty rate exceeds 40 percent.

13. U.S. Bureau of the Census, Census of Population and Housing, 1980, 1990, 2000.

14. Ibid.

15. Jon Jeter, "In Minnesota, Political Views Change with Minority Influx," *Washington Post,* March 3, 1998, A1.

16. Thomas E. Cronin and Robert D. Loevy, *Colorado Politics and Government:*

Governing the Centennial State (Lincoln: University of Nebraska Press, 1993); William E. Lass, *Minnesota: A History* (New York: W. W. Norton, 1998).

17. Cronin and Loevy, *Colorado Politics and Government.*

18. Martiga Lohn, "The Election Comes Home," *Southwest Journal* 10, no. 1 (January 13–26 1999): 1, 4.

19. Lass, *Minnesota: A History.*

20. Jean Hopfensperger, "Lawmakers Give Huge Boost to Affordable Housing," *Star Tribune,* May 15, 1999.

21. Art Branscombe and Bea Sutton Branscombe, "Park Hill History—A Treasury of Memories," *Greater Park Hill News* 31, nos. 6–13; 32, nos. 1–8, 10–12; 33, nos. 1–3 (1993–1995).

22. Smith and Lipsky, *Nonprofits for Hire.*

23. Art, "Social Responsibility in Bank Credit Decisions"; Fishbein, "The Community Reinvestment Act after Fifteen Years"; Khademian, *Checking on Banks.*

24. Federal Reserve Board, Public meeting regarding Norwest Corporation and Wells Fargo and Company.

25. Yinger, *Closed Doors, Opportunities Lost.*

CHAPTER 7. ADVANCING THE STRUGGLE FOR HOUSING EQUALITY

1. Mary C. Waters, "Multiple Ethnic Identity Choices," in *Beyond Pluralism: The Conception of Groups and Group Identities in America,* ed. Wendy F. Katkin, Ned Landsman, and Andrea Tyree (Urbana: University of Illinois Press, 1998), 28–46.

2. Claire Jean Kim, "The Racial Triangulation of Asian Americans," *Politics and Society* 27, no. 1 (March 1999): 105–138; Rogers M. Smith, "Beyond Tocqueville, Myrdal, and Hartz: The Multiple Traditions in America," *American Political Science Review* 87, no. 3 (September 1993): 549–566.

3. Martin Gilens, *Why Americans Hate Welfare: Race, Media, and the Politics of Antipoverty Policy* (Chicago: University of Chicago Press, 1999).

4. Hochschild, *Facing Up to the American Dream.*

5. Hero, *Faces of Inequality.*

6. Hochschild, *Facing Up to the American Dream.*

7. Rufus P. Browning, Dale Rogers Marshall, and David H. Tabb, eds., *Racial Politics in American Cities,* 3d ed. (New York: Longman, 2003); Cathy J. Cohen, *The Boundaries of Blackness: AIDS and the Breakdown of Black Politics* (Chicago: University of Chicago Press, 1999); chap. 3; John R. Logan, Jacob Stowell, and Deirdre Oakley, "Choosing Segregation: Racial Imbalance in American Public Schools, 1990–2000," March 29, 2002, Lewis Mumford Center for Comparative Urban and Regional Research, SUNY–Albany; Paula D. McClain and Joseph Stewart Jr., *"Can We All Get Along?" Racial and Ethnic Minorities in American Politics* (Boulder, Colo.: Westview Press, 1999).

8. Neil Kraus and Todd Swanstrom, "Minority Mayors and the Hollow-Prize Problem," *Political Science and Politics* 24, no. 1 (March 2001): 99–105.

9. Abravanel and Cunningham, "How Much Do We Know?"

10. Ibid.

11. Ibid.

12. Lee, "An Issue of Public Importance"; Fair Housing Center of Metropolitan Detroit, "$115,000 and Counting: A Summary of Housing Discrimination Lawsuits That Have Been Assisted by the Efforts of Private, Non-Profit Fair Housing Organizational Members of the National Fair Housing Alliance," June 26, 1999.

13. Abravanel and Cunningham, "How Much Do We Know?"

14. Turner, Ross, Galster, and Yinger, *Discrimination in Metropolitan Housing Markets.*

15. Ibid.

16. Joint Center for Housing Studies, "The 25th Anniversary of the Community Reinvestment Act: Access to Capital in an Evolving Financial Services System," prepared for the Ford Foundation, March 2002, *www.jchs.harvard.edu/crareport.html.*

17. The Lewis Mumford Center, "Ethnic Diversity Grows, Neighborhood Integration Lags Behind."

18. Ibid.

19. Ibid.; Nancy A. Denton, "Half Empty or Half Full: Segregation and Segregated Neighborhoods 30 Years after the Fair Housing Act," *Cityscape* 4 (1999): 107–122.

20. Logan, Stowell, and Oakley, "Choosing Segregation."

21. Glaeser and Vigdor, "Racial Segregation in the 2000 Census."

22. William H. Frey, "Melting Pot Suburbs: A Census 2000 Study of Suburban Diversity," Brookings Institution: Census 2000 Series, June 2001, *www.brookings.edu/urban.*

23. Peter Dreier, John Mollenkopf, and Todd Swanstrom, *Place Matters: Metropolitics for the Twenty-First Century* (Lawrence: University Press of Kansas, 2001), 50; Logan, "Separate and Unequal."

24. Ingrid Gould Ellen, *Sharing America's Neighborhoods: The Prospects for Stable Integration* (Cambridge: Harvard University Press, 2000).

25. Dreier, Mollenkopf, and Swanstrom, *Place Matters;* Ronald Schmidt Sr., Rodney Hero, Andrew Aoki, and Yvette Alex-Assensoh, "Political Science, the New Immigration, and Racial Politics in the United States: What Do We Know? What Do We Need to Know?" presentation at the American Political Science Association annual meeting, Boston, August 29–September 1, 2002.

26. Joint Center for Housing Studies, "The 25th Anniversary of the Community Reinvestment Act."

27. Sheri Berman and Kathleen R. McNamara, "CES Co-Sponsored Workshop on Ideas, Culture, and Political Analysis," *European Studies Newsletter* 27 (1998): 1–2.

28. Boris and Steuerle, *Nonprofits and Government.*

29. For example, McAdam, *Political Process and the Development of Black Insurgency, 1930–1970;* Meyer, "Social Movements and Public Policy"; Sidney Tarrow, *Power in Movement: Social Movements, Collective Action, and Politics* (Cambridge: Cambridge University Press, 1994); Mayer N. Zald, "Looking Backward to Look Forward: Reflections on the Past and Future of the Resource Mobilization Research Program," in *Frontiers in Social Movement Theory,* ed. Aldon D. Morris and Carol McClurg Mueller (New Haven: Yale University Press, 1992), 326–348.

30. Meyer, "Social Movements and Public Policy."

31. National Fair Housing Alliance, *www.nationalfairhousing.org,* accessed December 4, 2002.

32. This description drawn from Yinger, *Closed Doors, Opportunities Lost,* 190–193.

33. Joint Center for Housing Studies, "The 25th Anniversary of the Community Reinvestment Act."

34. Thanks to Peter Dreier for putting it this way.

35. Cathy Malmstrom, "Financial Modernization: A CRA Organizer's Worst Nightmare," *Shelterforce Online,* November/December 1999, *www.nhi.org/online/issues/108/malmstorm.html,* accessed November 19, 2002.

36. Thanks to Greg Squires for pointing out these areas in which fair housing and community reinvestment groups have begun to collaborate.

37. C. Alter, "Bureaucracy and Democracy in Organizations," in *Private Action and the Public Good,* ed. W. W. Powell and E. S. Clemens (New Haven: Yale University Press, 1998), 258–271; Susan E. Clarke, "The Prospects for Local Democratic Governance: The Governance Roles of Nonprofit Organizations," presentation at the Norwegian Institute for Urban and Regional Research–European Urban Research Association Workshop on Innovations in Urban Government, Oslo, Norway, April 1999; J. C. Jenkins, "Nonprofit Organizations and Policy Advocacy," in *The Nonprofit Sector: A Research Handbook,* ed. W. W. Powell (New Haven: Yale University Press, 1987): 296–320; J. L. McKnight, "Professionalized Services: Disabling Help for Communities," in *The Essential Civil Society Reader,* ed. D. E. Eberly (Lanham, Md.: Rowman and Littlefield, 2000), 183–194.

38. Frank R. Baumgartner and Bryan D. Jones, *Agendas and Instability in American Politics* (Chicago: University of Chicago Press, 1993); Rochefort and Cobb, "Problem Definition: An Emerging Perspective"; Maarten A. Hajer, "Discourse Coalitions and the Institutionalization of Practice: The Case of Acid Rain in Great Britain," in Fischer and Forester, eds., *The Argumentative Turn in Policy Analysis and Planning,* 43–76; John W. Kingdon, *Agendas, Alternatives, and Public Policies* (New York: HarperCollins College Publishers, 1995).

Index